{ Acknowledgments }

Thank you to Sourcebooks, especially Peter Lynch, for allowing me to create a follow-up to *Word Nerd*. Special thanks for support and editing assistance goes to my husband, Paul Magoulas.

~ The Definitive Compendium ~

PHRASEOLOGY

THOUSANDS *of* BIZARRE ORIGINS,
UNEXPECTED CONNECTIONS, *and* FASCINATING FACTS
about ENGLISH'S BEST EXPRESSIONS

BARBARA ANN KIPFER, PhD

SOURCEBOOKS, INC.®
NAPERVILLE, ILLINOIS

Published by Sourcebooks, Inc.
P.O. Box 4410, Naperville, Illinois 60567-4410
(630) 961-3900
Fax: (630) 961-2168
www.sourcebooks.com

Cataloging-in-Publication data is on file with the publisher.

Printed and bound in the United States of America.

DR 10 9 8 7 6 5 4 3 2 1

Introduction

Phraseology is a collection of really interesting things you probably do not know about thousands and thousands of phrases. This book is the result of a hobby of gathering observations about words, something that has just come naturally during my nearly thirty years as a professional lexicographer. It is a delightful hobby, writing down what I find to be truly interesting definitions, fascinating origins or histories, details of usage, surprising trivia, useful synonyms, or unexpected connections between phrases. In **Phraseology**, I have "caught" the interesting details about thousands of phrases and now present them to the wide world of word-lovers.

Phraseology contains notes from books about word history and etymology, unusual or lost or uncommon words, grammar instruction and usage, word trivia, differences between confusable words, how phrases are formed—from all the general and specialized dictionaries and language books that I have read. In **Phraseology**, I have distilled many, many bookshelves' worth of books in each of these areas, and now they are presented together for others to enjoy.

Readers will be inspired by **Phraseology** to explore further. They will find that any trip through **Phraseology** is a really cool way to learn things about phrases, things that may be useful, or things that they can then turn around and describe to their friends and families. In opening to any page, readers can have experiences like "wow, I had forgotten that," or "that is certainly something I did not know," or "aha! that is what that means!" or "oh, that is where that came from!" These phrases, including idioms and slang, greatly enhance the reader's knowledge and understanding by filling in his vocabulary with interesting information about phrases.

{ A }

A.1. steak sauce is so named for its being "the very best," and it was created in 1824

a cappella is Italian for "in chapel style"

the phrase **à coups de dictionnaire** means "with blows of a dictionary, with constant reference to a dictionary"

a cup too low means to not have drunk enough to be in good spirits

a fortiori means "stronger reason, still more conclusively" (from Latin)

à la is a compound preposition before nouns, and the corresponding masculine preposition is au, as in au pair

à la carte is French, literally "by the card," in other words, "ordered by separate items"

à la Florentine means with spinach

à la mode for beef means "made in a rich stew, usually with wine and vegetables"

à la niçoise refers to hot or cold dishes with tomatoes, black olives, garlic, and anchovies; also called niçoise

A-list first meant "first in a series of lists" (1890)

the phrase **a number of** is used with plural nouns (it is a determiner) and the verb should therefore be plural: "**A number of people** are waiting to buy tickets"

a posteriori, Latin "from the latter," refers to an argument which proves the cause from the effect

to cook something **à point** means "just enough, not overcooked or undercooked"

a priori is from Latin, literally "from what comes first"

ab ovo, "from the beginning," is from Latin, literally "from the egg"

an **abat-jour** is a skylight or device for deflecting light downward

an **Abbott and Costello** is frankfurters and beans in diner slang

abbreviated piece of nothing is slang for a worthless or insignificant person

{ **ABC gum** is gum that has already been chewed }

Abderian laughter comes from Abdera, in Thrace, whose citizens were considered rustic simpletons who would laugh at anything or anyone they didn't understand

abel-wackets are blows given on the palm of the hand with a twisted handkerchief, instead of a ferula; a jocular punishment among seamen, who sometimes played at cards for wackets, the loser suffering as many strokes as he has lost games

ablation is the evaporation or melting of part of the outer surface of a spacecraft, through heating by friction with the atmosphere

abominable snowman (1921) is a literal translation of the Tibetan term *Meetoh Kangmi,* "foul snowman," and Tibetan *yeh-the,* "little manlike animal," gave us yeti in the 1930s

about-face is a shortening of "right about face," a cavalry instruction since around 1800

above snakes is a way of saying "above the ground"

above the fold is the content of a Web page that can be seen without scrolling down; also called above the scroll

Abraham's bosom is another word for heaven

absence of mind is the failure to remember what one is doing

there are **adjectives** that are **absolute** and cannot take more/most, less/least, or intensives like largely, quite, or very: absolute, adequate, chief, complete, devoid, entire, false, fatal, favorite, final, ideal, impossible, inevitable, infinite, irrevocable, main, manifest, only, paramount, perfect, perpetual, possible, preferable, principal, singular, stationary, sufficient, unanimous, unavoidable, unbroken, uniform, unique, universal, void, whole

absolute music (abstract music, pure music) is music for its own sake—concerned only with structure, melody, harmony, and rhythm

absolute zero is calculated to be -460 degrees F, the point at which it is impossible to get colder, the lowest temperature that is theoretically possible

absolution day is the Tuesday before Easter

the **absolutive case** is used to indicate the patient or experiencer of a verb's action, the subject of an intransitive verb, as well as the object of a transitive verb

absorbent ground is a ground prepared for a picture, chiefly with distemper, or watercolors, by which the oil is absorbed, and a brilliancy is imparted to the colors

abstract expressionism is a description generally applied to aspects of modern American painting in the late 1940s and early 1950s which were concerned both with the various forms of abstraction and with psychic self-expression

abstract language describes words that represent concepts rather than physical things

abstract nouns are things like goodness, evil, beauty, fear, love; **concrete nouns** are physical objects like table, apple, moon

an **abstract number** stands alone (1,2,3) while a concrete number refers to a particular object(s), as one horse, two feet

an **abstracted form** is a word affix or element of a familiar expression that is borrowed to form analogous words, such as -gate for Koreagate (from Watergate) and -aholic for workaholic from alcoholic

the **abyssal plain** of the ocean is 6,600–20,000 feet and covers most of the ocean floor

an **academic press** (or university press) is a publishing house associated with a university or other scholarly institution, specializing in the publication of scholarly books and journals, particularly works written by its faculty

an **academic procrastinator** is a student who, lacking poor time-management skills and feeling stress, chooses to put off work or studying that needs to be done

academic question is a query that has an interesting answer but is of no practical use or importance

Academy Award (Oscar) refers to the Motion Picture Arts and Sciences

academy board is inexpensive board, made of cardboard, used as a surface for oil painting since the early nineteenth century, primarily for small paintings and sketches

an **academy figure** is a drawing usually half life-size, in crayon or pencil, done from a nude model

the **Academy leader** is the standardized film beginning showing a backward countdown from ten to three

Acapulco gold dates to 1965, for a local grade of potent marijuana grown around the resort town of Acapulco de Juarez, western Mexico

the **acceleration principle** is the principle that an increase in the demand for a finished product will create a greater demand for capital goods

accent acute is a synonym of acute accent

accent grave is a synonym of grave accent

the **acceptable face** of something is its positive or reasonable side

accepted pairing is advertising that concedes the merit of a competitor's product while promoting a contrasting feature of its own product

an **access road** is a road that provides access to a specific destination, as to a main highway or to a property that lies within another property

an **accessory apartment** is an apartment within a single-family dwelling, as for an in-law, aging parent, or college graduate returned home

an **accessory fruit** is one containing much fleshy tissue besides that of the ripened ovary; as apple or strawberry

accidental or subjective color is a false or spurious color seen in some instances, owing to the persistence of the luminous impression upon the retina, and a gradual change of its character, as when a wheel perfectly white, and with a circumference regularly subdivided, is made to revolve rapidly over a dark object, the teeth of the wheel appear to the eye to be of different shades of color varying with the rapidity of rotation

accidental lights are secondary lights or the effects of light other than ordinary daylight, such as the rays of the sun darting through a cloud, or between the leaves of trees—as well as the effect of moonlight, candlelight, etc.

the ladder on the side of a boat or ship to allow access from a smaller boat is the **accommodation ladder**

an **accomplished fact** is an irreversible accomplishment

according to Hoyle refers to Edmond Hoyle (1672–1769), an authority on card games

an **Ace bandage** is a trademark for an elastic bandage used to wrap joints when sprained or strained

ace in the hole first referred to in stud poker, is a place of concealment for the ace, the most valuable card

anyone caught with **an ace up one's sleeve** in a gambling context would be assumed to be cheating, yet this common Americanism has come to mean "hold something useful or powerful in reserve" without any suggestion of dishonesty

an **ace-boon-coon** is a very close friend

Achilles' heel should have the apostrophe, but is often written without it; **Achilles tendon** has no apostrophe

achromatic colors are white, black, and gray

acid jazz (derived from acid house) is a type of music combining jazz, soul, rhythm and blues, funk, and hip-hop and is also called jazz vibes

account receivable is an amount owed to an entity or a payment for goods or services; an **account payable** is an amount owed by an entity to others for goods or services

accountable mail is a shorter term encompassing registered, numbered, insured, and certified mail

accounting cost in economics is the total amount of money or goods expended in an endeavor, money paid out at some time in the past and recorded in journal entries and ledgers

acid rain was first used as a term in the nineteenth century to describe polluted rain in Manchester, England

acid snow is acid precipitation in the form of snow

acid test, for a test which is conclusive of the value or success of something, derives from the original use of nitric acid as a test for gold

acidic foods include most fruits, pickled vegetables, jams, and jellies

ack-ack (1939) represents A.A., the military abbreviation for anti-aircraft

acknowledge the corn originally meant to admit to being drunk, and then by extension to admit to any mistake, fault, or impropriety

acorn nut (hardware) is a closed nut having a domelike cover over the back, protruding part of the engaged screw or bolt

acorn squash really does resemble an acorn

the **acoustic meatus** is the ear opening through which sounds collected by the pinna reach the tympanic cavity

acoustic shock is a complaint of damaged hearing as a result of telephone workers' wearing headphones or earphones being subjected to excessive, continuous, or high-pitched noise

among foods, caviar is the dish most often cited as an **acquired taste**

across the board is an allusion to the board displaying the odds in a horse race

across the pond means "on the other side of the Atlantic Ocean"

acrylic paint is an emulsion paint employing a synthetic medium (acrylic resin); first used in the 1940s, it has proved a serious rival to oil paint with many modern artists

action painting as a term was introduced in 1952 by art critic Harold Rosenberg in preference to the term abstract expressionism

action potential is a brief electrical signal transmitted along a nerve or muscle fiber following stimulation

action verb is a word belonging to the part of speech that is the center of the predicate and which describes an act or activity

active capital is money or property that may readily be converted into money

an **active front** is the boundary between two different air masses, or a portion thereof, which produces appreciable cloudiness and precipitation and is usually accompanied by significant shifts in wind direction

active ingredient is the chemically active part of a chemical compound

acupuncture point is any of various places on the human body on a line of energy (called a meridian) into which an acupuncture needle can be inserted to exact a benefit; also called acupoint

an **acute angle** is less than 90 degrees, a right angle is 90 degrees, an obtuse angle is more than 90 degrees but less than 180 degrees, a straight angle is 180 degrees, and a reflex angle is more than 180 degrees but less than 360 degrees

ad creep is the gradual addition of advertising to non-traditional places and objects

ad hoc is Latin "for this (specific purpose)"

an **ad hominem attack** or criticism is aimed not at what someone has produced but at the producer

ad infinitum can mean "lasting a long time" or "endless, interminable"

ad interim means "temporary"

ad lib can mean "as much and as often as desired," as **ad libitum** is literally "according to pleasure"

know people who are easily influenced by advertising? call them **admass**

ad nauseam is rarely if ever used about anything that would provoke genuine sickness

ad valorem is a type of customs duties, from Latin "in proportion to the value"

in U.S. diner slang, **Adam and Eve** is shorthand for two fried or poached eggs; Adam and Eve on a raft is two poached eggs on toast

Adam's ale is a humorous term for water

the **Adam's apple** is so named for a piece of the forbidden fruit that became stuck in Adam's throat

a version of **add insult to injury** originated in the fables of the Roman author Phaedrus (15 BC–AD 50), who quoted a fable by Aesop

transport is an **added value** that many people ignore; they want products available in a store/shop, so that is a value added to its **intrinsic value**

a calculator usually has an **add-in memory key** (M+), a subtract from memory key (M-), memory recall (MR), and memory cancel (MC)

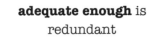

adequate enough is
redundant

adessive case is a noun case used to indicate adjacent location, and in English, this is usually expressed by the prepositions *near*, *at*, or *by*, as in "by the house"

Adirondack chairs are so called because they were first designed and used there

the knobs on an easel are called the **adjustment keys**

an **adjutant general** is a senior military administrative officer, especially an army general responsible for administration and personnel

adjuvant therapy is any secondary treatment for cancer (such as chemotherapy) given after the primary treatment (such as surgery) in order to remove residual microscopic disease

an **admiral's watch** is "a good night's sleep"

adolescent they is Roy Copperud's term for the use of the plural pronouns "they" and "their" with a singular verb, an ungrammatical but common practice, e.g., "Whoever does that will find their job in jeopardy."

an **advance directive** is a written legal document in which the signer asks not to be kept alive by extraordinary medical effort when suffering from terminal illness or severe disability; a prior statement of refusal to permit certain types of medical treatment; also called living will, health-care directive, directive to physicians

advance man was first recorded in 1879

advancing colors describe the perceived tendency of warm colors to appear at the forefront of a painting while cool colors recede

advent candles are marked into twenty-four sections and burned daily during Advent, including the four Sundays before Christmas

adverbial dressing gown is Ernest Gowers's term for modifying a verb or adjective phrase with an adverb, e.g., "frightfully boring"

an **aebleskiver pan** is for making Danish pancake balls, which are really apple dumplings

affirmative action was seen in print by 1935 but did not come into widespread use until the 1960s

affix-clipping is a word formed by moving a letter to or from a frequent companion word, e.g. a napple—an apple; this is also called **folk etymology**

A-frame, a "type of framework shaped like the letter A, " dates to 1909

an **after-party** is a more exclusive social gathering that takes place after a scheduled party or event such as a concert

Aeolian rocks are rocks that have been deposited or eroded largely by the wind

the huge ladders on fire trucks are called **aerial ladders**

an **aerial runway** is equipment for recreation or climbing where a rider traverses from a high point to a lower point on a pulley suspended on a cable

aesthetic emotion is any emotional response to works of art produced when thought and emotion come together to create meaning, also known as working emotion

any psychological disorder arising from the emotions is an **affective disorder**; affective disorder is another term for mood disorder

an **affinity card** is a credit card sponsored by an organization, such as a university or business, that receives part of the card user's fees

afternoon men is slang for drunkards having had a liquid lunch

wisdom or cleverness that comes too late is **after-wit**, also called **staircase wit**

an **agent noun** is the person or thing that performs the action of the verb and typically ends in -er or -or

Agent Orange, the powerful defoliant used by U.S. military in the Vietnam War, was so called from the color strip on the side of the container, which distinguished it from Agent Blue, Agent Purple, Agent White, etc., other herbicides used by the U.S. military

originating in the nineteenth century, an **agent provocateur** was a policeman who infiltrated suspect groups and encouraged them to commit crimes

an **agglutinizing language** is one in which words are typically made up of sequences of elements (the opposite is fusional language)

agree to disagree dates to 1770

ahead of the game dates to the 1970s

aide memoire usually refers to something concrete carried to jog the memory, often written material

the term **air conditioning** has existed since 1909

the **air fern**, which is billed in stores and some garden centers as a plant that needs no water or fertilizer, is actually the skeletal remains of a tiny sea animal called Sertularia, a distant relative of coral; the skeletons look like ferns and have extremely fine foliage; in stores they are also sold as air plants and air moss

the term **air force** was originally applied to the newly formed **Royal Air Force** of Britain (1917) and then became a general term for this type of organization

air fresheners are of U.S. origin

air guitar is an imaginary guitar that one pretends to play; the action of pretending to play an imaginary guitar

an **air gun** propels a projectile via compressed air

the loud annoying horn often blown at sporting events is an **air horn** or **signal horn**, a horn activated by compressed air

an **air pocket** is a region of low or uneven pressure destabilizing an aircraft

air quote is the use of one's index and middle fingers on each hand to gesture quotation marks for a word or saying

air raid (1914) was one of the key terms of twentieth-century warfare

air support is another term for bombing

air time is the time a basketball player stays in the air while attempting a slam dunk

the small trucks that push and pull aircraft around a terminal are the **aircraft tugs**

the **Airedale dog** was originally called a **waterside terrier**

an **airport novel** is a light piece of fiction sold in airports and railway stations

al dente is Italian, literally "to the tooth," and can be applied to other kinds of food besides pasta

al fresco implies the presence of some nearby structure (one does not hike **al fresco**)

alang-alang is a type of Philippine grass

the Alcan (Alaska and Canada) Highway is now the **Alaska Highway**

{ **Alaska strawberries** is slang for bacon and beans }

sturgeon was once so plentiful in New York's Hudson River that it was humorously called **Albany beef**

an **Albert chain** is a chain used to anchor a pocket watch or other fob to a waistcoat

album nigrum is a term for the excrement of mice and rats

alcohol flush reaction is a condition where the human body cannot break down ingested alcohol completely, due to a missing enzyme, causing a flushing or blushing of the face, neck, etc. when alcohol is consumed

algal bloom is a proliferation of algae in water

Alice in Wonderland is a term for someone who is perpetually confused or amazed by the world around them

the **alimentary canal**, based on the Latin *alimentum* "food" (also digestive tube), is the entire tube extending from the mouth to the anus; the **esophagus** is between the pharynx (at back of throat) and the stomach, while the trachea (windpipe) is alongside it

A-line, a dress or skirt shaped like an A, was created by Christian Dior

alive and kicking goes back to the eighteenth century, when London fishmongers referred to fresh fish flapping about in their carts

the call **all aboard** was used on riverboats before it was used on trains

is your life in a state of disorder? then you are **all aflunters**

in the phrase **all balled up**, the balls are ones of ice on horses' feet in the winter

all cats are gray in the dark means that in the dark, physical appearance is unimportant

All Fools' Day is another term for April Fool's Day

all Greek to me comes from Shakespeare's *Julius Caesar*

from a gusseted dress being thought to improve a woman's appearance, we get the phrase **all gussied up**

all hat and no cattle is someone who acts rich or important but has no substance

{ **all intents and purposes** is redundant }

all mouth and trousers means "boastful and blustering; all talk and no action"

all of a sudden is correct (not all of the sudden)

all of a twitter means to be very excited

all-purpose flour is the finely ground and sifted meal of a blend of high-gluten hard wheat and low-gluten soft wheat, which can be used in most food recipes calling for flour

all ready means "prepared;" **already** means "previously"

use "**all right**," not "alright"

that's **all she wrote** started as college jargon in 1948

in **all systems go**, go means "correctly functioning"

all the way in diner slang is a sandwich with everything, often lettuce, tomato, mayo, etc.

all together means "collectively," "in one place," "all at once"; **altogether** means "in sum, entirely"

all told basically means "all (being) counted" or "in summation"

alla prima is a technique of painting in which the picture is completed in one session

the **allative case** is used to indicate movement onto, or to the adjacency of something, and in English, this is usually expressed by the prepositions "to" or "onto," as in "to the house," "onto the house"

All-Bran Cereal arose as a convenient way of using up the bran left over from other products

the **Allegheny River** got its name from Delaware *welhik-heny*, "most beautiful stream"

alluvial deposits are sediment (mud, sand, gravel, pebbles) transported and deposited by a watercourse

an **alluvial fan** is a deposit of sand, silt, gravel, or rocks that fans out at a mountain or slope's base

all-wheel drive means the vehicle always (full-time) operates in four-wheel drive

alma mater "bounteous mother" originally referred to the Roman goddesses of abundance and later was applied to universities with the notion that they are the "mother" of intellectual and spiritual nourishment of students

 almighty dollar is an expression first used by Washington Irving

the **Allen key**, screw, and wrench got their names from Allen Manufacturing Company in Hartford, Connecticut

an **alley apple** is a brick, rock, or stone when used as a missile

alley-oop may come from French *alles!* "go on!" and the French pronunciation of "up"

the ends of automobile jumper cables are called **alligator clips**

an **alligator pear** is another name for avocado

feeling **all-overish** means you are physically or mentally uneasy

all's right with the world comes from a Robert Browning poem

marzipan is also called **almond paste**

aloe vera is literally Latin for "true aloe" in contrast to the agave, which is very much like it

a Yale graduate, Ellery Chun, coined the term **aloha shirt**

alpha and omega signifies the first and last or God's eternity, as well as "the most important part"

alpha male is a domineering man; the dominant member in a group of males, especially animals

alpha taxonomy is the science of finding, describing, classifying, and naming living things; this retronym is used in those cases where the word taxonomy may be ambiguous: where the word taxonomy is (also) used in the sense of a classification in a hierarchical system

alpha version describes a development status that usually means the first complete version of a program or application, that is most likely unstable, but is useful to show what the product will do to, usually, a selected group—and is also called preview version

alpha waves are the slow electrical waves produced in the human brain of someone who is awake but inactive

alphabet soup describes an extravagant use of initialisms or acronyms

alter ego is Latin for "other self"

an **altered state** is any state of mind that differs from the normal state of consciousness or awareness of a person, especially one induced by drugs, hypnosis, or mental disorder

alternative energy is that which does not deplete natural resources

alternative medicine is also called complementary medicine

altocumulus undulatis are the clouds in a herringbone sky

{ tinfoil was replaced by **aluminum foil** in the 1920s }

a great synonym for excrement is **alvine dejections**

Alzheimer's disease was named in 1912 but remained in the vocabulary of medical specialists until the 1970s when it became a higher-profile disease (abbreviated form Alzheimer's was recorded in 1954)

the **Amazonian epoch** is the most recent of the Martian geologic epochs, from 1,800 years ago to the present

an **Amber Alert** is an emergency broadcast or notification system used when there has been an abduction, especially of a child

amber heart refers to amber's warm hue and poor heat conductivity transposed to emotional traits, meaning a particularly warm, loving, or kind heart

an **ambient device** is any simple wireless object that unobtrusively presents information

ambient food is food that can be stored at room temperature

ambient light is the light surrounding an environment or subject, especially in regard to photography and other artwork; also called available light, existing light

ambient music is that which has no persistent beat and is styled to create or enhance an atmosphere

ambient temperature is the temperature of the surrounding environment; technically, the temperature of the air surrounding a power supply or cooling medium

the **amen corner** constitutes the seats near the pulpit in church

American beauty is the name of a red, white, and blue playing marble (also called American fried, fried marble)

{ **American cheese** hails from England }

American dream was first written in 1931 by U.S. historian J.T. Adams

American Indian is just as acceptable as Native American

American plan is room, services, meals; European plan is room and services

American run is the unit of thickness of yarn

amicus curiae is Latin, literally "friend of the courts," and the plural is *amici curiae*

an **amour de voyage** is a temporary infatuation as is experienced during a cruise, airplane flight, etc.

one's **amour-propre** is one's awareness of what is right and proper for oneself

amplitude modulation is the written-out form of AM (radio)

amuse-bouche or **amuse-gueule** both mean literally "something to please the mouth" and are used for an appetizer or pre-meal tidbit

anabatic wind is an upslope wind, usually applied only when the wind is blowing up a hill or mountain as a result of local surface heating and apart from the effects of the larger scale circulation; the opposite is **katabatic wind**

anadama bread is a loaf bread made from corn meal, flour, and molasses

an **anagram dictionary** is a list of words, or groups of words, ordered according to the number of each letter in the word; used for solving crosswords and similar puzzles

the term **anal retentive** appears in text by the late 1950s

analysis paralysis is the condition of being unable to make a decision due to the availability of too much information which must be processed in order for the decision to be made

the area of the hand connecting the thumb and first finger is the **anatomical snuffbox**

ancien régime is French "old rule," referring to the government and social order of France before the French Revolution

and one denotes getting fouled while shooting a basketball, qualifying for a free throw

Andes Mountains is from Quecha *andi*, "high crest"

anecdotal evidence is nonscientific observations or studies, which do not provide proof but may assist research efforts

an **angel food cake** has no fat and is a cake an angel could not resist

angels on horseback are oysters wrapped in bacon, grilled, and served on buttered toast, while **devils on horseback** are prunes doing the same

Anglo-Saxon is the language from which English developed; from the Angles, Saxons, and Jutes from northern Germany and Denmark in the fifth century AD

angora wool is a mixture of sheep's wool with angora rabbit hair

angostura bitters' source is Angostura, Venezuela

an **angry white male** is a political conservative

angry young man was used by a reporter in 1957 to refer to John Osborne, who wrote the play *Look Back in Anger*

anima mundi is Latin for "soul of the world"

animal companion is a euphemistic term for a pet

anon and presently originally meant "immediately" and changed to "in a while"

anorexia nervosa is an attempt to lose weight by chronically not eating

answer on a postcard refers to giving a brief answer or opinion

an **answer-jobber** is one who makes a living by writing answers

ant killers is jocular slang for the feet, especially very large feet

{ **animal crackers** were first made in the home and then by the National Biscuit Company }

before the sixteenth century, **animal functions** were those of the brain and nervous system; vital functions were the heart, lungs, and other essential organs; while natural functions involved assimilation and nutrition

in surfing, **ankle slappers** are very small waves

anything filled with neat (punched out) holes can be called an **Annie Oakley** (the Wild West sharpshooter)

in **anno Domini**, only capitalize the D (lord)

annus horribilis is Latin for dreadful year

annus mirabilis is a wonderful year

anointing of the sick is the Catholic sacrament when a priest anoints a dying person with oil and prays for salvation

an **ant lion** is not an ant or a lion; it is the larval form of the lacewing fly

ante meridiem is "before the middle of the day"

antipasto and **hors d'oeuvre** are different terms—first Italian, second French—for the same thing, appetizers or starters

antique brass is a brownish yellow color, like that of brass

antique white is a broken white color

Antoniadi scale is a scale of seeing conditions used by amateur astronomers; its categories are: I perfect, without a quiver, II slight undulations, but with calm periods lasting several seconds, III moderate, with some greater air movements, IV poor, with the image in constant movement, and V very bad, making observation difficult

from the 1920s, **ants in one's pants** is a rhyming idiom calling up a vivid image of what might cause one to be jumpy

any more if you mean "any additional"— **anymore** if you mean "nowadays" or "any longer"

an **anytime minute** is a minute of use on a cellular phone that is charged at a flat rate rather than charged according to the time of day

anyway is correct if you mean "in any case"; otherwise, use **any way**

an **Anzac biscuit** is made from wheat flour, oats, coconut, and golden syrup and named for its use by Anzac soldiers in World War I

> **A-OK** (1961) is an abbreviation of all (systems) OK, originally in the jargon of astronauts

the **aorist aspect** is a feature of the verb which denotes an action or condition that is completed and singular; an example of the aorist is the verb pair "to listen" and "to hear," with "to listen" having a continuous action and thus imperfective and "to hear" having the same meaning but being a singular, momentary, finite action and thus being aorist in aspect

an alcoholic drink before a meal is an **aperitif** or **preprandial libation**

a baby's well-being measured by the **Apgar score** looks at respiratory effort, skin color, heart rate, muscle tone, and sense of smell (named for U.S. anaesthetist Virginia Apgar)

an **apothecary chest** is a low one with lots of small drawers for holding medicines

the **Appian Way** was the road between Rome and Capua, so called because it was begun (302 B.C.E.) by the consul Appius Claudius Caecus

apple brown betty is another term for apple crisp

apple butter is not really butter but spreads like real butter and probably originated with the Pennsylvania Dutch

don't upset the **applecart** is an allusory phrase first recorded by Jeremy Belknap in *The History of New Hampshire*, 1788

apple charlotte was probably named for Queen Charlotte (1744–1818), wife of George III

apple juice is pressed, processed, and pasteurized; **apple cider** is just pressed and, strictly speaking, apple cider is redundant as cider is traditionally made from apples

the pupil of the eye was called the "apple" in earlier English because it was thought to be a solid sphere; it gives us the phrase **apple of his eye**

the earliest record of the term **apple pie** does not occur until the late sixteenth century

apple strudel is an Austrian pastry of apples, spice, raisins, etc. in phyllo pastry

apple-pie bed is a folk etymology as it's actually from French *nappe pliée*, "folded cloth" (means a bed with the sheets folded so one cannot stretch out)

apple-pie order is a corruption of French *nappes pliées*, "folded linen"

{ **apples and oranges** replaced the earlier apples and oysters }

apples to oranges denotes an unfair comparison, as between things that cannot be evaluated according to the same criteria

applied arts are arts that apply aesthetic principles to the design or decoration of useful objects—industrial design, bookmaking, illustration, printmaking, and commercial art

an **approach light** is one of a series of lights installed along the projected centerline of an airport runway to assist a pilot in aligning the aircraft during the approach to landing at night

après ski refers to recreation after skiing, as in dancing and drinking

April Fool's Day is also called All Fools' Day

an **apron piece** is the ornamental shaped portion below the seat-rail of a chair—or the underframing of tables and stands

apropos of nothing means "without any apparent reason or purpose"

aptitude tests claim to measure how much you are able to learn, and achievement tests test how much you have already learned

aqua fortis was the old name for nitric acid, literally "strong water"

Arabic numerals (0–9) are so called because they were introduced to Europe by the Arabs, who brought them from India; they did not supersede Roman numerals until the sixteenth century

arbor in **Arbor Day** is Latin for "tree"

arbor vitae, a type of evergreen shrub, was the name given by French physician and botanist Charles de l'Écluse, from Latin "tree of life"

the **Archean eon** is the first eon in Earth's history, 4.6–2.5 billion years ago

Archimedes principle is that when an object is immersed in a fluid, it has a loss in weight equal to the weight of the fluid it displaces

an **architects' scale** is a ruler with two or more faces, marked off in various scales proportional to a foot—and used for making scale drawings

the **Arctic Circle** is an imaginary ring, as is the **Antarctic Circle**, at 66 degrees north and south, respectively

the **arctic front** is the semipermanent, semicontinuous front between the deep, cold arctic air and the shallower, basically less cold polar air of northern latitudes

ardent spirits are strong alcoholic liquors made by distillation, as brandy, whiskey, or gin

Area 51 is a military base in Nevada, rumored to be where the U.S. government hides extra-planetary alien visitors

arena football is an adaptation of American football to an indoor 50-yard field

the **arithmetic mean** is a value obtained by calculating the sum of a set of quantities and then dividing that sum by the number of quantities in the set (also called average)

an **arithmetic operator** is any of the four basic operators in arithmetic: addition, subtraction, multiplication, and division

an **arithmetic progression** is a sequence in which each term is obtained by the addition of a constant number to the preceding term, as 1, 4, 7, 10, 13

American cowboys and lumberjacks called beans: **Arizona strawberries, Arkansas strawberries, Mexican strawberries,** and **prairie strawberries**

Arkansas toothpick is a bowie knife or similar mid-size pocketknife

arm candy is a companion chosen for his or her physical beauty, especially as chosen by a celebrity for attending a social event

phrases that mean just about the same things are **armchair critic, backseat driver, armchair traveler, Monday-morning quarterback**

originally **armed to the teeth** meant barely armed at all

Armistice Day is the former name of Veterans Day

with **arms akimbo** means with hands on the hips, elbows out, often in disdain

{ the term **arms race** dates to 1936, when the world was again arming itself for future conflict }

aromatic rice is any rice with an aroma and flavor like roasted nuts or popcorn, such as Basmati, Jasmine, and Texmati

on an aircraft carrier, the device that abruptly stops the landing aircraft is the **arresting gear**

the antonym of **avant garde** is **arrière garde**

the **arrow-finger** is the forefinger

arsenic hour is the time of day when both children and parents have come home but dinner has not yet been served, seen as being difficult due to everyone being tired and hungry

an **art cabinet** has a glass front, display shelves or niches, and sometimes a mirrored back for showing off ornamental items

art deco is shortened from art *decoratif,* "decorative art," from the 1925 *Exposition des arts decoratifs* in Paris

an **art horse** is the traditional art school bench used in drawing classes, usually having grooves for holding drawing boards

an **art journal** is a collection of words and images kept by an artist as a scrapbook

art mobilier is the name for small portable works of art found in archaeological or prehistoric sites

an **art movie** is a movie intended to be an artistic work rather than a commercial movie of mass appeal

art nouveau, "new art" (1901), was in and out of fashion in the 20th century and extremely popular in the late 1960s

art rupestre is the French term for prehistoric cave art

artesian well is a well in which the water is forced to the surface by natural pressures; named for Artois, a former province in northern France where such wells were common

article of faith simply means "firmly held belief"

artificial intelligence is a process of connecting programs needing the human touch with humans, such as the simple task of identifying objects in photographs, which humans can do better than computers

artificial intelligence was a concept by 1956, but AI (1971) did not take off as a field until the 1970s

artificial horizon is an instrument in an aircraft displaying a line on a flight indicator that lies within the horizontal plane and about which the pitching and banking movements of the aircraft are shown

an **artificial language** is an invented language, as opposed to a hereditary one, intended for a special use, as in international communication, a secret society, or computer programming

an **artist's dummy**, the lay figure, was first layman, from Dutch *leeman*, "joint man"

as and when means "when possible; eventually" as in "I'll be in touch with you as and when"

as easy as pie refers to the eating of pie, not the making of one

as pleased as punch refers to Mr. Punch, who is self-satisfied with his actions

as the crow flies means "by the shortest, most direct route"—but it is actually the rook, not the crow, that does this

ashtanga yoga is a form of hatha yoga based on Patanjali's Yoga Sutras and its eight stages or "limbs" and involving ujjayi breathing and a swift series of poses

Asian elephants are smaller than African elephants

asphalt jungle is the city as a place of danger

assault is an attempt or threat to do physical harm; battery is unjustified application of force; assault and battery is carrying out of threatened physical harm or violence

the term **assembly line** is recorded by 1914

assisted living is housing for the elderly or disabled that provides housekeeping, meals, and nursing care as needed

the **asteroid belt**, located between Mars and Jupiter, is also the boundary between the inner and outer planets

Asti Spumante originated in Asti, Italy

A-story is the crown or top story of the tallest trees in a jungle (there's also B-story through E-story)

astral body is an encompassing term for any star, planet, comet, or other heavenly body

at first blush refers to an earlier sense of blush, "a glimpse, momentary view," when it is a reference to the rosy light of dawn

at full chisel is synonymous with **at full tilt**

the @ is sometimes called cabbage, curl, gizmo, snail, strudel, rose, shmitshik, twist, or whirlpool—as well as **at sign** and at symbol; the American National Standards Institute has called it "commercial at" and a new, seemingly authoritative name for the ubiquitous @ is atmark.

at the drop of a hat alludes to the western frontier practice of dropping a hat as a signal for a fight to begin

at the first hop means immediately

{ **Atlantic salmon** actually belong to the trout family }

atomic bomb (1914) was a term discussed while World War I was in progress, though not built in reality until the mid-1940s (atom bomb, 1945; atomic power, 1914; atomic energy, discovered by Ernest Rutherford, 1906)

an **atomic clock** is regulated by the vibrations of an atomic or molecular system such as cesium or ammonia

an **attenuating circumstance** is an intervening event, including the passage of time, that weakens the connection between two other events

attested language is a language for which evidence has survived to the present day, either in the form of inscriptions or literature, or because the language is still spoken

an **attributive adjective** is usually directly in front of the noun, e.g. lonely planet; an adjective placed next to a noun is attributive (red sky)

an **attributive noun** is a noun used like an adjective—as in government policy or administration policy or portrait painter

au contraire can be used in place of "on the contrary"

au courant is French, literally "in the (regular) course"

au fait means one is knowledgeable or well acquainted with something specific—as a situation or set of facts

au fond is a synonym for "basically"

au gratin literally translated means "with scrapings"—which originally involved scraping dried or toasted bread from the bottom of a pan and mixing it with grated cheese

au jus, "with the juice" or "in broth," should be pronounced oh-ZHOO

au naturel is French, literally "in the natural state," originally meaning "uncooked" or "prepared without a fuss," but used euphemistically for "undressed"

au pair is from French for "on equal terms" and pertains to arrangements paid for by mutual services

an **Augean stable** is an accumulation of corruption or filth almost beyond the power of man to remedy

August ham is a jocular term for watermelon

an **aula magna** is a great hall or large classroom used for special occasions at a university

auld lang syne is a phrase that literally means "old long since" or "old long ago" and became famous in Robert Burns's 1788 song

auto-da-fé, a sentence passed by the Inquisition" (pl. autos-da-fé), is from Portuguese, "judicial sentence or act of the faith," especially the public burning of a heretic

automatic writing is that directed by a spirit or the unconscious mind—as with a **Ouija board** (*Oui* "yes" in French and *ja* "yes" in German makes the meaning "yes yes")

auxiliary verbs are be, do, have—as well as can, could, may, might, must, shall, should, will, and would

avant-garde is from French and first meant vanguard

Ave Maria is Latin for Hail Mary

Avenue of the Americas is the official name given in the 1940s to Sixth Avenue, New York, to honor the Latin American Countries

aversion therapy is teaching someone to avoid a negative behavior or changing someone's behavior by punishing them (also called **aversive conditioning**)

{ **avocado green** is a dull green resembling the flesh of the fruit }

avoirdupois, or **Imperial weight**, is commonly used to measure food, people, and merchandise

an **awareness band** or **awareness bracelet** is made of rubber or fabric on which a slogan is written, usually sold to raise awareness for charitable causes

the expression **ax to grind** originated in the days when many people still sharpened axes (nineteenth century)

Ay caramba is from Latin-American Spanish ¡ay! (interjection denoting surprise, but also used instead of "ouch") and *caramba*, lace worn on the head (euphemism for *carajo*, an exclamation of disgust in South American Spanish language)

the interjection **ay**, **chihuahua** expresses surprise or shock—even dismay, annoyance, or resignation

Aztec two-step for upset stomach and diarrhea dates only to 1953

azure stone is another name for the lapis lazuli

{ B }

B movie (1930s) was so called from being the second, or supporting, film in a double feature, but some film industry sources say it was so called for being the second of the two films major studios generally made in a year, and the one made with less headline talent and released with less promotion

baba ganoush translates to Arabic "father of coquetry" in reference to its supposed invention by a member of a royal harem

babies-in-the-eyes is a miniature reflection of oneself seen in the pupils of another's eyes

baby back ribs are the pork ribs that come from the blade and center section of the loin; the meat between the ribs is called **finger meat**

in **baby bunting**, bunting means "chubby one"

baby corn are immature ears of corn less than 3 inches long and harvested after just forty to forty-five days of growth; also called **cocktail corn**

baby grand is the smallest size of grand piano

baby talk is the way adults talk to very young children, not vice versa

baby teeth are also called **deciduous teeth**, **first teeth**, **milk teeth**, or **temporary teeth**

Bacchi plenus is a Latin synonym for "blazing drunk"

BACH motif is a sequence of four notes (B flat, A, C, B natural) included in a piece of music as a homage to Johann Sebastian Bach

bachelor girl is a dated term for a young unmarried woman, usually one who is self-supporting

a **bachelor seal** is a young male seal that has not mated

the **bachelor's button** is also called the cornflower

bachelor's degree (1362) refers to one who has taken the first or lowest degree at a university, who is not yet a master of the arts

bachelor's fare is bread and cheese and kisses

back bacon is a British term for Canadian bacon

back to square one may have originated from early board games, such as Snakes and Ladders

a **back-friend** is a pretended or false friend

back-of-the-envelope means "approximate, rough, simplified" as in "Do some back-of-the-envelope calculations before all the facts come in."

 the **back burners** on a stove are used to keep things simmering, while the **front burners** are usually the hottest and used for cooking or heating quickly

a **back channel** is a secret, indirect, or irregular means of communication, especially for sensitive government and diplomacy matters

back formations are words formed by removing suffixes from longer words that are mistakenly assumed to be derivatives, as emote from emotion

a **back issue** is a previous issue of a periodical, especially a magazine

a **back number** is a person who, like a back issue of a magazine or periodical, is no longer in demand

back of beyond originated in Australia to describe the vast interior or outback

back of the house is the kitchen and kitchen staff of a restaurant

back to basics is a U.S. catchphrase from 1975

backroom boy dates to 1941, for someone engaged in essential but unpublicized work, especially research

the white lights on the rear of a car, which turn on when the car is in reverse gear, are the **backup lights**

the term **bacteriological warfare** (1924) preceded **germ warfare** (1938) and **biological warfare** (1946)

you can remember the difference between **bactrian** and dromedary camels because B has two humps

bad egg for someone who turns out to be rotten came about only in the mid-1800s

bad hair day is now applied by either gender to a day on which nothing seems to go right

a **bad hat** is a rascal or good-for-nothing

bad juju is harmful magical power attributed to something or someone; a bad vibe or aura

badge engineering is the practice of marketing a motor vehicle under two or more brand names

bad-mouth (1941) probably ultimately came from the noun phrase bad mouth (1835) "a curse, spell," translating an idiom found in African and West Indian languages

bag and baggage originated in the 1400s and at first meant an army's property

bags of mystery is slang for "sausage"

bain marie is another term for a double boiler (two pots)

baked Alaska was created at Delmonico's to commemorate the purchase of Alaska; the French equivalent of baked Alaska is omelette à la norvégienne

baked beans' "cousin" is pork 'n' beans; in 1895, HJ Heinz first put beans with tomato sauce in a can

baked meats or **bake meats** are meat pies

{ **baked wind** is another term for hot air }

a **baker's dozen** or thirteen loaves, the extra called the in bread or vantage loaf, was to avoid a fine if the twelve were not the expected weight

a **baker's peel** is a flat, shovellike, usually hardwood implement used to move pizzas and breads in an oven; also called peel, pizza peel

baking soda is a principal ingredient in **baking powder** (with either starch or flour, etc.)

baking stone is a thick, heavy stoneware plate used to simulate the baking qualities of a brick oven; a stone first preheated on the oven floor and then upon which the item is actually baked

balance of trade is an equilibrium between the money values of the exports and imports of a country; or more commonly, the amount required on one side or the other to make such an equilibrium

a **balanced sentence** in grammar is a sentence with two clauses or phrases of fairly equal length and strength for clarity

bald in **bald eagle** means "white," not "hairless"; eagle comes from the Latin word *aquila*, "black eagle," from *aquilus*, "dark-colored," which the bald eagle is until it gets the white head plumage as an adult

bale of hay is a combination of peas, string beans, and potatoes

ball and chain dates from the early 1800s and alludes to chaining a heavy iron ball to a prisoner's leg

in a flushing toilet, the ball part inside the tank is called the **ball cock**

from the literal beginnings of **ball of wax** (something to which almost anything will stick but also a material which will retain an impression of things it contacts), it is not hard to understand the metaphoric extensions the phrase has undergone to its meaning of "all things included"

ball the jack, "hurry," originated in railway jargon in which a "highball" was a signal to get underway or increase speed, and a "jack" was a locomotive

a **ball washer** is a device found near the tee of some golf holes on a golf course, used for cleaning dirt off of golf balls

a **balloon glass** is a large, rounded drinking glass for brandy, etc.

in a comic's speech balloon, the point is the **balloon pointer**

ballpark figure relates to the practice of estimating attendance at a baseball game

balsamic vinaigrette is an oil-based dressing made with balsamic vinegar, a dark sweet liquid aged in wooden barrels

the **Baltic Sea**'s name is from Latin *Balticus*, either from Lithuanian *baltas*, "white," or Scandinavian *balta*, "straight"

a **Baltimore Chop** in baseball is a ball hit just in front of the plate and bouncing high enough to allow the runner to make it to first base

a **Baltimore wrench** is the use of a chisel and hammer to do something

in golf, a **banana ball** is a sliced ball that travels on a long arc

banana belt is any region with a relatively warm climate; a tropical region

a **banana clip** is a large, curved hair clip

in soccer, a **banana kick** is one that is off-center, making the ball curve or bend in flight before suddenly dropping

banana oil, "hogwash, nonsense," may be a variation on **snake oil**, a term for quack medicine that was extended to mean nonsense; bananas produce no commercial oil and banana oil comes from amyl alcohol, not bananas

banana paper is paper made from part of the stem of the banana plant, or paper made from banana fiber

to have one foot on the **banana peel** means to be severely ill or slipping toward death

a **banana republic** is a small Central American country dependent on one crop or foreign capital

the **banana seat** of a bicycle is tapered at the front and curves upward at the back

banana skin is a term for "a cause of upset or humiliation"

a **banana split** is so named for the split banana

banana-peel variety means broad farce

bananas Foster is a dessert of lengthwise-sliced bananas sauteed in rum, banana liqueur, and brown sugar and served with vanilla ice cream

{ **bangers and mash** is sausage and mashed potatoes }

a **banjo hit** is an 1800s baseball term meaning a weakly hit fly ball which just goes over the infielders

a **banjo hitter** is a baseball batter who lacks power, usually hits bloop singles, and has a low batting average

banoffi pie (or banoffee) is a blend of banana and toffee—its two main ingredients

banyan trees were named for the merchants (banians) who sold their wares beneath them; these trees can cover an area large enough to shade thousands of people

the **baobab tree** is so thick (up to 30 feet across) that some African tribes hollow them so families can live inside

baptism of fire first meant the grace of the Holy Spirit imparted through baptism, as distinguished from the sacrament or rite

the **baptismal name** is the name that precedes a person's family name, especially the first name—given during a Christian baptism

a **bar code** includes code terms for the country of manufacture, the manufacturer, and the type of product—a combination specific enough to ordinarily identify any product

a **bar cookie** is a type of cookie made by baking batter in a sheet pan, then cutting it into bars or squares

bar mitzvah is for a boy; *bat* or *bas* mitzvah for a girl

the two small rubber rollers on the bar over a typewriter roller (the paper bail) are the **bar rolls**

bar sinister is a popular and erroneous term for bend sinister—a broad diagonal stripe on a shield and a supposed sign of bastardy

a **barani roll** is a difficult one-and-a-half rotation twist in the air in gymnastics

barbecue mode or **barbecue maneuver** is the rotation of a spacecraft to allow the heat of the sun to fall on all sides

the **Barbie doll** (1959) was named for the creator's daughter, Barbara

{ **barking squirrel** is another name for the prairie dog }

barking up the wrong tree comes from nineteenth century raccoon hunting, where dogs were used to chase the varmints up a tree

the **Barnum effect** is the tendency to accept certain vague or worthless information as true, such as character assessments, horoscopes, or exaggerated claims

baroque music is a genre of classical music of c. 1600–1750, which included composers such as Bach, Handel, and Vivaldi and has a heavy use of counterpoint and polyphony, conveyed drama, and elaborate ornamentation

barrel of laughs has a connection to beer barrels, conducive to merriment

a **barrel vault** is the simplest type—a continuous vault, typically semicircular in cross-section

monkeys are usually a source of merriment, so if one had a **barrelful of monkeys**, one supposes this to be quite hilarious; a group of monkeys is actually called a troop

a **barrier beach** is a narrow ridge of sand or pebbles bordering a shoreline

a **barrier reef** is a coral reef running parallel to the shore but separated from it by a channel of deep water

the **Bartlett pear** was not developed by Enoch Bartlett (1779–1860) but promoted and distributed by him

baryonic matter is the "ordinary" matter of our universe—protons and neutrons, collectively called baryons

a **bas bleu** is a learned woman; also called a **femme savante**

basal means "belonging to the bottom layer"; therefore, **basal cells** are the innermost layer of the epidermis and the basal metabolic rate is that of the body at rest (0) which keeps vital functions going

a **bascule bridge** operates like a seesaw

base ball is the 1800s spelling of baseball

a **BASE jump** is from a building, antenna tower, span, or earth

a **base metal** is one considered precious—like copper, tin, or zinc—or any one of the metals—as iron, lead, etc.—that are readily tarnished or oxidized, in contrast with the noble metals

baseball stadiums were first called ballparks around 1900; before then they were called ball grounds, baseball grounds, ball fields, and baseball parks

Basic English is 850 selected words intended for international communication

{ **basket case** was originally slang denoting a soldier who had lost all four limbs, thus unable to move independently }

as smiling as a **basket of chips** means showing great happiness

basmati rice literally means fragrant rice (Hindi)

bas-relief (1667) is from Italian *basso-rilievo*, "low relief, raised work"

the large drum in a set is the **bass drum**

basset hound is from French—basset is a diminutive of bas "low," from Latin *bassus*, "short"

bat in **bat an eyelid** is derived from the now obsolete bate, "to beat the wings" or "to flutter"

bat one's eyes alludes to a term from falconry, the action of a hawk rapidly beating its wings

bat wings are the flabby underside of the upper arms

the expression **bated breath** is based on bate, meaning "to moderate, restrain" or "to lessen, diminish"; though bated was once rather common, it is now rare except in this set expression

bathtub gin (1930) is homemade gin, especially that made illegally

in **bats in the belfry**, belfry is the human head

batten down the hatches derives from a time when tarpaulins were fastened with battens (strips of wood) over a ship's hatches before a storm

batter bread (also **egg bread**, **spoon bread**) is cornbread made with eggs and milk

the top of a (snare) drum is called the **batter head**

batterie de cuisine is another way to describe pots, pans, and utensils used in cooking

battery acid is an epithet for bad or cheap wine, bad coffee, etc.

battle axe was originally meant as a rallying or war cry

battle honors refers to the names of battles and actions in which a warship (or a previous namesake) has taken part, usually displayed on a board in a prominent position

in the vocabulary of cockfighting, a **battle royal** was a contest in which a number of gamecocks were put in the pit to fight at the same time until only one remained

battleship gray is a medium grey color tinted with blue, like that of a battleship

a **balustrade** is a railing held up by balusters; a **banister** is a handrail held up by balusters; the post at the top or bottom is the **newel** or **newel post**

bawdy house is an old term for brothel

bay window comes from French, meaning "gape, stand open" as such a window has an outward projection

Bayonne ham is a mild, smoked boneless French ham that is cured in wine and similar to prosciutto; also called jambon Bayonne

BB guns have ball-bearing pellets, hence the name

bean counter, for an accountant, only dates to 1975

bean curd is another name for tofu

bean time is time for the evening meal, dinner

a **bean-feast** started as an annual dinner given by employers for their workers—either from the serving of beans or a bean goose

a **bear claw** is a large, sweet pastry shaped like a bear's paw

a **bearing** or load-bearing wall is one that holds the weight of a ceiling, floor, or roof above it

hunters had beaters beat bushes to startle game birds into the air so they could be shot, giving us the phrase **beat about/around the bush**

the term **Beat Generation**, coined by Jack Kerouac in the 1950s, came from beatitude according to him

to **beat the band** is based on the idea of making more noise than the band

it is likely that the slang expression **beat the rap** originated in another expression, take the rap, in which rap is slang for "punishment"

to **beat the tar out of** may first have literally meant to beat a sheep's side to remove tar which was put there to heal a cut or sore from shearing

the part of a vacuum cleaner that rotates to move dust and dirt into the vacuum is the **beater bar**

Beau Brummel refers to an extremely or excessively well-dressed man

beau geste is French, literally "splendid gesture"

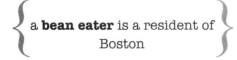

a **bean eater** is a resident of Boston

beau ideal is the conception of perfect beauty or a model of excellence

beau monde is a seasoning spice that adds a hint of onion and celery to a dish

the **Beaufort scale** was named for Sir Francis Beaufort, the naval hydrographer who devised this wind speed scale

Beaujolais Nouveau is a dry, fruity, light red wine bottled right after fermentation without aging

beautiful people first referred to the colorfully dressed hippies of the 1960s

beauty contest (1899) begat **beauty queen** (1922)

the terms **beauty shop** and **beauty parlor** originated in the United States around 1901 and the synonym **beauty salon** came in around 1922

beauty sleep was first defined as sleep taken before midnight, regarded as the most refreshing portion

because it's there was the reply given in 1923 by George Mallory

the dark green cloth of a pool table is the **bed cloth** or felt

bed clothes usually refers to blankets and sheets, while **night clothes** is pajamas and gowns

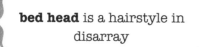

bed head is a hairstyle in disarray

a **bed push** is a fund-raising event, sometimes run by hospitals, where a wheeled bed is pushed through the streets to raise awareness of the campaign

a **bed skirt** is a decorative covering that is placed under a mattress and hangs to the floor, especially hiding what is under the bed

bee bread is a term for pollen collected by bees as food for their young

beef jerky and **jerked beef** come from Spanish *charqui*, which Spanish borrowed from Quechua *c'arqui*; nothing is "jerked" in the preparation of the dried meat, as folk etymology sometimes assumes

beef on weck is a sandwich made of beef in a hard roll covered with grains of salt and caraway seed

beef Stroganoff is named for nineteenth-century Russian Count Paul Stroganoff

beef Wellington, a filet enclosed in pastry, was named for the Duke of Wellington

beer and sandwiches means "informal negotiations"

beer cheese is a soft, ripe German cheese with a sharp flavor like Limburger; also called Bierkäse

beer goggles is the condition of excess beer making people look more attractive than they are

a **beer nut** is a peanut served with its husk but not its shell

bee's knees once existed in the more ribald version bee's nuts, and bee's knee was used from 1797 for "something insignificant"

the strict meaning of **beg the question** is to base a conclusion on an assumption that is as much in need of proof or demonstration as the conclusion itself (the formal name is *petitio principii*)

the phrase **beggar description** derives from Shakespeare's *Antony and Cleopatra*

bell, book, and candle describes the instruments formerly used in the ceremony of excommunication from the Roman Catholic Church: a bell was rung, the book was closed, and the candle was extinguished

a **bell pepper** is also known as a sweet pepper

to **bell the cat** is to undertake a dangerous mission

the **belladonna lily** is also known as the amaryllis

dust and dirt that accumulate under furniture due to negligence is **beggars' velvet**

in basketball, **behind the arc** means a shot or occurrence outside the three-point line

behind the eight ball derives from the pool game where one is penalized if another ball touches the eight ball

in boxing, **being on one's bicycle** is constantly moving around the ring to avoid the opponent

bel canto (1894) is Italian for "fine song"

the rare person who has a fine, cultivated mind, social grace, and brilliant wit is a **bel esprit**

bel paese is a type of mild, creamy cheese, an Italian proprietary name, literally "beautiful country or region"

Belle Époque (fine period) is the time before World War I

belles-lettres, "elegant or pure literature, aesthetics," dates to 1710, from French meaning "fine letters"

bell-penny is money one saves for his/her own funeral

bells and whistles is an allusion to a fairground organ with lots of bells and whistles

bellysinkers, doorknobs, and **burl cakes** are nicknames for doughnuts

below stairs is a synonym for basement

belt and suspenders means "having several layers of protection" or "redundant or overly cautious"

bench tolerance is a baker's term for the property of dough that allows it to ferment at a rate slow enough to prevent overfermentation while it is being made up into bread on the bench

to **bend one's elbow** means to drink liquor (1937)

the **benthic realm** is the sea bottom and all the creatures that live on or within it

bento box is a partitioned, lacquered, or decorated box made of wood or other material in which a meal consisting of various types of Asian food (bento) is served; also called obento

icebergs often break apart to form smaller, separate bergs called **bergy bits** or **bitty bergs**

beri-beri (1703), a paralytic disease prevalent in much of India, is an intensifying reduplication of Sinhalese **beri,** "weakness"

Bermuda green is a pale, slightly blue shade of green

Bermuda onions originated in the Bermuda Islands

Bert and Ernie is a term used to describe two inseparable friends whose personalities are vastly different—from the Muppet characters on the television series *Sesame Street*

ancients believed that under great emotional stress, the soul would actually leave the body, and a person would be **beside himself**

the expression **beside the point** is from ancient archery and literally means one's shot is wide of the target

the **Bessemer process** is named for engineer and inventor Sir Harry Bessemer (1813–98), who invented it; it is the process for decarbonizing and desiliconizing pig iron by passing air through the molten metal

best bib and tucker refers to the sixteenth century bib-front of a man's shirt and a woman's tucker, a piece of fine lace or muslin tucked around the neck of a dress

the **best boy** is the first assistant to the chief electrician (gaffer) on a film set

best man originated in Scotland where the groom kidnapped his bride with the aid of friends, including the toughest and bravest—the best man

beta waves are comparatively high-frequency electrical waves in the brain of a human who is awake and active

a **bête blanche** is a slight cause of aversion or a minor annoyance

bête noire translates from French to "black beast" and means "the bane of someone's life" or "pet aversion"

originally, **better half** had no hint of male chauvinism, applying to a husband as well as a wife and meant seriously

between a rock and a hard place "a predicament when one is forced to choose between two equally undesirable or dangerous alternatives," seems to be a paraphrase of the classical expression "between Scylla and Charybdis," a huge rock and a perilous whirlpool in the *Odyssey*

between grass and hay is the period between adolescence and adulthood

between hawk and buzzard means "very anxious"

between Scylla and Charybdis is like saying between a rock and a hard place

between the jigs and the reels is a phrase for "during odd times"

beware Greeks bearing gifts is an allusion to the famous Greek gift of the Trojan horse

the Normans fenced off their possessions with pales or stacks and pale became the territory or district under a particular jurisdiction; hence, the phrase **beyond the pale** being an anathema to society

B-girl (1936) is an abbreviation of bar girl, U.S. slang for a woman paid to encourage customers at a bar to buy her drinks

the **Bhagavad Gita** is a dialogue between Krishna and Arjuna inserted in Mahabharata, from Sanskrit, literally "Song of the Sublime One," from Bhaga, a god of wealth, and *gita*, "song"

a **bib necklace** is one consisting of three or more rows

the **bib nozzle**, **sill cock** (or bibcock) is an outside faucet on a house

Bibb lettuce was developed by nineteenth century amateur gardener John Bibb in his Kentucky backyard

bichon frise is from French *barbichon*, "little water spaniel," and *frise*, "curly-haired"

bide one's time is based on abide, meaning "remain" or "to wait awhile"

the term **Big Apple** was adopted in 1971 as the theme of an official advertising campaign to lure tourists back to New York City; horse-racing journalist John Fitzgerald used it in the 1920s and jazz musicians used the term after that

a **big band** has to have at least fourteen different instruments

big bang was first described by Fred Hoyle in 1950

Big Ben is not the clock in the tower of the Houses of Parliament but the bell itself

George Orwell coined **Big Brother** in 1949

big business is a term of U.S. origin, by 1905

big cheese is an Americanism derived from the British expression, the cheese meaning "the correct thing; the best"

the **Big Crunch** in astronomy is a hypothetical state of extremely high density and temperature into which a closed universe will recollapse in the distant future, a reversal of the big bang in which the current expansion stops, reverses, and results in all space and all matter collapsing together

the **big dance** refers to an important event characterized by a time of buildup or preparation

Big Dipper is the name for the seven-star asterism (known in England as Charles's Wain) in the constellation Ursa Major, first attested 1869

Big Drink was a term for any large body of water, including the Mississippi, which is more commonly called the **Big Ditch** or **Big Water**; **Big Muddy** is the Missouri River, and the **Big Pond** is the Atlantic Ocean

Big Mac (1970) is a proprietary name registered in the United States in 1973 but claimed by McDonald's as theirs since

pool or pocket billiards—with eight ball and snooker being forms of pool

a **binary relation** is a relation, such as "is less than" or "is the daughter of," that makes statements about pairs of objects, these statements being true or false depending on the objects

big kahuna originally meant "priest" or "wise man"

1957; it is two all-beef hamburger patties, special sauce, lettuce, cheese, pickles, and onion on a sesame seed bun

the **big rip** is one hypothetical end of the universe in which it expands at an increasing rate until all matter is torn apart

big voice is a public address and siren system used for warnings

bigging it means someone's exaggerating

Bikram yoga is a style of hatha yoga developed by Bikram Choudhury, comprised of twenty-six poses and two breathing exercises done in a room heated to 95–105°F

bill of health was first a document given to the master of a ship by the consul of the port in order to certify that when the ship sailed there were no infectious diseases on-board

billet-doux, "love letter," is from French, literally "sweet note"

billiards is from French billard "cue" or "bent stick" or "stick to push balls"; billiards is the general name; Americans mainly play

binary stars are two stars revolving around a common center of mass

the **Bing cherry** was developed in 1875 by a Chinese man named Bing in Oregon

the **binomial name** is the name of an organism in two parts, the genus and species, e.g., Homo sapiens

bipolar disorder has replaced the term manic depression

a **bird strike** is a collision between a flying bird(s) and an aircraft

bird's nest soup is a spicy Chinese soup considered a luxury, made from the outer part of the nests of a certain genus of swift

birth control as a term was recorded by 1914; **family planning**, 1931

birthday cards first appeared in 1902

in probability theory, the **birthday paradox** states that in a group of twenty-three (or more) randomly chosen people, there is more than 50 percent probability that some pair of them will have the same birthday

a **biscuit cough** is caused by mere irritation or a tickle in the throat

a **biscuit shooter** is a waitress at a lunch counter or a cook on a ranch

bisque firing is the first firing of a ceramic, and **glost fire** is the second firing

the name of the day that is added during a leap year is **bissextile day**; a **bissextile month** is a month with an extra day in a leap year (February)

bitch switch is an informal term for a power button that does not immediately cut the power to a computer, but must instead be depressed continuously for five seconds before the computer powers off

bite the bullet was probably a military expression literally stemming from the practice of giving a wounded soldier a lead bullet to clench his teeth on when there was no anesthetic

bite the dust is a literal translation of a line found in Homer's *Iliad*

{ **bitter cold** is an age-old set phrase in which bitter functions adverbially }

bitter end comes from the timber to which the anchor rope or chain of early sailing ships was fastened (the bitt); the anchor was left out as far as the rope/chain would go, that was the bitter end

a **black and tan** is a blend of dark and pale beers, as pilsner and porter

black bottom pie is a pie shell made from chocolate cookies and filled with dark chocolate custard and topped with rum custard

the **black box**, an aircraft's flight data recorder, is usually orange, not black

a **black cow** is a root beer float containing chocolate ice cream; it is also called a **mud fizz**

Black Death is the modern name for the bubonic/pneumonic plague epidemic of 1347–51 in Europe; introduced in England (1823) by Elizabeth Penrose's history of England and the exact sense of "black" is not clear

coal is **black diamonds** (diamonds and coal are forms of carbon)

black dog is a metaphor for depression or melancholy

a circumorbital haematoma is a **black eye**

Black Forest ham is a smoked boneless German ham with blackened skin and a light smoky flavor

Black Friday is the Friday after Thanksgiving, when crazy Christmas shopping ensues

black gold is slang for "oil" or "petroleum"

the scientific term **black hole** did not become part of the language until 1968, probably somewhat inspired by the 1756 incident the Black Hole of Calcutta; we misuse black hole colloquially (as an absence) just as we misuse quantum leap, but only physicists are likely to be upset

black ice is thin, hard ice, especially transparent or invisible on a road surface

black magic is a translation of Latin *nigromantia*, "corpse conjuring"

Black Maria for police car came from a black woman, Maria Lee, who helped police in escorting her drunk or disorderly boarding house customers to jail

black market was coined around 1931 but didn't come into full use until World War II

black out "to extinguish or conceal lights as an air-raid precaution" existed by 1919 (the noun blackout, 1935)

black sheep have the connotation of being bad from their wool being harder to dye

black tea is fully fermented before drying

black tie is black bow tie with a tuxedo and means semiformal evening dress

a spell of warm sunny weather in late September/early October is **blackberry summer**

BlackBerry thumb is a musculoskeletal disorder from repeated BlackBerry or PDA use, with pain and tenderness at the thumb base restricting use and dexterity of the thumbs

a **blackberry winter** is a cool May when blackberries bloom

blackboard bold is a typeface used for representing bold characters, mainly used in mathematical texts, that allows these characters to be easily distinguished from non-bold characters when written

{ **black-coated worker** is a humorous name for a prune }

black-collar pertains to employment in the black market, engagement in illicit trade or distribution of untaxed goods and services

black-eyed peas are so named for their black hilum (scar where it attaches to ovule) and they go by many other names: crowders, black bean, black-eyed bean, black-eyed susan, bung belly, China bean, cow bean, cream pea—but they are not "peas," they are "beans"

a **blank cartridge** is one with powder only—no ball, bullet, or shot

blank verse is verse without rhyme

blaze a trail originally referred to markings a trail by chipping part of the bark off a tree—the resulting bare wood being the "blaze"

the **bleeding edge** is the forefront of a technological development

a **blind alley** is blind because it has no "eye" or passage through it

blind as a bat is a simile based on the erroneous idea that the bat's erratic flight means it cannot see properly, and this phrase has survived even though it is now known that bats have a sophisticated built-in sonar system

blind baking is cooking a pie crust or pastry shell before adding the filling; this is also called **baking empty**

blind copy is a copy of a document sent to a third party, with no evidence to the original correspondent that it was sent to a third party

the Greek statue for justice is wearing a blindfold so she cannot see the bribes being offered to her, hence **blind justice**

the **blind leading the blind** first appeared in the Bible's Matthew 15:14

blind spot can refer to the point in the retina of the eye where the optic nerve enters, and which is insensitive to light

a **blind stitch** is a sewing stitch that is visible on one side only

blindman's bluff was originally blindman's buff, as in "a blow"

blindman's dinner is a dinner unpaid for

{
a package with the merchandise displayed in a plastic bubble(s) is a **blister pack**
}

a **blob-tale** or **ong-tongue** is a tattletale or gossip

block capitals or block letters are letters printed or written separately and without serifs (plain)

a **blonde moment** is an instance of being silly or scatterbrained

blood pudding is a black sausage containing pig's blood and other ingredients

the **Bloody Mary** is named for Mary Tudor, the English queen (Queen Mary I) remembered for her bloody persecution of Protestants; it was called the Red Snapper before it came to New York from Paris

the end of the banana that attaches to others in the bunch is the **blossom end**

blow hot and cold comes from one of Aesop's fables

blue blood is a translation of the Spanish *sangre azul* attributed to some of the oldest and proudest families of Castile, who claimed never to have been contaminated by Moorish, Jewish, or other foreign admixture; the expression probably originated in the blueness of the veins of people of fair complexion as compared with those of dark skin

the first appearance of **blue chip** in relation to stocks occurred after the 1929 stock crash (Black Tuesday)

blue collar is physical labor, and blue workshirts are supposedly characteristic wear

in a boxing match, there is a **blue corner** and a **red corner**

a **blue heeler** is an Australian blue cattle dog breed

blue ice is the clean, compact, and vividly blue ice formed in glaciers (and on the surface of some lakes and seas) by the recrystallization of snow

the **blue jay** inspired the name of jay for "country folk" and later the word "jaywalk"

blue laws comes from the color of paper used for writing down strict colonial New England laws which restricted or banned certain behaviors

a **blue moon** is one of two full moons in a month

the name **blue movie** is derived from the custom of Chinese brothels being painted blue

blue plates divided into compartments were once used for fixed-price restaurant meals; now **blue plate** means "pertaining to a full restaurant meal ordered as a single item, often as a special of the day"

blue sky laws are laws protecting the public from securities fraud

the **blues scale** in music generally consists of tonic, major second, minor third, fourth, fifth, major sixth, and minor seventh, in which notes, particularly the third, fourth, and fifth may be bent

blue-sky thinking is original or creative thinking, unfettered by convention

B'nai B'rith is a Jewish fraternal organization founded in New York City in 1843, from Hebrew "Sons of the Covenant"

bo or **bodhi tree** comes from Sanskrit words *budh*, "understand thoroughly," and *gaha*, "tree"—the Buddha's enlightenment having occurred under such a tree

the term **boat people** was originally applied (1977) to refugees from Vietnam and other Southeast Asian countries

Bobbsey twins is a facetious name for two people who are often seen together and look or act alike

bobby pins got their name because originally they were used with bobbed hair

bobby socks are so called because they are short like a bob hairstyle; **bobcat** got its name because of its short tail

a **bob-house** is a small mobile shack used on frozen lakes for ice-fishing

body art is when the artist's own body is the medium

body language (1966) is apparently a translation of French language *corporel*

body odor and B.O. are first recorded in print in 1933

boeuf bourguignon translates to Burgundy beef

a **boiling point** is technically the temperature at which a liquid's vapor pressure equals external pressure

bois clair is another term for unstained and unvarnished wood

> **bok choy** is Chinese for "white vegetable" and is also called Chinese cabbage

in **bold relief** means is giving the appearance of standing out from the background

boll weevil is from Old English *wifel*, "beetle," and boll, the pod of the cotton plant, which this beetle attacks

bolo tie (1960s) is a necktie of thin cord fastened in front with an ornamental clasp or other device

bolt bucket is slang for a machine, especially an automobile, that is clunky or unreliable

bon mot is used to mean "clever or witty remark" and has the plural *bons mots*

a **bon vivant** is a person who lives well, a companionable type who enjoys good wine and fine food

bona fide, pronounced BO-nuh-fide, is Latin for "in good faith"

bond paper is a superior quality of strong, durable white writing paper

bone china is fine porcelain that contains bone ash

bookkeeper is the only English word with three consecutive repeated letters (not including its other forms) in which omission of the medial hyphen is a practical option, which it is not in, for example, hoof-footed or sweet-toothed

boomerang kid is any young person past high-school age who returns home to live after college or a period of independence; also called boomeranger

{ **Bombay duck** is a fish, not fowl, and its name refers to its being easy to catch during monsoon season }

bone of contention originated in the sixteenth century, relating to two dogs fighting over a bone

a **bone orchard** is a graveyard

to **bone up on** suggests a "stiffening" of one's knowledge as a piece of whalebone strengthens a corset

boo-boo, "mistake" (1954), is apparently a reduplication of boob, which had acquired a secondary sense of "foolish mistake"

booby hatch was first a kind of wooden hood over a hatch, readily removable

booby prize comes from German *bubenpries*, "boy's prize"

the **book award** in law school is an award or recognition for receiving the highest grade in a class (traditionally an actual book, but recently more likely a letter or certificate acknowledging the achievement)

boon companion means "good convivial" (from French *bon*, "good")

the nicknames for states are also called **booster names** (as on license plates)

boot camp (1944) is from Marine inductees being called "Boots" and the Marine Corps custom to send them all through this grim process

boo-yah (or boo-ya, c. 1990) is an exclamation used to express extreme pleasure, approval, etc.; also written booya, boo-yaa, booh-yeah, booyah

Border collies originated near the border between England and Scotland

born with a wooden ladle in one's mouth means "unlucky"

any place, as along a highway, where soil has been dug and borrowed, is a **borrow pit** indirect illumination—as from another room —is **borrowed light**

bossa nova is Portuguese for "new bump"

in diner slang, **bossy in a bowl** stands for beef stew

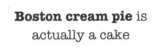

Boston cream pie is actually a cake

the **Boston Tea Party** apparently was not so called before 1864

bottle age is the time spent by a wine maturing in its bottle

the small plaque hung around the neck of a bottle or decanter, usually of silver, is a **bottle ticket**

a **bottom feeder** is one who benefits or profits from things cast off or leftover by others

bottom line is a reference to the line at the bottom of a financial statement which shows its profit or balance

the bottom of a door is the **bottom rail**

bottoms up is a drinking toast of naval origin

Botts' dots are the raised bumps that divide road lanes (named after their inventor)

bought the farm originally meant to die in an airplane crash

a **boulder train** is a line of boulders that follow the historical path of a glacier

the grassy part between a road and the sidewalk is a **boulevard strip**

we sometimes recognize words from their word shape or silhouette—called their **bouma shape**

bounced check refers to its not sticking but rather being returned to the writer of the check

a **bound form** is a meaningful linguistic element like pre- or -ing that occurs only attached to another form (which may be free or bound); a **free form** may and often does stand by itself but need not—such as under or like

boutique farmer is a specialist farmer raising one particular product for a niche market

the big handle on scissors is the **bow handle**; the smaller one is the **ring handle**

bow tie pasta is also called **farfalle**, "butterflies"

the **bowie knife** got its name from Colonel Jim Bowie (1796–1836), who used this knife designed by his blacksmith brother

bowl of red is a serving of chili

the **bowler hat** was named after English hatter William Bowler

bow-wow, imitative of a dog's barking, was first recorded in 1576

a **box cutter** is a type of hand tool consisting of a holder and a retractable razor blade; also called utility knife

names for the accordion include **box of teeth, bricklayer's piano, groan box, pleated piano, and stomach Steinway**

box office is an office in a theater for booking seats, originally "hiring a box"

a **box seat** was originally a square pew in a church or a seat on the box of a coach

a **box social** is a social event at which boxes of food are auctioned to male bidders, who win the privilege of eating and dancing with the woman who prepared the box lunch

a **box turtle**'s lower and upper shell form a closed box into which the head and legs are withdrawn

boxcar is a freight car covered with a roof and enclosed on the sides to protect its contents

boxer shorts are so named for their resemblance to those worn by boxers

Boxing Day has nothing to do with the sport but with a traditional Christmas box given to tradesmen in Britain on this day

Robert Baden-Powell founded the **Boy Scouts** in 1908

brain cloud is the temporary inability to think properly, or to remember something

brain drain is the emigration of highly trained or intelligent people from a country

brain food (1930s) is any food that is considered to aid intelligence, memory, or creativity; by extension, any intellectual sustenance

brain freeze is a sudden feeling of pain in the forehead or temples, especially when eating or drinking cold items, caused by the temporary narrowing of the arteries as a result of the rapid cooling of the hard palate; also called ice cream headache; the term brain freeze was registered by 7-Eleven in 1994—meaning that people have to pay to put it on any products and the same is true for the term three-peat, registered by basketball coach Pat Riley

brain on a stick is an intelligent person who is emotionally or socially immature or inept

a **brain trust** is a group of experts that advise a politician or government

a **brain wave** is a sudden inspiration or a happy thought

{ **brain worker** is a term for a teacher or educator }

branch water is that from a brook or stream—or ordinary water when added to alcoholic drinks

brand equity denotes all of the distinguishing qualities of a commercial brand that results in personal commitment to and demand for the brand; the intangible value-added aspect of particular goods otherwise not considered unique

the term **brand name** originated with whiskey as the producers branded their names on the barrels

brand-new has nothing to do with modern commerce, but returns to the original meaning of brand "burning wood"; brand-new was brand-new in 1570

a **Brandy Alexander** cocktail is named after Alexander the Great

the device used to measure feet for shoes is the **Brannock device** a **brass hat** is a high-ranking officer in the armed forces

brass monkey is slang for very cold weather

Aldous Huxley's **Brave New World** (1933) ultimately derives from use of this phrase in Shakespeare's *Tempest*

Brazil nuts are seeds, not nuts

bread and butter is a collective noun calling for a singular verb

a **bread and butter letter** is a letter of thanks for hospitality

bread and butter pickles may be so called because they are "basic" pickles (pickled cucumber)

bread and circuses refers to a diet of entertainment or political policies fed to the masses to keep them happy and complacent

a **bread bag** is a plastic wrapper in which a loaf of bread is sold, intended to keep the bread fresh for longer than it would be if unwrapped

bread flour is unbleached, specially formulated flour with a high level of gluten, which contributes to the structure and elasticity needed for yeast bread dough

the **bread guides** are the metal gratings for holding bread slices in place in a toaster

a **bread knife** is a long one with a serrated edge for cutting bread

bread pudding is a dessert made of bread slices, fruit, milk, eggs, sugar, and spices

in a toaster bread slot, the part that lowers and raises the bread is the **bread rack**

break camp means to pack up gear and leave a camp or campsite

break dancing was so called as it was designed to fill a break or gap in a piece of rap music

the line where a collar folds is the **break line**

{ the allusion in **break the ice** is to breaking a path in ice for a ship to pass }

break the mold refers to the artist breaking a mold so the artwork could not be replicated

breakfast of champions is coffee and a cigarette upon waking

breakfast tea is a robust blend of black tea that is more full-flavored and full-bodied than a single tea, appropriately drunk in the mornings when trying to awaken

breaking and entering is illegally going into someone else's property, even if the intruder does not literally beak anything to do it; opening an unlocked door does not change the fact that it is a crime

a person who **breaks the road** is the first to pass over it after a snowstorm

a **breech-cloth** or **Indian waist-band** was once called a **gee-string**

breeze of luck is a period of prosperity

a **brew pub** is defined as a commercial establishment that brews its own beer for sales on and off the premises and is typically combined with a restaurant

bric-a-brac (1840) is from an obsolete French phrase à bric et à brac," at random, any old way"

in Sikh and Buddhist weddings, brides and grooms are tied together with scarves or cords and in western ceremonies, the **bridal bouquet** is tied with ribbons—the knots symbolizing a bond, love, and unity

bridge mix is so called from its typically being served during card games

Bright's disease, "chronic nephritis," was so called for English physician Richard Bright (1789–1858), who in 1827 first described it

a **brilliant cut** for a diamond is two many-faceted pyramids joined at their bases with the upper one truncated near its apex

a **brilliant full cut** is a diamond with thirty-two crown facets, twenty-four pavilion (underside) facets, an octagonal table (top), and a culet (facet that is the point of the pavilion)

at a country fair, a person who successfully caught the greased pig could keep it and **bring home the bacon**; the term originated in 1909 in a Tad Dorgan cartoon

the **bristlecone pine** is also called the hickory pine, Jack pine, Cattail pine, and foxtail pine; the oldest specimen is more than eight thousand years old

Bristol board is a fine, smooth pasteboard that is sometimes glazed (named for Bristol, England)

the **British Isles** comprise Great Britain, Ireland, and about five hundred nearby smaller islands

the **British pound** got its name because it was originally equal to the value of a pound of silver

in athletics, the track and field **broad jump** was changed to the **long jump** c. 1967 because of the negative association with "broad" for a low-class woman

when something is described as **broad-spectrum**, it is effective against a wide variety of organisms, e.g., antibiotics and pesticides

Broca's area of the brain is concerned with the production of speech and was named after P. Paul Broca, a French surgeon

broccoli rabe is a leafy green vegetable with broccoli-like buds and bitter-flavored greens

in music, a **broken chord** is one in which the notes are played successively

a **broken link** is a connection in an HTML document to a URL that is not working properly, especially because it goes to a Web page that is no longer available or that has moved to another server

music played together by different families of instruments (e.g., brass and woodwinds) is **broken music** and the instruments so mixed constitute a broken consort

in football, **broken-field** describes an area where the defenders are relatively scattered

the **bronchial tree** is the branching system of bronchi and bronchioles conducting air from the windpipe into the lungs

the **Bronx Cheer** is the sound of derision made by blowing through closed lips with the tongue in between

the **Bronze Age** began in the late fourth and early third millennium BC

bare spots on the underbelly of a bird, used to warm eggs, are **brood spots**

a door is **brought home** when closed

brown ale is a type of beer characterized by its brown color and rich malty and hoppy flavor with hints of caramel

brown envelope is an anonymous-looking envelope for delivering personal or intimate information or illicit payments

brown fat is the tissue involved in rapid production of heat in hibernating animals and human babies

brown goods are electronic goods other than kitchen and laundry appliances, especially entertainment equipment; brown goods are also any brown-colored liquor, such as bourbon, brandy, and whiskey

gloomy meditation or melancholy is known as being in a **brown study**, a translation of French *sombre reverie*

brown sugar is unrefined or partially refined; brown rice is unpolished with only the husk removed

brown thumb means a lack of skill at growing plants

browned off, "fed up, disgruntled," is probably a reference to a dish that has been overcooked

Brownian movement (1871) is named for Dr. Robert Brown, who first described it

Brownie points is a U.S. saying, probably a development from brown-nose

one of the first blend words was brunch, and for a time after its introduction, all blend words were referred to as **brunch words**

Brussels sprout is a relatively new vegetable, only about four–five hundred years old; the parts of a Brussels sprout are called buds (it is Brussels sprout, not Brussel sprout; the plural is Brussels sprouts) and the French call Brussels sprouts *choux de Bruxelles,* "Brussels cabbages"

brutum fulmen is a term for "harmless thunderbolt" or an "empty threat"

bubble and squeak is cooked cabbage fried with potatoes and meat

bubble tea is a frothy Chinese drink of iced tea, milk, and flavorings and served over gummy black balls (pearls) of tapioca and is also called pearl tea, pearl milk tea, black pearl tea, tapioca tea, Boba tea, Boba milk tea

bubble wrap was originally a trademark

in the **bubonic plague** of the seventeenth century, buboes—inflamed swelling or abscesses in glandular parts of the body, especially the groin or armpits—were the main symptom

buck and file are two pickpockets operating together

buck fever is the nervousness experienced by first-time hunters when they first sight game

a **buck party**, like a **stag party**, is one without ladies

buck teeth, large front teeth protruding over the others, may be from buck, the adult male of some animals, such as rabbits—which have this type of front teeth

a **bucking kier** is a large circular boiler, or kier, used in bleaching

buckle down to work refers to a knight's being buckled into his armor before battle

Buddha nature is the true pure nature and emptiness of every being; the original nature present in all beings which when realized leads to enlightenment; also written Buddha-nature

buffalo mozzarella is a cheese made of water buffalo and cow's milk, the most prized of fresh mozzarella cheeses; also called *Mozzarella di bufala*

Buffalo wings are small deep-fried **chicken wings** cooked in spicy hot cayenne pepper sauce, so named from first being served in Anchor Bar, Buffalo, New York (1964); buffalo wings are spicy; chicken wings are not

poor quality liquor is sometimes called **bug juice**

a **bugle-beard** is a shaggy beard like buffalo hair

build a fire under may come from an action taken by mountain people to get mules to move when they refuse to budge

bulimia nervosa is binge eating followed by self-induced vomiting, purging, or fasting and is also called the **binge-purge syndrome**

bulk large is an equivalent of loom large

a **bulkie roll** is a soft, round sandwich roll

a male cook at a mining or lumber camp can be called a **bull cook**

a **bull market** has rising stock prices, which encourage buying

a **bull moose** is simply a male moose; solitary moose in North America often band together in winter and tramp the snow firm in a small area to form a **moose yard**

bull session (1920) is an informal conversation or discussion, starting out being one strictly involving males

British stock bulletins were called "bulls," and when the trading was low, they were "bare"—hence, now, **bulls and bears**

bull's-eye can refer to a hemispherical piece or thick disc of glass inserted in the side or deck of a ship, or elsewhere, to light the interior

bull-speaking is boasting language

bum rap dates to 1927

in **bum steer**, steer is used in the sense of "advice, guidance"

bumper crop is unusually large crop growth and harvest

the **bung hole** is the aperture through which beer enters a cask

the **bunny hug** was a lively ragtime-rhythm ballroom dance popular in the United States in the early twentieth century

the **Bunsen burner** was introduced by German chemist Robert Bunsen (1817–1899)

buoyancy aid is a term for a waterproof device in the form of a jacket, which stops one from sinking in water—formerly called life jacket

a **burial mound** is an elevated earthen grave

to **burn off** can mean to broadcast unaired episodes of a canceled television program

burn rate is how fast a business spends money like venture capital, in excess of income

burn the British means toasted English muffins in diner slang

a **burning bush** is an ornamental shrub bearing a crimson berry

burnt sienna is an earth color with an opaque, red-brown mass tone—made by calcining raw sienna

burnt umber is a pigment made by burning raw umber, which is changed by this process from an olive brown to a bright reddish brown

a **burp gun** is a lightweight, portable submachine gun

to **bury a story** in journalism is to place it on an inner page of a newspaper

bury the hatchet comes from Native Americans—when they smoked the calumet or peace pipe, they would bury their hatchet, scalping knives, and war clubs in the ground

bush bacon is rabbit

bush as in "wilderness" contributes to **bush league**—first used for minor league baseball teams located in the wilderness

business class is a travel class lower than first class, but higher than coach or economy class

business lunch is found as a term in American English by 1926

a **busted flush** is a person or thing that shows great promise but fails anyway

busy as a bee comes from bees being known for their industry

the end of a tennis racket is the **butt cap** (a fishing pole has one, too)

butter beans are the same as lima beans

single-serving butters are called **butter cups**

{ **buttered eggs** in Britain are scrambled eggs in America }

the **butterfly effect** describes the phenomenon whereby a minute localized change in a complex system can have large effects elsewhere—from the notion that a butterfly in Rio de Janeiro could change the weather in Chicago

in the **butterfly stroke** in swimming, both arms are raised out of the water and lifted forward together

buttermilk sky is a cloudy sky resembling the mottled appearance of buttermilk

butternut squash bears some resemblance to a nut of the butternut tree

the **butter-teeth** are the two upper middle incisors

a **button ear** is a dog ear that folds forward toward the eye and hides the inside of the ear

a **button mushroom** is a young, unopened one

the notch on the bottom edge of an iron is the **button nook**

by and large comes from the sailing expressions "by the wind" and "sailing large"—and the phrase implies a balance between two extreme positions or consideration of things in a general way

feudal rights to firewood are the source of the expression **by hook or by crook** (1380); the words actually mean about the same thing as crook refers to a staff with a hooklike end

by planets means "irregularly, capriciously"

by scissors! is a mild oath

by-child is a kinder word for illegitimate child

a name for a subordinate goal is **by-end**

{ C }

C rations, which stands for combat rations, was the canned food formerly served to U.S. soldiers

cabbage patch is a small, unimportant thing or place—like a small town

a **cabbage pounder** is an inept golfer who spends a lot of time in the rough

cabin class is the intermediate accommodation on a passenger ship

a **cabin cruiser** is a large motorboat that has a cabin and plumbing and other conveniences necessary for living on board

cable stitch is a knit done to resemble twisted rope

cabriole is a ballet jump or a leg position of a leaping animal, which is what a **cabriole leg** (of furniture) resembles

the **cacao tree** produces beans, cacao or cocoa, which are used to make chocolate (from Aztec, Nahuatl word *xocoatl*)

cacoethes loquendi is an itch for speaking, an irresistible urge to talk (*scribendi* is the counterpart for writing)

Cadmean victory is from Greek *Kadmeia nike*, "victory involving one's own ruin," from Cadmus, legendary founder of Thebes in Boeotia and bringer of the alphabet to Greece

cadmium red is a pigment used in painting, consisting of the sulfide and the selinide of cadmium, characterized by its strong red or reddish color

cadmium yellow is a bright yellow pigment containing cadmium sulfide

Caesar salad was invented by Caesar Cardini, a Tijuana, Mexico, restaurant owner

Julius Caesar was allegedly the first person delivered by **Caesarean section**

Caesar's wife is a person who is required to be above suspicion

café curtains are ones that hang from rings on a round rod

café filtre is coffee made by pouring hot water through ground coffee beans in a filter, often served black in demitasse cups

café latte (coffee-milk) is espresso poured into steamed milk; café au lait (coffee with milk) is equal parts steamed milk and strong brewed coffee (not espresso) or one-third dark roast coffee and two-thirds scalded milk

café macchiato is espresso coffee topped (marked) with teaspoons of foamed milk, often with added flavoring like caramel

café mocha is steamed chocolate with espresso poured into it, topped with a sprinkle of cocoa

café noisette (French for hazelnut) is an espresso with a little bit of hot milk—the equivalent of the Italian macchiato

café society are those who frequent fashionable restaurants and nightclubs

Cajun seasoning is a blend of seasonings that generally includes chiles and other spices such as celery, garlic, mustard, onion, and pepper

a **cake slice** is a knife with a wide, triangular, unsharpened blade, designed to cut and serve slices of cake

cakes and ale first appeared in the metaphorical sense in Shakespeare's *Twelfth Night*

a **calamari ring** is a circular slice of squid, usually one of several, deep-fried as an antipasto

a **calendar year** or **civil year** is January 1–December 31

{ a **California blanket** are newspapers used for sleeping purposes by the homeless }

California roll is a popular form of sushi made of avocado, crabmeat, carrot, and cucumber and wrapped in vinegared rice and nori (red algae)

a **California widow** is a married woman whose husband is away for extended periods

a **caliper brake** is that used on bicycles in which a pair of arms carrying brake pads move inwards and press on the rim of the wheel

to **call a spade a spade** is based on an ancient Greek expression, literally "to call a fig a fig, a trough a trough," which became another Greek word for digging tool, which was then translated to "spade"

a **call drink** is a mixed drink for which one specifies (i.e., calls) the exact brand or brands of liquor to be used; the opposite is a **well drink**

the **call number** is that on the spine of a library book that indicates its location

to **call the shots** is an allusion to the game of pool in which the player names which ball must go into which pocket—or an allusion to dice gambling

the **calla lily** has a white funnel-shaped flower with an orange spadix

cambric tea is a beverage for children containing hot water, milk, sugar, and a small amount of tea

Cambridge blue is a light bright blue

camel hair or **camel's hair** really is made from the hair of a camel—though a camel's hair artist brush is often from a squirrel's tail

a **camel's nose** is a small part of something very large, especially when difficult or unpleasant to deal with

cameo lighting is a sort of spotlight that accentuates a single person and maybe a few props in the scene

a **camera lucida** is an optical device consisting of an attachment that enables an observer to view simultaneously the image and a drawing surface for sketching it

a **camera obscura** is a darkened boxlike device in which images of external objects, received through an aperture, as with a convex lens, are exhibited in their natural colors on a surface arranged to receive them: used for sketching, exhibition purposes, etc.

can hardly is standard English; **can't hardly** is dialect

a **can of corn** in baseball is an easy fly ball, referring to the days when cans at a grocery store were tipped off high shelves with a broom handle

can of worms is based on an image of a container of maggots for use as fish bait

Canadian football is a type of football played in Canada that resembles American football but derived from rugby and is played with twelve-person teams

the **Canary Islands** are actually named for the large dogs roaming there—*canaria* in Latin, a linguistic relative of canine

the **can-can** (dance) is from French, possibly from *can*, the child word for "duck," via some notion of waddling, or *cancan* "noise, disturbance," echoic of quacking

canicular days is another term for the dog days of summer

a **canker sore** (aphthous ulcer) is inside the mouth; a **cold sore** (fever blister or herpes simplex) is outside the mouth

canned copy refers to prewritten material such as press releases, publicity releases, and features from news syndicates

canned in **canned laughter** (1904) refers to mechanically or artificially reproduced laughter

canon law is ecclesiastical law, that laid down by a church

canonical form is the simplest or most symmetrical form to which all functions of the same class can be reduced without loss of generality

the times for daily Christian prayer are the **canonical hours**—matins with lauds, prime, terce, sext, nones, vespers, and compline

the **canopic jar** used in preparing mummies is named for Canopus, a city in ancient Egypt

cap and bells is the insignia of the professional jester

a **cap nut** (hardware) is a closed nut having a domelike cap over the back, protruding part of the engaged screw or bolt

cap-à-pie is from French, literally "head to foot"

in architecture, **Cape Cod** refers to having a simple, rectangular, one-and-a-half stories of clapboard, with low central chimney and steep shingled roof

{ **Cape Cod turkey** is dried salt cod }

a **capful of wind** is a light puff of wind

capital goods are goods used in making other goods, as opposed to **consumer goods**

capital messuage describes a house together with its yard, outbuildings, and land

capital punishment is the imposition of the death penalty for crime (from Latin *caput*, "head")

capri pants were named after the island of Capri, off the western coast of Italy, and were once tight calf-length pants with slits at the bottom hem; now this name is applied to all calf-length pants

a **captain's chair** is one having a rounded back formed by a heavy rail resting upon vertical spindles and coming forward to form the arms, and the term dates to around 1945

carbon dioxide is the gas we exhale and **carbon monoxide** is the gas in car exhaust

carbon footprint is a measure of the amount of carbon dioxide produced by a person, organization, or state in a given time

carbonated water is an effervescent beverage artificially charged with carbon dioxide

card counting is a strategy in pontoon or blackjack in which a player keeps a mental tally of the cards played in order to calculate the probability of certain cards being dealt and therefore obtain an advantage

a **card shark** is a proficient, cutthroat, but honest card player—and a **cardsharp** is a swindler

a **cardinal adjective** is a cardinal number used as an adjective, e.g., one in "one meatball"

cardinal numbers are one, two, three; **ordinal numbers** are first, second, third

the four main compass points are the **cardinal points**

cardinal red is a deep scarlet, named for a religious cardinal's cassock (robe)

Plato and Aristotle said the **cardinal virtues** are justice, prudence, temperance, and fortitude

Care Bears were fictional cartoon bears created as greeting card characters by American Greetings in 1981

CARE packages were originally from the Cooperative for American Relief Everywhere

carnal knowledge is sexual intercourse, literally "knowledge of the flesh"

carnauba wax is the hardest of the vegetable waxes, obtained from the leaves of a Brazilian palm

around 1828, Mexicans living in Texas invented **carne con chili**, "meat chunks with chili"

carpal tunnel syndrome describes a compression of a nerve over the carpal (eight small bones of the wrist) bones through a passage (tunnel) at the front of the wrist

carpe diem is a quotation traced back to Horace ("Odes"), meaning "seize the day!"

carpenter bees—large solitary bees with purplish wings—bore nests into dead wood

a **carpenter's square** is a tool used in carpentry to measure out right angles and is larger than a try square

a **carpet knight** is a knight who spends his time in luxury and idleness (knighted on the carpet at court rather than on the field of battle)

the **carpet moth** is related to the clothes moth

a **carpet sweeper** is manual as compared to a **vacuum sweeper/cleaner**, which is mechanical

a **carriage clock** is so called because it is portable and was first used by travelers

{ **carriage dog** is an archaic term for a Dalmatian }

the **carriage trade** is a reference to the wealthy and socially prominent members who arrived for shopping by private carriage

carried by acclamation is passed by a shout of approval

carrot-and-stick refers to an offer of reward countered by the threat of punishment

a long time ago, a man of importance would entrust his closest subordinates with blank sheets or correspondence cards (**carte blanche**) with only his name at the bottom, for use in a crisis; carte blanche, "blank paper," had the figurative sense of "full discretionary power" from 1766

cartilaginous fish are those with skeletons of cartilage instead of bone—including rays and shark

a **case badge** is a small sticker, usually placed on the front of a personal computer, stating the name of the company who produced the personal computer

case furniture is a generic term for furniture intended to hold or store things

case grammar is a type of grammar in which the deep structure of sentences is analyzed for the semantic roles of the words and phrases

case law (1861) is the law settled by decided cases

a **casement window** has a frame containing one or more panes of glass hinged at the side, top, or bottom; a sash or **double-hung window** has two frames of one or more panes of glass that fit into grooves at the side, top, or bottom and slide past or to meet one another

if something is **case-sensitive**, then there is a different meaning or interpretation based on upper- and lower-cased letters

just as a cow goes on giving milk placidly without causing problems, so can a product go on producing profits—a **cash cow**

to **cast aspersions** is to make damaging or spiteful remarks

cast iron is an impure variety of iron, containing from 3–6 percent of carbon, part of which is united with a part of the iron, as a carbide, and the rest is uncombined, as graphite

to **cast pearls before swine** is to offer something valuable to someone who does not appreciate it

insects, like termites, actually have **caste systems**

Castile soap is named for Castile, Spain, where it was originally made

casting out nines is a procedure for checking whether additions, subtractions, and multiplications are probably correct or certainly incorrect; this method takes its name from the fact that nines may be ignored when checking an equation: Each digit in each value is added, except that nines and digits that sum to nine are discarded. When a single digit is reached for each value, the original operations are performed again. If both sides of the equation balance, the equation is deemed correct.

castor oil is the only nondrying oil that is completely miscible with alcohol

castor sugar is very finely granulated sugar that was formerly sprinkled from a castor

casus belli, "act justifying war," is Latin *casus,* "case," and *belli,* "war"

{ **cat beer** is milk }

a **cat burglar** is so called because one usually enters by extraordinarily skillful feats of climbing

a **cat flap** or **cat door** is a hinged door as part of a larger door or wall, which allows a cat to go outside and come back in without assistance

cat gut is actually the dried, twisted intestines of sheep or horses, not cats

very thin, weak ice is called **cat ice**

The **Cat in the Hat** has 220 words

in the Middle Ages, pork was thought unclean and pigs were in a poke/bag to be disguised; sometimes a cat was put in the bag and the new owner fooled—when the **cat was let out of the bag**

a **catalytic converter** is a device with a catalyst for converting pollutant gases into less harmful ones

catbird seat derives from a James Thurber short story

catch and release is a variety of angling where the fish are released after capture, as a conservation measure

Catch-22 by Joseph Heller (1962) was an anti-war satire that has become a commonly used phrase in the English language, signifying something absurdly impossible to achieve or Kafkaesque in proportion. It started out, though, as *Catch-18,* and Simon & Schuster would have published it as such had not rival publisher Doubleday stepped in. Doubleday was planning publication of best-selling author Leon Uris's *Mila 18,* and when they heard that a first novel by an unknown was coming out at the same time with a similar number title, they firmly protested. Simon & Schuster in the end acquiesced, and Heller changed his title to avoid trouble.

catchword, **guideword**, or **running head** are the word(s) at top of reference book pages

the **cathode-ray tube** was used in twentieth-century television sets and the term originated around 1905; a **cathode ray** describes a beam of electrons emitted from the cathode (negatively charged electrode) of a high-vacuum tube

Catholic twins are siblings born within twelve months of each other

cat's light is dusk or twilight

cause celebre is literally (French) "famous case"

knobby calcite growths on the walls and floors of once-submerged caves are called **cave coral** or cave popcorn

caveat is Latin for "let him beware"; **caveat emptor** being "let the buyer beware," and **caveat venditor** is "let the seller beware"

the **CE key** or clear entry key on a calculator clears the most recently entered number from the display and from memory without removing the rest of the calculation

celery seed is the seed of a plant related to the celery plant—and it has a celerylike flavor and aroma

you should write **cell phone, e-mail**, and **video game**—keeping the separation

> **cat's pajamas** and **cat's meow** for someone or something superlative are said to have been coined by the cartoonist and sportswriter Tad Dorgan

cat's paw is a pattern of ripples on a surface of water

catty-cornered (1838) is from now-obsolete cater, "to set or move diagonally"

cauliflower, collard greens, kale, and **kohlrabi** are all derived from Latin caulis, "cabbage"; **cauliflower** is, literally, "flowering cabbage"; the original English form of cauliflower was colieflorie or cale-flory

a **causative verb** causes an action and usually has the suffix "en" (brighten, shorten, tighten)

a synonym for **cement mixer** is **concrete mixer**

a **center back** is a player in the middle of the back line in a sport like volleyball

one's **center of gravity** is a point from which the weight of a body is considered to act

something can **center on** but not "center around" because center is technically a single point

the dots between syllables in a dictionary are called **center points** the **center spread** is the two facing middle pages of a newspaper or magazine

central heating as an idea dates from Roman times but the term is dated 1906

centrifugal force acts in a direction away from the center of rotation or curvature of a rotating or orbiting body; centripetal force acts toward the center of rotation or curvature

cereal grain or **cereal grass** is any plant from the grass family that yields an edible grain, such as barley, corn, oats, rice, rye, wheat

certified mail is when the sending and receiving of a letter or package are recorded

{ **cerulean blue** is a light greenish-blue pigment consisting essentially of oxides of cobalt and tin }

cha-cha, a type of Latin-American ballroom dance (1954) that evolved from the mambo, is echoic of the music

a **chadless punch** is a paper tape punch that does not produce little pieces of paper (chads)

chafing dish derives from the now obsolete sense of chafe, "become warm, warm up"

a **chain story** is a story with each section written by a different author picking up where the previous one left off

chair day is the evening of life, old and often infirm but passing time in ease and comfort

a **chair mat** is a sheet of durable, smooth material that is placed on a floor space occupied by a chair typically equipped with casters to prevent undue wear and reduce static on carpet

chair post is another way to say leg of a chair

a **chair rail** is a piece of molding attached to a wall, usually separating the dado or wainscot from the upper wall, which is used to prevent chair backs from damaging the wall

chaise longue is pronounced SHAYZ-LONG

chamber music was a type of music especially designed for performance in a private room as distinguished from a large space, us a church

a **chamber orchestra** is eighteen to forty members, while a **symphony orchestra** is sixty five to ninety musicians

a **chamber pot** is a bowl (pot) kept in the bedroom (chamber) and used as a toilet, especially at night

a **champagne socialist** advocates socialist beliefs while consuming the best things in life

champit tatties is Scottish for mashed potatoes

Chanel No. 5 perfume is made from ylang-ylang from the Comoro Islands, jasmine from Grasse in the south of France, and May rose

Chantilly lace is named for a town near Paris

Chapter 11 is named after the U.S. bankruptcy code 11; **chapter 11** is a form of bankruptcy that involves a reorganization of a debtor's business affairs and assets; it is generally filed by corporations which require time to restructure their debts

> **chapter and verse**
> originally referred to the
> Bible as a precise authority

the **chapter of accidents** is any series of unpredictable events that greatly influences the life of each of us—things, for example, that if they had not happened, one might not exist

character actors specialize in portraying eccentric or unusual people

a **charitable word** is one that remains a word when one of its letters is removed (like "seat")

Charley horse is a common name for an old horse, especially one afflicted with stiffness

charm bracelets were first thought to protect the wearer on the one hand and attract admirers on the other

a **charnel** (from Latin *carnale*, "flesh") is a burial place or cemetery, not a place where bones are burned; a **charnel house** is a building for burials

chartered plane is correct, not charter plane

chasseur sauce is made from mushrooms, white wine, and butter

a **chatter mark** is a mark left on a surface by a tool

the **chattering classes** denote educated people with liberal opinions and attitudes

che sarà, sarà is Italian for "what will be, will be"

a **check box** in computing is an element or widget of a graphical user interface corresponding to a small square on a paper form that is either left blank or ticked; ticking the box enables the function with which it is labeled

check minus is an acknowledgment that a school assignment, such as a paper, was completed but is not satisfactory

check out the plumbing is a euphemism for "go to the toilet"

checkered flag figuratively means victory in a race

Cheddar cheese originated in the town of Cheddar Gorge, England

cheek by jowl is "in close intimacy" or "side by side"

cheeping-merry is being half-drunk

cheerful robots are those people who accept their place and status in society, no matter how lowly, without complaint

cheese steak is an American sandwich of sautéed beef and onions with melted cheese in an Italian or French hard roll; also called Philadelphia cheese steak

cheese straws are strips of pastry, sometimes twisted, topped with cheese and baked until crisp

cheesed off, "fed up," may not come from cheese in the regular sense (the souring that occurs in cheesemaking) but from nineteenth-century thieves' slang, where cheese meant "stop," and **cheese it** still means "stop what you're doing"

chef d'oeuvre is French, literally "chief (piece) of work"—a masterpiece

chenin blanc is named for Mont-Chenin in Touraine, France

cherchez la femme, literally "seek the woman," is based on the notion that a woman is the cause for whatever crime has been committed, first used by Alexandre Dumas père in "Les Mohicans de Paris" (1864)

a **cherry tomato** is orb-shaped and about one inch in diameter; a **grape tomato** is grape-shaped, red, and 1/2–3/4" long

chess pie is a pastry shell filled with a mix of eggs, sugar, butter, some flour or corn-meal, and various flavorings, a southern U.S. specialty that becomes dense when baked, with a crisp top

a **chest freezer** has a lid that opens from the top rather than front-opening

the **cheval de bataille** is a "favorite subject" or "favorite argument"

a tall mirror swung on an upright frame is a **cheval glass** and takes its name from French *cheval*, "horse"—a synonym for "supporting framework"—which describes this mirror

to **chew the carpet** is to lose emotional control

to **chew the fat** is to argue a point—with the allusion to mouth movements when trying to chew through fat; chew the fat dates to

1885 and originally meant "to grumble or complain," while the sense of idle conversation is only from 1907

{ **chewing gum** originated in the United States in the middle of the nineteenth century }

Chia Pets take their name from the chia plant seeds that come with the figurines; chia is a member of the sage family and it grows only in porous surfaces with an abundant water supply

Chicago-style pizza means it has a thick crust

chicken à la king was said to be named after E. Clark King, proprietor of a hotel in New York

In Herbert Hoover's 1928 presidential campaign, he used slogans including terms like "full dinner pail" and "full garage," but Hoover never promised a **chicken in every pot**; the phrase has its origins in seventeenth-century France with Henry IV saying that peasants would enjoy "a chicken in his pot every Sunday." Although Hoover never uttered the phrase, the Republican Party did use it in a 1928 campaign advertisement touting a period of "Republican prosperity" that had provided a chicken in every pot. And a car in every backyard, to boot.

chicken Kiev was originally chicken cutlet Kiev, "cutlets in the Kiev manner"

a **Chicken Little** is a pessimist/alarmist (after the children's tale)

chicken-flutter is undue excitement

chicken-fried steak is thin tenderized steak dipped in batter and fried like chicken, served with country gravy

chicken-pecked is being under the rule of a child, as hen-pecked is under the rule of a woman

chick-pea is a false singular back-formation from chich-pease (1548), from French *pois chiche*

chiles rellenos (stuffed chile pepper) is a Mexican dish of mild green chiles filled with cheese, dipped in batter, and fried

for the name of the fiery vegetable, the U.S. spelling is **chili** (plural chilis) while the British spelling is **chilli** (plural chillies); the name of the Mexican dish is **chili con carne** (United States and United Kingdom), which is literally (Spanish) "chili pepper with meat;" guesses at the etymology include that it comes from an Aztec word meaning "bowl of red" or derives from a Nahuatl word meaning "sharp, pointed"

chili peppers are no relation to the condiment pepper

to **chili-dip** is to swing a golf club, hitting the ground before hitting the ball

the **chimney pot** is the topmost part of the chimney and is covered by a piece of metal

the **chimney stack** is the part of a chimney that projects above a roof, containing multiple flues, each one terminating in a chimney pot

chin music is idle chatter

the **China Syndrome** is a hypothetical sequence of events following the meltdown of a nuclear reactor, in which the core melts deep into the earth, so named because China is on the opposite side of the earth from a reactor in the United States

Chinese checkers were invented in nineteenth-century England and originally called Halma

Chinese gooseberry is the original name of the kiwi fruit

Chinese Pinyin literally means "spell sound"

a **Chinese wall** is a strong barrier or a rule prohibiting the exchange of confidential information between different departments of an organization

Chinese whispers refers to mistakes caused by faulty communications

> **chipped potato** is another name for a potato chip

chips and salsa is a term for computer hardware and software, respectively

chock-a-block is nautical, said of two blocks of tackle run so closely they touch

chock-full (c.1400 chokkeful) is possibly from choke, "cheek," or it may be from French *choquier*, "collide, thrust"

one's **chocolate foot** is the foot favored to use or to start with when running, kicking, etc.; one's dominant foot (perhaps from a German term)

choo-choo is an echoic nursery name for "steam-engine locomotive" (1903)

chop suey is an alteration of Cantonese *tsaap sui*, "various or mixed bits"

chop-chop for "quick, quickly" is pidgin English based on Chinese dialect *kuai-kuai*

a **choropleth map** is a map in which areas are shaded or patterned in proportion to the measurement of the statistical variable being displayed on the map, such as population density or per-capita income

choux pastry is the light pastry used for making eclairs and profiteroles

chow mein (an alteration of Chinese ch'ao mein, "to fry flour" or "fried dough") is parboiled noodles to which other ingredients are added after being stir-fried separately; lo mein is parboiled noodles mixed with stir-fried stuff

chow-chow was pidgin English for "mixture," probably from Mandarin Chinese *cha*, "miscellaneous"

the term **Christian name** has largely given way to first name, forename, or given name

a **Christmas cracker** is a cardboard tube containing a party favor and wrapped in colored paper that opens with an explosive noise when both its ends are pulled

chump change dates to the mid-1960s

early bottle openers did resemble large, old-fashioned keys, possibly like those that opened the large doors of churches; **church key** started out as slang for bottle opener in the early 1950s and it was considered mildly shocking, even sacrilegious

ciabatta bread is Italian, meaning "slipper" for its shape

apple juice if unfermented is **cider** or **sweet cider**; if fermented, it is **hard cider** (apple cider is redundant)

cider oil is cider concentrated by boiling or freezing and infused with honey

circle the wagons is to unite in defense of a common interest, agreeing on a defensive strategy against criticism or a similar attack

circular breathing is the type of constant exhalation used by players of wind instruments

a **circular gateway** in a wall is a moon gate

Christmas creep is the inexorable tendency for the commercial aspects of Christmas to appear earlier every year

chrome yellow is any of several yellow pigments consisting of normal lead chromate and other lead compounds; there is also chrome orange and chrome red, made under slightly different conditions

chuck wagon is from the colloquial sense of chuck, "food, provisions"

a **circulating decimal** (or repeating decimal) is a decimal in which a pattern of one or more digits is repeated indefinitely, for example, 0.353535

circulating medium is anything used as money, e.g., a valuable commodity, paper money, or illegal drugs

cire perdue, "lost wax process," is a metal-working technique used to cast figurines and statues in which the desired form was carved in wax, coated with clay, and baked; the wax runs out through vents left in the clay for the purpose, and molten metal is then poured through the same vents into the mold

a **citizen journalist** is any person who collects, analyzes, reports, or disseminates news and information outside of traditional professional journalism organizations

civil disobedience was coined by Henry David Thoreau (essay, 1849)

civil liberties is a broad term referring to the liberties guaranteed people by law or custom

civil rights generally refers to the individual rights guaranteed by the Bill of Rights and the 13th, 14th, 15th, and 19th Amendments—as well as legislation such as the Voting Rights Act

civil service first denoted the British East India Company staff who were not in the army or navy

the **Civil War** was once called the War of Secession

civil wrong is an infringement of someone's civil rights

clair de lune, French for "moonlight," is a pale gray-blue glaze applied to some Chinese porcelain

New England **clam chowder** is made with clams, bacon (or salt pork), potatoes, and milk or cream thickened with some flour; Manhattan clam chowder is a chowder intensely flavored with tomato

a **clam-butcher** or **oyster-butcher** is one who opens these

{ **claret-colored** indicates a deep purplish red }

clarified butter is unsalted butter that has been heated to remove the milk solids

the colors of cigars are: green (**clarissimo**) to blonde (**claro claro**) to café au lait (**claro**) to light-brown (**colorado claro**) to reddish-brown (**maduro colorado**) to dark brown (**maduro**) to black (**oscuro**)

classic pull-back is long hair pulled back in a fastener, such as a barrette

classical Japanese is the language as spoken and written during c. 900–1200 CE; it continued to be commonly used as the written language until about 1900 CE

classical music more specifically applies to European conventional or serious pieces written between 1750–1830

classically sculptured, for wine, means having a well-balanced vintage

classified advertisement (1889) is so called from being arranged in classes

a hammer with two prongs on the opposite side of the striking head is a **claw hammer**

clean as a whistle comes from a whistle's need to be clean to make a pure sound

clean bill of health derives from bill of health, a certificate carried by a ship attesting to the presence or absence of infectious diseases among the ship's crew and at the port from which it has come

clean potato is slang for something that is excellent, a person of faultless character

clean someone's clock refers to a clock's "face"

clear coat is a nonpigmented protective coating that improves a base paint's durability and gloss

clear grit means "real stuff" or "true nature"

cleft lip is the accepted term, as harelip is thought to be offensive

a **cleft sentence** is that in which an element is emphasized by being put in a separate clause, introduced by an "empty" word such as "that" or "it," e.g., that was the president you were talking to

a **click language** is any language of the three-branch family (Khoisan, Sandawe, and Hatsa), which uses tones to distinguish meanings and show case, gender, and number for nouns

clicking-fork't, of a sheep, means having its ears marked by having two triangular-shaped pieces cut out

a **client state** is a country that is dependent on the economic or military support of a larger, more powerful country

climate control is another way of saying air conditioning

to **climb Parnassus** is to create poetry

a **climbing bolt** is a bolt permanently fixed to a rock face to allow climbers to attach ropes, etc.

clinical death is not just the cessation of heartbeat and respiration, but usually also involves brain death

a **clinical psychologist** has a PhD or PsyD and has completed an internship, and a **psychiatrist** is a medical doctor who is specializing in mental disorders; **psychotherapist** is a generic term for anyone who provides psychological therapy while a **psychoanalyst** provides psychoanalytic therapy (must have a master's degree)

{ ready-made artwork that can be shared is **clip art** }

clip joint is based on clip meaning "swindle, rob"

clock speed is the megahertz at which a computer or microprocessor performs internal operations

clockwork orange is any person or organism with a mechanistic morality or lack of free will (from a 1971 film adaptation of a 1962 novel of the same name)

close but no cigar is an interjection alluding to awarding a cigar to the winner of some competition, such as hitting a target

a **close encounter** is a supposed observation, or observation of evidence, of extraterrestrial beings or their craft

a **closed compound** is a compound word without spaces in it, e.g., dishcloth, keyboard, pancake, waterproof

closed shop (trade union only), where membership in a labor union is required for employment, is a U.S. term from 1904 that became established in industrial relations

a **closet drama** or **closet play** is one that is to be read rather than acted

clothes horse originally referred to a frame on which washed clothes are hung to dry indoors

it is the larvae of the **clothes moth** that eats holes in fabric

on a **clothing snap**, there is a ball and a socket

clotted cream is cream made thicker and richer by cooking; until the nineteenth century, clotted cream was known as clouted cream

cloud base is the undersurface of a cloud; the level or altitude of the lowest part of a mass of clouds

a **cloud forest** is a wet mountain or jungle forest frequently shrouded in mist

in **clove hitch**, clove is the past tense of cleave, because the rope appears as separate parallel lines at the back of the knot

the **clover hitch knot** is so named because the rope appears as separate parallel lines at the back of the knot

a **cloze test** is one in which a person must fill in missing words to measure their comprehension of text (cloze being a spoken abbreviation of closure)

club trains, WWII long-distance commuter trains, gave us the term **club car**

a **club chair** is so called because it is a style often found in clubs

relatives of the **club mosses** were the first plants to colonize the land during the Silurian period

club sandwiches (c. 1900) either got their name from first being popular at country clubs or were named after the double-decker club cars of early American railways or the word club implies "combination to make a total"

club soda (also sometimes called soda water) is a flavorless soft drink that also gets its effervescence from an infusion of carbon dioxide; the distinction between seltzer and club soda is that club soda also contains a bit of sodium bicarbonate

club steak is synonymous with Delmonico steak (named for a Swiss-born restaurateur)

the **club-sandwich generation** is the one responsible for the care of their children and parents

a **clutch of eggs** or **clutch of chicks** is based on Germanic and Scottish *cleck*, "to hatch"

CNN effect is the negative results (mainly economic) of people staying at home and watching twenty-four-hour-a-day news channels, especially during a crisis or military situation

coals to Newcastle is something brought or sent to a place where it is already plentiful

coarse salt is somewhat refined and sometimes used in cooking; **sea salt** is derived from seawater through evaporation

{ the first **coats of arms** were light garments worn over armor with a symbol printed or woven on them }

cobalt blue is a blue to green pigment consisting of a variable mixture of cobalt oxide and alumina; there is also a cobalt green, cobalt violet, and cobalt yellow

a Los Angeles restaurant owner, Bob Cobb, threw together a salad of leftovers and named it after himself, **Cobb salad**

cock-a-doodle-do (1573) is an imitative, cognate of French *cocorico*, German *kikeriki*, Latin *cucurire*, Russian *kikareku*, and Vietnamese *cuc-cu*

cock-a-hoop is "exalting"

{ **cock-a-leekie** is Scottish soup made of chicken and leeks }

cock-and-bull story (1660) is so called from its origin, apparently in referring to some story or fable

cocked in **cocked hat** means "turned up," as this term is about a hat with two or three turned-up edges

the **cocker spaniel** was so called because it was bred to flush game birds, such as the woodcock

cockles of the heart is redundant

a **cock-robin** is a male robin, and a **cock-sparrow** is a male sparrow

cocktail party is a term from 1928, though "cocktails" have been drunk in the United States since at least the early 19th century

cocktail party effect is another term for the ability (or the difficulty) of focusing one's attention on a single auditory source in a jumble of noises, the process of selective listening

to be **cock-throppled** is having a large Adam's apple

coconut butter is a solid fat obtained from the lining of a coconut and used in making candles, lotion, soap, etc.

co-ed, short for co-education, was first used in Louisa Mae Alcott's *Jo's Boys* (1886); the meaning "girl or woman student at a co-educational institution" was first recorded in 1893

coffee art is any design created on top of espresso, latte, or other coffee drink by a barista, especially with milk or cream

the term **coffee bar** was actually first recorded in 1905, but the concept did not take off until the 1950s

coffee cake is so called because it was first served with coffee

coffee culture is a lifestyle or society in which coffee consumption and coffeehouse establishments are integral activities

coffee klatsch is from German *Kaffeeklatsch*, "coffee" and "noise" or "gossip," and means "gossip over cups of coffee"

a **coffee spoon** is equal to ¼ teaspoon

coffee-table books date to the early 1960s and were once called grand-piano books

a **coffin nail** (or tack) is a cigarette

a **cog railway**'s purpose is to ascend very steep slopes

a **cognate object** is a direct object that has the same derivation as the verb that it goes with, e.g., sing a song, live a full life

cognitive dissonance is a condition of conflict or anxiety resulting from inconsistency between one's beliefs and one's actions, such as opposing the slaughter and treatment of animals for making fast food and then eating meat at fast-food restaurants

cola nuts contain caffeine and can be chewed or made into a drink

Colby jack cheese is a combination of Colby and jack cheese

cold bread is either stale bread or bread that is simply not hot

cold comfort is from Shakespeare's *King John*

cold cream (1709) is a cooling unguent for the skin

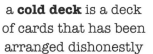

a **cold deck** is a deck of cards that has been arranged dishonestly

cold dope is a synonym for statistics

cold duck is a mixture of sparkling burgundy and champagne and it is from a German term

a **cold frame** is a miniature greenhouse for plants during frost season

a **cold front** is characterized by a wedge-like slipping of cooler denser air beneath warmer, forcing it to rise

the snub of a **cold shoulder** started when people overstayed their welcome and were served cold beef shoulder rather than hot food

a **cold sore** or **fever blister** is usually caused by herpes simplex; a **canker sore** is usually caused by food allergy or stress

cold turkey is an allusion to the unpleasant after-effects of not drinking alcohol or indulging in drugs, including cold sweats and gooseflesh; cold turkey had an early adverbial usage, "suddenly, without preparation or warning," before the noun meaning the treatment for an addict

the **cold war** (coined in 1945) experienced changes in temperature until the Communist regimes of Eastern Europe collapsed in the late 1980s

cold-fire is fuel laid for a fire, but unlit

cole crops are those of the cabbage family—including broccoli, cabbage, cauliflower, collards, kale, and kohlrabi

collateral damage is U.S. military jargon dating to 1975

a book of biographies is a **collective biography** or prosopography

collective farming was found in a 1919 text by Lenin

collective fruit is that which is formed from a mass of flowers, as the mulberry, pineapple, etc.; it is also called multiple fruit

a **collective noun** is one referring to a group, like a school of fish

the **collective unconscious** is the unconscious mind derived from ancestral memory and experience—common to all mankind

college try is a zealous or serious all-out try, on behalf of one's school, team, alma mater

in the "Twelve Days of Christmas," it is four **colly birds**, not four calling birds

a **color code** is a system of marking things with different colors to ID them

a **color phase** is a seasonal variation of the skin, pelt, or feathers of an animal

color shifting ink is used in dollar bills to prevent counterfeiting; the ink changes color when viewed from various angles

the first demonstration of **color television** was given in 1928 by John Logie Baird

color therapy is a system of alternative medicine in which colors and their energy frequencies are used to correct psychological or physical imbalances; also called chromopathy, chromotherapy, color healing

a **color wheel** shows the relationship between colors

column inches is a way of saying "press publicity"

combat fatigue is a more recent term for shell shock

a **combination oven** has conventional heating and microwave capabilities

the **combine harvester** (1926) was probably the biggest single technological development in twentieth-century farming

a **combining form** contributes to the particular sense of words as distinct from a prefix or suffix that adjusts the sense or determines the function of words; it is a base and suffix combination that is added to another base; back in the late nineteenth century, the editor of the monumental Oxford English Dictionary (OED), Sir James Murray, proposed that a word that occurs only in combination with other words should be called a **combining form**, to distinguish it from traditional suffixes and prefixes, which are grammatical forms of words

a **combining vowel** is sometimes used to link a base with subsequent elements

come to a head is a term from gardening—waiting for cabbage leaves to come together and form a head

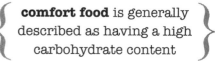
comfort food is generally described as having a high carbohydrate content

a **comfort station** is another name for public lavatory

comfortable words are ones of encouragement and sustenance—hopeful and strengthening

comma chaser is slang for **copy editor**

comme il faut, French for "as it should be" or "as it is necessary," defines the territory between what is correct and what is fashionable

a **comment clause** adds a parenthetic statement to another clause, e.g., you know, you see

a **comminuted fracture** is one that results from the bone's having broken into several pieces

common law is often contrasted with statutory law, as it is based on custom and judicial precedent rather than statutes

a **common market** is a group of countries that imposes few or no duties on each other's trading and establishes a common tariff on outside countries

a plant's **common name** is the one by which it is known to the public, as opposed to its **botanical name**

common nouns pertain to the class of objects or concepts as opposed to particular individuals (proper nouns)

common plugs is a term for the common rut of mankind

common stock is stock other than preferred stock; it entitles the owner to a share of the corporation's profits and a share of the voting power in shareholder elections

common touch is the ability to get along with or appeal to ordinary people

a **commonplace book** is a notebook of extracts from other works kept for personal reference

a **commuter belt** is an area surrounding a city from which a large number of people travel to work each day

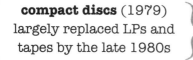

compact discs (1979) largely replaced LPs and tapes by the late 1980s

companion animal is a humorous term for a pet

companion planting is the arrangement of different plants close to each other that enhance or protect each other

when a comparison is of such a nature that it comprises three terms, then **comparable** is the word to use; when it comprises four terms, the relation requires the word analogous

compare to should be used to liken things; compare with should be used when considering similarities or differences

the **compass card** is the star indicating the cardinal points and intermediary directions

the **compass rose** is the symbol on a map that shows which direction is north, south, east, and west

compassion fatigue is an indifference to charitable appeals as a result of the frequency of such appeals

complementary colors are those opposite each other on the color spectrum

a **complete game** is one credited to a baseball pitcher who starts and finishes the game

a **complete protein** is one containing all of the essential amino acids in the correct quantity and ratio for humans, found only in a few animal foods, such as the egg

a **complex sentence** has one principal clause and one or more subordinate clauses; a compound sentence has two or more independent clauses

complex words are formed via derivation, which is the process by which a word like unbelievable is built up from the root or base *believe* or by which expedite is built up from the base *ped* (Latin for "foot")

the **complimentary close** or closing is the Sincerely, Yours Truly, etc. of a letter

compliments of the season is another way of saying Merry Christmas and a Happy New Year

you **comply with** but **conform to**

a **composed salad** is one in which the components are elaborately put together or arranged, rather than tossed

a **compost pile** is made up of garden and/or kitchen refuse that decomposes

compound butter is a chilled mixture of whole butter and flavoring ingredients such as herbs, used to flavor and color dishes

the **compound eye** is an array of many small visual units, found in insects and crustaceans

a **compound fracture** is when the bone pierces the skin

a **compound leaf** has two or more separate blades or leaflets on a common leafstalk

in American English, **compound nouns** usually begin life as two single-syllable words separated by a space, then are joined by a hyphen, and finally coalesce into one word, as we see in words like bathroom, blackboard, footstool, typewriter, girlfriend; by contrast, compound nouns made up of three or more words will tend to remain hyphenated, like: son-in-law, daughter-in-law, mother-of-pearl, attorney-at-law, happy-go-lucky

a **compound number** is one expressed with more than one unit—like 6 feet 5 inches or 10 pounds 6 ounces

a **compound sentence** has more than one subject or predicate

compound words are formed by composition or compounding, which is the process by which blackboard is formed from the simple words black and board, and geography is formed from the combining forms geo- and graphy; a compound can also be defined as a lexeme containing two or more potential stems or roots

{ **computer "bug"** was coined by a person whose computer was shorted out by a moth }

a **concave lens** is thinner at the center; a convex lens is thicker at the center

concavo-convex is more curved on the concave than the convex side

concentration camp was originally applied to camps set up by Lord Kitchener during the South African/Boer War of 1899–1902, the underlying idea being that the inmates were "concentrated" in one place where they could not help fighting forces

a **concept album** expresses a particular theme

a **concert grand** is the largest grand piano, up to 2.75 meters long

a word that is created by folding or collapsing together other words is a **concertinaed form**

the white cloud left by a jet is the **condensation trail** or **contrail**

a poem whose words form a shape is
called **concrete poetry**

condensed milk is thickened by evaporation and then sweetened

conditional tense denotes the occurrence of an action under certain conditions, e.g., "I would run the marathon, if my leg weren't broken."

Conestoga wagons were named for Conestoga, Pennsylvania

Coney Island is not an island, but it used to be

confectioners' sugar is preferred but the spelling confectioner's is also fine; confectioners' sugar is icing sugar in British English

there were eleven **Confederate States of America**

a **confidence trick** (con) was first a swindle in which the victim was persuaded to entrust money or valuables to the swindler

conger eel comes from Greek *gongros*, "sea eel"

in the **Congreve poem**, it is "music has charms to soothe a savage breast, to soften rocks, or bend a knotted oak" (not beast)

conjoined twins is a technical term for Siamese twins

a **conjure woman** or man is one who practices voodoo

the **conning tower** is the superstructure of the submarine which contains the periscope

conscientious objector was coined at the end of the nineteenth century for someone who objects on principle to being inoculated—but by 1916 was applied to people who refused to fight in World War I

consensus gentium fallacy is arguing that an idea is true because most people believe it or because it has been said throughout history

consist in refers to abstract elements or qualities or intangible things

consist of is used in reference to materials, preceding elements that compose a tangible thing

a **consonant cluster** is a group of consonants pronounced in immediate succession—as *str* in strong

conspiracy theory was originally a neutral term, but since the mid-1960s it is somewhat derogatory

Constitution State is the nickname for Connecticut

constructive memory refers to an apparent memory of an event that did not actually happen

consulting room is the term for the place where a doctor or other therapeutic practitioner exams patients

contact flying is navigation of an aircraft by using landmarks

contact juggling is the art of moving a single ball or multiple balls, as by rolling or spinning, with the defining characteristic being that the artist stays in contact with the ball or balls rather than throwing them

an aeronautical landing made with the landing place in full view is a **contact landing**; a landing made in fog, rain, snow, darkness, or other obscuration in which the landing place cannot be seen is an instrument landing

it is called a **contact lens** because it is in contact with the eyeball surface

contact prints are photographs made by placing a negative directly onto sensitized paper (contact sheet)

contagious magic is the assumption that a lock of hair or something physically associated with a person, such as a garment, can directly affect that person if removed or something is done to the artifact

content words are the nouns, verbs, adjectives, and adverbs which contain most of the referential or cognitive meaning of a sentence

a **context clue** is a method by which the meanings of unknown words may be obtained by examining the parts of a sentence surrounding the word for definition/ explanation clues, restatement/synonym clues, contrast/antonym clues, and inference/ general context clues

the **continental crust** of the earth is generally older and more complex than the oceanic crust

continental drift was first described in 1915 by Alfred L. Wegener in *The Origins of Continents and Oceans*, but it has been replaced by the theory of plate tectonics

Continental Navy was the name of the United States Navy between 1775 and 1794

a **continental shelf** is an underwater extension of the continent going from the coast to the continental rise (where the slope starts)—no more than 660 feet; the continental slope is 660 to 6,660 feet deep

continuous clock in sports is, especially in American football, a rule where the clock operates continuously in a one-sided game, so as to hasten the end of the contest

the **contour feathers** of a bird are those involved in flying and regulating body temperature

contra dance is a type of folk dance style in which couples dance in two facing lines of indefinite length

in **contract bridge**, the bidder receives points toward game only for the number of tricks he bid; in auction bridge, tricks made in excess of the contract are scored toward game

control characters are ASCII characters to indicate carriage return or tab or backspace, typed by depressing a key and the control key at the same time; the control key is the one on a computer keyboard that is used (in combination with some other key) to type control characters

controlled substance is a term referring to a drug or chemical substance whose possession and use are controlled by law

a **convection oven** heats/cooks food by the circulation of hot air

in computing, **conventional memory** was the first 64K of memory, where programs were loaded to be run

the ladybug most common to us is the **convergent ladybug**

conversation fluid is a term in the West for whiskey

conversation piece was first a type of genre painting in which a group of figures were posed in a setting

convert into means to change from one thing to another; convert to means to switch allegiance, loyalty, or obligation

converted rice is white rice prepared from brown rice—by soaking, steam pressure, drying, and milling

convexo-concave is more curved on the convex than the concave side

the **conveyor belt** dates to 1906 and became a key element in the mass production of twentieth-century industry

cooking wine is any inexpensive wine used for cooking rather than drinking; some wines are especially made for this purpose, often with salt added

a **Cook's tour** is a very fast tour of a location, from Thomas Cook (travel agent)

cool as a cucumber refers to a cucumber's high water content, which makes them cool

cool beans means "okay"

cool colors are the blues and greens of the color spectrum, associated with water, sky, ice, and cooler temperatures; also called cold colors

the broad conical Asian hat is a **coolie hat**

> a **cooling-board** is the board on which a dead body is laid out

co-opt, "to select (someone) for a group or club by a vote of members," is from Latin *cooptare,* "to choose as a colleague or member of one's tribe"; sense of "take over" came by 1953

a **coordinating conjunction** is placed between words, phrases, clauses, or sentences of equal rank—and these include: and, but, and or

a **coping saw** is a saw with a very narrow blade stretched across a u-shaped frame—for cutting curves (cope as in "vault, arch")

a **copper beech tree** has purplish-brown leaves

a **copular verb** is one that links a subject to a complement that refers to the subject, e.g., "That soup smells delicious"

copy sort in advertising research is a technique measuring individual phrases and verbal ideas in a commercial by the audience's levels of attention or recall, relevance, and feelings

cor anglais is French for English horn

cordon bleu is literally "blue ribbon"

a **corduroy road** is one made of tree trunks laid across a swamp

core asset and core competency describe something essential to success and distinguishing advantage, respectively

core competency is a defined level of expertise that is essential or fundamental to a particular job; the primary area of expertise; specialty; the expertise that allows an organization or individual to beat its competitors

core fruits include the apple, pear, Japanese plum, and quince

core hours are the fixed block of time during which an employee is expected to be at work

the **Corinthian order** is the most richly decorated in classical architecture

the **Coriolis force** is the cause of clockwise water currents in the northern hemisphere and counterclockwise in the southern hemisphere

a **corn dog** is a hotdog covered in cornmeal batter that is fried and served on a stick

> maize cob in the United Kingdom is **corn on the cob** in the United States

in **corn pone,** "small oval loaf of corn bread," pone is from a Native American word for "bread"

corn salad is a name given to several species of annual herbs sometimes used for salad

corn snow has a rough granular surface due to thawing and freezing

corn syrup is made from cornstarch and has dextrins, dextrose, and maltose

corned beef has no corn and means "preserved in salt," getting its name from corn's sense "particle" for the particles of salt that permeate the beef as it soaks in brine; it comes from cattle that spend their final months in a feedlot eating a grain-rich diet; the meat has more flavor and marbling than grass-fed beef

Cornish hen or **Cornish game hen** is the same as **Rock Cornish**

a **corn-stealer** is a hand

coronary thrombosis or **heart attack** is a blockage of the flow of blood to the heart caused by a blood clot in the coronary artery; whereas, cardiac arrest is a sudden, often temporary, cessation of heart function

corporal punishment, from Latin *corpus,* "body," means "bodily"; **capital punishment** originally involved losing one's head, from Latin *capit,* "head"

corps de ballet means "body of ballet" as distinct from solo dancers

corpus fetishism in linguistics is an insistence that the only valid source of illustrative examples of words or language constructs is from the corpus (existing body of literature) of the language

correlative conjunctions are those used in pairs to join structurally identical sentence parts, e.g., neither fish nor fowl

cos lettuce is named for the Aegean island of Kos, where it originated

Cosa Nostra is Italian for "our thing or affair"

cosmic microwave background is the cooled remnant of the hot big bang that fills the entire universe and can be observed today with an average temperature of about 2.725 kelvin

cosmic rays are highly energized atomic nuclei or particles traveling at the speed of light through space; physicist A.A. Millikan discovered cosmic rays in 1925

the **cosmological argument** claims that all things depend upon something for their existence, so the cosmos must depend on an independent being (God)

{ **cost-benefit** refers to assessing the benefits of an undertaking in relation to its cost }

cost-effective is anything effective and productive in relation to its cost

costume jewelry as a term refers to its being made up of inexpensive or imitative gems

cottage cheese is also Dutch cheese, pot cheese, smear cheese, clabber cheese, or curd cheese; cottage cheese was supposedly named for its origins in farm-cottage kitchens and first referred to any spreadable cheese

a **cottage garden** is an English style characterized by somewhat haphazard plantings of flowers, herbs, vegetables, and climbing vines

a **cottage industry** is working from home, using one's own equipment

cottage pie is another name for shepherd's pie

cotton bolls are the round, fluffy clumps in which form cotton grows on a cotton plant

cotton candy is also called **spun sugar**

to **cotton to**, "to begin to like," alludes to cotton thread that attaches itself and sticks to something

couch potato, a pun on boob tube, as the potato is a tuber, came into use in the late 1970s and was registered as a proprietary term in the United States in 1984

could have might sound like "could of," but "could of" is not OK

the correct phrase is "I **couldn't care less**," not "I could care less"

to **count kin** with someone is to compare one's pedigree with that of another

count nouns are physical objects that can be counted (people, things); mass nouns are for physical things that are not usually counted (air, rice, steel, water)

to **count the ties** is to idly walk railroad tracks

a **countersunk hole** is a hole which is drilled into a surface, so that when a screw is inserted, the screw head is level with the surface

counting sheep may have come from the verbal association between "sheep" and "sleep"

country gravy is a white sauce made from pan drippings, flour, and milk; popularly served with country-fried steak

country music has the sub-genres of country and western, hillbilly, and bluegrass

a **country rock** is one that encloses a mineral deposit or igneous intrusion

a **county agent** is an advisor employed by the government to assist people in rural areas with methods of farming and home economics

coup de foudre is a sudden unforeseen event or instantaneous and overwhelming passion, such as love at first sight; it is French, literally, "stroke of lightning"

coup de grace is literally "blow of mercy" from the blow that ends a prisoner's torture

coup de main is a sudden and unexpected movement or attack

an attack in print is a **coup de plume**

coup de savate is a kick with the flat of the foot

coup d'etat is literally "blow of state" (pronounced koo-day-TAH)

court cards (king, queen, jack) were originally coat cards, as all these figures are dressed up

court martial was originally martial court, a judicial court consisting of military or naval officers for the trial of military or naval offenses or the administration of martial law

the light that comes on in a car when the door is opened is the **courtesy light**

courtesy titles are given through social custom and do not carry legal status

a **cousin-in-law** is the husband or wife of one's cousin

a **cover artist** is a musical artist who makes a cover version of a song that was originally recorded by another artist

cover crop is planted to keep weeds down and add humus to the soil between seasonal plantings

the **cover slip** is the small piece of thin glass that covers the specimen on a microscope slide

a **cover-slut** was an apron or other item of clothing tied on to cover untidiness underneath

cow college is a slang term for agricultural college

cow tipping is a somewhat mean-spirited activity whereby one knocks over a sleeping cow (which sleeps standing up) by pushing on its side

a **cow town** originally (1885) was a local center in a stock-raising district and later referred to any small, isolated town

cowboy caviar is baked beans

cow's breakfast is a term for a straw hat or mattress

crab apple was influenced by crabbed "sour"

crab Rangoon is not a dish that originated in Asia

crab-skuit was a small open fishing boat with sails

cracked wheat is grains of whole wheat that have been crushed or broken roughly into tiny pieces before being used in a food product

cracker-barrel philosophy is home-spun philosophy—as the barrels in old-time country stores were where people would sit and talk philosophy

to be **crample-hamm'd** is to be stiff in one's lower joints

a **cranberry morpheme** is a morpheme within a complex word whose meaning is opaque to the present speakers of the language; the English word cranberry seems morphologically complex, since it must be distinguished from words such as raspberry, blackberry, and gooseberry—still, cran has no meaning and does not function as an independent word: cranberry is the only word in which cran appears

cranberry-eye is a bloodshot one

crazy paving is that using irregularly shaped stones or slabs

creamed cheese became **cream cheese**

cream puff dates to the 1880s and **cream soda** to 1854 (both U.S. terms)

credit card first had the meaning of "traveler's check" in the late nineteenth century, then its current meaning by 1952; credit cards were first called "shoppers' plates" and then "charge cards"

the difference between **crème brûlée** ("burnt crème") and **crème caramel** is in the method of achieving the caramel topping

crème de cacao is pronounced KREEM duh KO-ko

colorless **crème de menthe** is also made, in addition to green

crème fraiche is literally "fresh cream"—heavy cream soured with buttermilk, sour cream, or yogurt

crenellated molding is a kind of indented molding used in Norman buildings

the **creosote bush** is now regarded as the world's oldest living plant, with one specimen being 11,700 years old

crêpe de chine, a fine crêpe/silk fabric, is literally "crêpe of China"

a **crêpe suzette** can also be called a **Suzette pancake**; crêpes suzette are rolled in an orange sauce and served with flaming brandy

the sun's rays that shine down through the clouds are called **crepuscular rays**

crew cut (1942), a style worn by the crews of Yale and Harvard University, was foreshadowed by crew-cropped (1938) and crew haircut (1940)

the **crew sock** got its name from its use by rowers

a **cri de coeur** can be a protest or a plea for help, describing an action as much as a statement

cribbed logs are the notched horizontal logs that overlap at the corner of a building

criminal conversation is another term for adultery

critical mass is the minimum amount of material needed to set off a nuclear bomb or make a nuclear reactor create significant energy

crock pot is redundant

the saying **crocodile tears** is from the belief that they weep while devouring or luring their prey

Crohn's disease was named for U.S. pathologist B.B. Crohn (1884–1983), one of the team that wrote the article describing it in 1932

cross seas is when two opposing waves meet head-on and form a towering crest

cross the Rubicon means to commit oneself irrevocably to a course of action

someone **cross-grained** is hard to please

a **cross-index** or **cross-reference** is a reference at one place in a work to information at another place in the same work

in basketball, a **crossover dribble** is a maneuver in which a dribbling player rapidly switches the ball from one side to the other in order to move around a defender

a **croque monsieur** is a French toasted ham and cheese sandwich that is dipped in beaten egg before being prepared, often with a grilling iron. A croque madame is a croque monsiour with a fried egg on top

Cro Magnon (1869) is from the name of a hill in Dordogne province of France, where in a cave prehistoric human remains were found in 1868

Cro-Magnon man (1869) was named for a hill of Cretaceous limestone in the Dordogne province of France in a cave at the base of which skeletons of Homo sapiens were found in 1868 among deposits from the Upper Paleolithic age; it had previously been supposed that modern man did not exist in Paleolithic times

crookneck squash are familiar orange types sold at farm stands around Halloween

a **crop circle** is any area of grain or crop that has been flattened or cut into a circular geometric pattern, sometimes thought to be made by flying saucers; also called corn circle

a drawing of a slice of something is a **cross-section**; a drawing with the casing removed is a **cutaway**; a drawing with the parts separated out is an **exploded view**

to **cross-train** is to learn another skill, especially one related to one's current job

a **crossword puzzle** was first called a word-cross

the phrase **crowd the mourners** means to be in a hurry

crowd-surfing is when someone is passed in a prone position over the heads of an audience, such as at a rock concert

a metal bottle cap with a crimped edge is a **crown cap**

crown molding is the same as cornice

a **crown roast** is a roast of lamb or pork with the ribs arranged like a crown

the **crow's nest** is the platform near the top of the mast of a ship

Shakespeare's phrases include **cruel to be kind** (*Hamlet*), **not budge an inch** (*Taming of the Shrew*), **paint/gild the Lily** (*King John*), **too much of a good thing** (*As You Like It*), there's a rub (*Hamlet*), **it's Greek to me** (*Julius Caesar*)

cruising range is how far an aircraft or ship can travel without refueling

a **crumb-bum** is a truly filthy vagabond, with crumb referring to lice or bedbugs

the **crumple zone** is the part of a motor vehicle designed to crumple and absorb impact

a **crush room** is a room or area in a theater or opera house for the audience to walk about during intermissions

crushed velvet has its nap pointing in different directions in irregular patches

cry all the way to the bank is attributed to Liberace

cry uncle is regarded as an Americanism, but its origins go all the way back to the Roman Empire. Roman children, when beset by a bully, would be forced to say *"Patrue, mi Patruissimo,"* or *"Uncle, my best Uncle,"* in order to surrender and be freed

crystal from Greek *krustallos*, originally meant "ice" and it is, properly, **rock crystal**—describing ornamental pieces or items of crystallized quartz; fine glass, when cut or etched, is called crystal—often there

is no crystallized quartz, but it does contain lead and is then called lead crystal

crystal lattice is the symmetrical three-dimensional arrangement of atoms inside a crystal

cub in **cub reporter** simply implies youth and inexperience

a **Cuban sandwich** is a sub with ham, roast pork, Swiss cheese, mustard, and pickle

cubby house is a term for a child's play house

cube farm is an office filled with cubicles

to **cube out** is to reach the volume limit of a container

running cheaper cuts of meat through rollers to create a grid pattern inspired the name **cube steak**

cucking stool (1215) is from *cuck*, "to void excrement," from Old Norse *kuka*, "feces" (the chair was sometimes in the form of a close-stool); also known as trebucket and castigatory, it was used on disorderly women and fraudulent tradesmen, either in the form of public exposure to ridicule or for ducking in a pond

you **cue up** a videotape or CD, but you queue up to buy movie tickets

cuff and stuff is to physically place someone under arrest

a **cuff link** links the split cuff of a shirt

cui bono? means "for whose benefit?" (not "for what purpose?")

cul-de-sac was first an anatomical term "bag-shaped or tubular cavity, vessel, or organ, open only at one end" from French, literally "bottom of a sack"; its application to streets and alleys is from 1800

the **cultivated mushroom** is the whitish type most widely grown and sold for consumption; the **shiitake mushroom** is the equivalent of the cultivated mushroom in Japan

cultural anthropology is the same as **social anthropology**

summa **cum laude** is Latin for "with highest praise," magna cum laude for "with great praise," and cum laude for "with praise"

Cumberland sauce is red currant jelly flavored with orange, mustard, and port

cup of coffee is a short time in the major leagues by a minor league baseball player

cupboard love is gastronomic desire combined with emotional insincerity

cupcake liners are also called **baking cups**

cup-holder cuisine is food that is designed for eating during travel, especially by car in that the packaging fits in a cup holder

{ **cupid's bow** is the upper edge of the upper lip of the human mouth }

curate's egg describes something that is partly good and partly bad

curb weight is that of a vehicle without cargo or occupants

curds and whey is actually cottage cheese

curiosity delay is another term for rubbernecking

to **curl one's liver** is to experience

curriculum vitae is Latin, meaning "course of life"

a **curry comb** is a flat serrated comb used to groom a horse

to **curry favor** is believed to be a corruption of the older phrase "to curry favel," the general name for any horse that was roan, sorrel, chestnut, or yellow in color

curry powder is a mixture of such things as turmeric, ginger, and coriander for making curry

curtailed of one's fair proportions means deformed

a **custard pie** is more correctly an open flan or tart (containing custard)

cut and dried originally referred to herbs sold in herbalists' shops—which were more effective than fresh-picked (cut and dry is a variant)

to **cut eyes** is to meet someone's gaze and then look away quickly

to **cut heads** is to compare musical skill, as in a jam session

cut/split/slice melon means to distribute bonuses or extra profit among employees or investors

in **cut the mustard**, mustard is slang for "the best thing"

{ **cut to the chase** was first a silent film term }

the kitchen tool for pounding or flattening meat is a **cutlet bat**

if something **cuts no ice**, it makes no difference

a **cutting horse** is one trained to cut cattle out of a herd

Cyber Monday is the Monday after Thanksgiving, when online Christmas shopping begins in earnest

the control on a washing machine, dishwasher, or dryer is the **cycle selector**

{ D }

a **dabbling duck** feeds in shallow water by dabbling (moving the bill around in the water) and upending; the mallard, teal, shoveler, and pintail do this

the **daddy longlegs** is also known as the harvestman

a **dado rail** is a horizontal molding fixed to an interior wall about 4–5 feet above the floor

a **Dagwood sandwich** is a very thick sandwich made with a variety of meats, cheeses, condiments, and lettuce; also called Dagwood

a **Daikon radish** is a long, white, carrot-shaped radish with a mild taste

the **daily double** is a single bet on the winners of two named races in a day

the **daily dozen** originally was a set of twelve exercises devised by Yale University football coach Walter Camp around the early 20th century

a **dairy bar** is a commercial establishment serving dairy products that it makes, especially ice cream, and usually breakfast and/or lunch

a **daisy chain** is a string of daisies threaded together by their stems

Dalai Lama comes from Mongolian, meaning "ocean" and "teacher, guru," and he is regarded as the "ocean of compassion"

the **damask rose** is named for the Syrian city of Damascus

Damson plums were originally from Damascus, Syria

dancing grounds is the name of the place where birds perform mating rituals

dandy brush is the name of the coarse brush used for grooming a horse

a **dangling participle** is one intended to modify a noun, but that noun is not actually present in the text

Danish pastry dates to 1934 and the shortened form Danish is from 1963; Danish are popular and were perfected in Denmark, but are said to have originated in Austria

danse macabre originally described images in which a skeletal Death was shown dancing on a grave (Middle Ages)

{ to be **dansey-headed** is thoughtless or giddy, as from dancing }

dapple gray was originally apple gray

Darby and Joan refers to an old and extremely happily married couple

dark chocolate is a slightly bitter deep-brown chocolate with no added milk

the allusion in **dark horse** is to being "kept in the dark"

dark matter is any material that has not been directly detected but whose existence is postulated

dark meat (nineteenth century) is the thighs and legs of a cooked fowl

dark side is a distinctly negative ethical paradigm; short form of "dark side of the Force" coined by George Lucas in the making of the original *Star Wars* trilogy; a depressing or evil aspect; an unseen or unknown portion especially in reference to the far side of the moon

dragonflies are sometimes called a **darning needle** or **devil's darning needle**

data mining is a type of database application that looks for hidden patterns in large groups of data, like helping grocery stores target customers based on their recent purchases

data processing has been around since 1954

a **datum line** is the horizontal or base line, from which the heights of points are reckoned or measured, as in the plan of a railway, etc.

the **Davis Cup** was a national tennis championship trophy donated in 1900 by U.S. statesman Dwight Filley Davis (1879–1945) while still an undergraduate at Harvard

Davy Jones is a term for the evil spirit of the sea; Davy Jones's locker is the bottom of the sea

birdsong at daybreak is **dawn chorus**

day care can refer to care needed by children or the elderly

a **day lily** is so called because its flowers last only for a day

a **day sign** was any of 20 glyphs used, along with a number from 1 to 13, in traditional Mesoamerican calendars to identify their 260 days

day trading is the buying and selling of a security on the same day

daylight-saving time was the original form in the early twentieth century, but now a common form is **daylight-savings time**

day-spring is the first appearance of light in the morning

D-Day (1918) was the "date set for the beginning of a military operation," with D as an abbreviation—now refers almost exclusively to the day of June 6, 1944

de facto ("in fact; actually") is almost always used in actual or implied contrast with **de jure** ("according to law")

de rigueur is French, literally "in strictness" and means "required by etiquette or current fashion"

de trop is French for "one too many"

doornail in **dead as a doornail** is a large-headed nail of a door or the knob on which a knocker strikes

dead cat bounce is a slang term for an apparent recovery from a major decline in stock prices resulting from speculators rebuying stock that they previously sold rather than from a genuine upturn in the market; it's an allusion to free-fall descent and then a brief rally—if you threw a dead cat off a 50-story building, it might bounce when it hit the sidewalk, but you would not confuse that bounce with renewed life; it is still a dead cat

a **dead drop** is where you hide a secret message

if two horses tied in a heat, the heat did not count and was called "dead"; now any tie can be called a **dead heat**

to work (etc.) for a **dead horse** or to work the dead horse is to do work which has been paid for in advance, and so brings no further profit; to flog (or mount on) a dead horse is to attempt to revive a feeling or interest which has died out; to engage in fruitless effort

to be **dead in the shell** is to be utterly worn out

dead in the water is a nautical expression dating back to sailing ships and refers to a boat sitting motionless in the sea on a windless day

a **dead language** is one that is no longer in everyday (spoken) use

a calculation based on guesswork is called **dead reckoning**; it was first the method of determining the place of a ship from a record kept of the courses sailed as given by compass, and the distance made on each course as found by log, with allowance for leeway, etc., without the aid of celestial observations

the printed paper version of an online periodical or article or a printed book can humorously be called a **dead tree edition**

a **dead wall** is a blank wall unbroken by windows or other openings

a **dead zone** is an area where there is no signal reception or transmission for cellular telephones, radios, etc.

deafening silence is an oxymoron

the **death rattle** is the gurgling sound heard in a dying person's throat

> **death ray** (1919) was a staple of (pulp) science fiction in the mid-twentieth century

on a **debit card**, the merchant pays a flat fee per transaction, but for a credit card or debit card used as a credit card, the merchant's fee is a percentage of the amount of the sale

around 98 percent of the caffeine is gone from **decaffeinated coffee**

in surfing, **deck grips** are rubber non-slip pads glued to the top of a surfboard to stand on

a feathery or uncut paper edge is called the **deckle edge**

declarative memory is a type of long-term memory where facts and events are stored

decorative arts is any of the arts that create entities that are both useful and beautiful

to **de-dupe** is to remove duplicate entries from a list or database

Deely-bobber was a headband with springs carrying ornaments, a 1982 trademark name held by Ace Novelty Company; earlier it had been a patent name for a type of building blocks, manufactured 1969–1973

deep six referred originally to putting something under six fathoms of water

the **Deep South** includes Alabama, Georgia, Louisiana, and sometimes Texas and Mississippi

deep space is a synonym for outer space

deep-dish can mean "extreme" or "thoroughgoing"—as in "she's a deep-dish Jets fan"

deep-fry means to fry food in an amount of fat or oil sufficient to cover it completely (deep)

a **defective verb** can only be conjugated in certain persons and numbers, e.g., the verb "can" is defective, as it lacks an infinitive

deferred success is a euphemistic formulation for "failure"

defining vocabulary (lexicography) is a relatively small set of words used to define all other terms in a dictionary

"the" is the **definite article** of English

déjà lu ("already read") is the feeling that one may have read the present passage or one very like it before

déjà vécu is the most common déjà vu experience of realizing that something said or done occurred previously in one's experience

déjà vu is French, literally "already seen"; the phrase was originally a technical term in psychology

the **delative case** is one used to indicate movement from a surface, and in English this is usually expressed by the prepositions *from* or *off of*, as in "down off of the house"

a **Delmonico steak** is a small steak cut from the front of the short loin and is also called club steak, New York steak, New York strip, strip steak, strip loin steak, Kansas City strip steak (named for U.S. restaurateur)

an aircraft's single triangular wing is the **delta wing**

peninsulas were first called **demi-islands** or **demi-isles**

demi-veg, or **demi-vegetarian** is being mainly vegetarian but also sometimes including meat and fish

a **demonstrative adjective** (or demonstrative pronoun, demonstrative determiner) points out which person, object, or concept is being referred to (this, that, these, and those)

denatured alcohol is ethyl alcohol that is unfit for drinking but is still useful for other purposes

denizen labels is the term for "what do you call someone from," like Oregonian or Luxemburger

dental formula is a brief notation used by zoologists and dentists to denote the number and kind of teeth of a mammal

a **dental spa** is a dental practice incorporating spa facilities so as to attempt to make patients feel more comfortable and relaxed about having treatment

a **dental technician** is one who makes and repairs artificial teeth

Denver boot (1967) uses the name of the city of Denver, Colorado, for a kind of wheel clamp used to immobilize an illegally parked vehicle

a **Denver sandwich** is scrambled eggs with ham, green peppers, and onion on bread; also called western sandwich

desoxyribonucleic acid became **deoxyribonucleic acid** (1933) or DNA (1944)—but was not known outside the scientific world until 1953 when its double helical structure was explained

Depression glass was mass-produced tinted glassware made from the late 1920s to the 1940s and often used in giveaways to draw customers

depressive realism is a theory proposing that depressed people see the world more accurately

depth psychology is the study of unconscious mental processes and motives

a **derived adjective** is an adjective derived from a noun or verb, e.g., dreamy from dream, sterilized from sterilize

{ **dermagraphism** and **passion purpura** are the giving of love bites or hickeys }

dernier cri, "newest fashion," is more likely to be used tongue-in-cheek

derring-do was originally (c.1374) *dorrying don*, literally "daring to do," misspelled *derrynge do* in the 1500s and mistaken for a noun by Spenser, who took it to mean "manhood and chevalrie," then picked up from him and passed on to Romantic poets as a pseudo-archaism by Sir Walter Scott

a **descriptive adjective** describes a noun or pronoun (beautiful woman) and a **limiting adjective** limits it (ten apples)

desert in **desert island** refers to the meaning of "abandon" or "left empty"

words cut into hedges are called **design bedding**

baseball's **designated hitter** typically bats for the pitcher a **designer drug** was "designed" to circumvent drug laws as the structure used is not illegal but mimics the chemistry and effects of an existing banned drug

on a room thermostat, where you set it is the **desired temperature**

a **desk dictionary** is one volume, medium-sized (not unabridged)

a **dessert grape** is grown for eating rather than for making wine

a **dessert spoon** is equal to ½ tablespoon

dessert wines are 14–24 percent alcohol

deus ex machina is an unexpected power or event saving a seemingly hopeless situation

a **devil's advocate** is one who advocates the contrary or wrong side, or injures a cause by his advocacy

{ **devil's food** suggests its sinful richness and its dark color, as opposed to **angel food**, its white counterpart }

devils on horseback is angels on horseback, oysters wrapped in bacon, made with hot seasoning of Tabasco or red pepper, and served on toast points

devil's smiles are gleams of sunshine among dark clouds

a poetic way of describing a nervous hand or foot tapping is to call it a **devil's tattoo**

dew drop is either a small amount of morning moisture or an 1800s baseball term meaning a slow pitch

dew point is the temperature at which water vapor in the air begins to condense—and it is used to calculate humidity in the air

the **Dewey decimal system** was proposed in 1876 by Melvil Dewey (1851–1931) while acting librarian of Amherst College; he also crusaded for simplified spelling and the metric system

a **dextral shell** is a spiral shell with whorls that turn from left to right, or like the hands of a watch when the apex of the spire is toward the eye of the observer

diagnostic drawing series is a standardized art therapy assessment of how people tend to draw

dialect geography is the branch of linguistics concerned with the regional differences in accent, usage, and vocabulary

a **dialog box** on a computer screen is one that requires you to make a choice

diamente top is one covered with sequins, beads, or pailettes

a **diamond drill** is a rod or tube the end of which is set with black diamonds and used for perforating hard substances, especially for boring in rock

the **diamond wedding** anniversary can be the sixtieth or the seventy-fifth

a two-tone fog signal (breeoooo) is a **diaphone fog signal**

the **diatonic scale** is a scale consisting of eight sounds with seven intervals, of which two are semitones and five are whole tones

to **dice with death** is to take serious risks

to **die in the harness** is to work until the end of one's life or die during the performance of one's duty—similar to **die with one's boots on**

in biology, a **diel cycle** is a twenty-four-hour cycle

a **die-up** is when a bunch of cattle or other animals die of a drought, grass fire, blizzard, etc.

a **diffused neologism** is a newly coined word or phrase that has already reached a significant audience, but has not yet gained full mainstream acceptance

on a cat's paw, the "fingerlike" pads of the claws are the **digital pads** and the larger "palmlike" one is the plantar pad

a **diplomatic illness** is one, real or imagined, used to avoid a meeting or engagement

a **direct object** is the recipient of the action of a transitive verb

two valves are in **direct proportion** when an increase (or decrease) in one results in or is related to an increase (or decrease) in the other

a **direct verb** is a verb that agrees in person and number with the subject of a clause by conjugation, e.g., "He listens to the radio"

a **dirt farmer** is one who makes a living from poor land, usually without hired labor

dirty pool comes from the 1947 film *Gentleman's Agreement*

the **digital divide** is the gap between those who have computers with Internet access and those who do not, as well as the gap between those who are computer literate and those who are not

Dijon mustard, originally made in Dijon, France, is a spicy mustard made with white wine and seasonings

a **dill pickle** is a cucumber that is pickled and flavored with dill weed

dim sum comes from Cantonese *dim sam*, "touch the/your heart" or "dot heart, small heart"; it is a snack of different hot savory pastries

dimensional lumber is that which is finished/planed and cut to standardized width and depth specified in inches

a **dinner jacket** is white and a **smoking jacket** is velvet

dirty rice is white rice cooked with onions, peppers, herbs, Cajun spice, and chicken livers

a **dirty weekend** is one spent away, especially in secret, with a lover

a horse jockey operates horses, giving us **disc jockey** from someone who operates discs or records (1941; **dee-jay** in 1955, **DJ** in 1961)

discourse analysis is concerned with the larger units of communication, such as the relationships between and among sentences, and the structure of paragraphs or larger units

a **discourse marker** is a word or phrase used to organize segments of what is communicated; an example is "I mean"

the **discovery well** is the first successful oil well in a new field

discretionary income is that remaining after taxes and necessary expenses

a **dish cloth** is for washing or drying dishes; a **dish towel** is for drying only

a **disk flower** is any tubular flower that projects from the heads of daisies, sunflowers, and asters

disorderly house is an archaic term for a brothel

u **displaced person** is one forced to leave his or her homeland due to war, persecution, or natural disaster

disposable income is money you have left after paying taxes

the female side of a family is the **distaff side**, the distaff being a stick used for holding yarn when spinning; the male side is the **spear side**

the hand's heart line is also known as the **distal transverse**

distance work is employment carried out from a remote location; telecommuting

the **District of Columbia** occupies the same sixty-nine square miles as the nation's capital, Washington, DC

ditto marks are two apostrophes representing "ditto"

divided skirt is a synonym for culottes

diving ducks include the pochard, scaup, tufted duck, and goldeneye

to **do birds** is to serve a prison sentence

to **do someone brown** can mean to take advantage of someone

to **do something up brown** means to do something completely or thoroughly

to **do something with a wet finger** means to do it with great ease

the **Doberman pinscher** is named for Ludwig Dobermann, a nineteenth-century German dog-breeder of Thuringia

Doc Martens, the type of heavy walking shoe (1977, though use claimed from 1965), is the trademark name taken out by Herbert Funck and Klaus Martens

a **docking station** allows a laptop to serve as a desktop computer

the phrase **dog days** is said to have originated in Roman times as *canicularis dies*, "days of the dog," referring to the dog star Sirius or Procyon, the Romans thought the rising of the most brilliant star of the constellation Canis Major contributed to the heat of summer

a **dog in the manger** is someone who prevents others from having things even though they don't need or want them themselves

the **Dog Star** is named for its appearing to follow at the heels of Orion the hunter

dog watch, the two-hour watches on board a ship, is based on dog sleep, the light or fitful sleep typical of dogs (catnap being even shorter)

a **dog with a fiddle front** has bowlegged forelegs

dog year refers to a period of time in the life of dogs, defined such that the average life expectancy of a dog in "dog years" is numerically equivalent to the average life expectancy of a human: a four-year-old dog is about as mature as a human of twenty-eight to thirty years

dog's breakfast is a mess or muddle (also called dog's dinner) and originally may have referred to a cooking mishap with results fit only for dog consumption

dog-and-pony show (1914) started as American slang for a small circus or traveling show and, in extended use, a small-scale or poor quality entertainment or service

{ **dog-eat-dog** is an allusion to the proverb "dog does not eat dog" }

do-gooder appears in American English from 1927, presumably because do-good was no longer felt as sufficiently noun-like

a **dog's life** is an expression first recorded in a sixteenth-century manuscript and alludes to the miserable subservient existence of dogs during this era

dog's soup is rain water

a spell of cold weather when dogwood trees are in bud or blossom is **dogwood winter**

doing double horse is doing or being two things at a time

do-it-yourself is a post-1945 phrase

dolce far niente (1814) is from Italian, meaning "sweet doing nothing"

dolce vita is literally "sweet life," shorthand for hedonism or decadence

dollar diplomacy is the use of a country's financial power to exert international influence

dollars to doughnuts means "most certain or assuredly" and it comes from betting—being willing to bet dollars against doughnuts (viewed as basically worthless) means that you are totally confident you are right; variants are dollars to buttons, dollars to cobwebs, dollars to dumplings

a **dolly mixture** is a set of small sweets of various shapes and colors, such as a doll might eat

dolman sleeve is partly from Turkish *dolaman*, "robe," a long outer robe worn by Turks—and the dolman sleeve is much wider at the shoulder and narrow at the wrist

Dom Pérignon is a trademark name (1954, in use from 1936), from a monk of that name (1638–1715), the blind cellar-master of the monastery of Hautvilliers near Epernay, France, who was said to have discovered the advantage of corked bottles in fermentation; Dom was a title of authority

the **Domesday book** (1178) was the popular name of Great Inquisition or Survey (1086), William the Conqueror's inventory of his new domain, from Middle English *dom*, "day of judgment"

home economics is now called **domestic science**

the **domino effect** is a particular example of a chain reaction, as is the spread of a rumor

{ the **domino theory** is about the effect of a political event in one country on neighboring countries }

Don Juan, a rake, was the name of a legendary Spanish nobleman whose dissolute life was dramatized by Gabriel Tellez in his "Convivado de Piedra" and adopted by Lord Byron in his well-known poem

donkeys are used as beasts of burden, so **donkey work** is the harder, unattractive aspect of an undertaking

donkey's years dates to around 1900, probably originally donkey('s) ears, as rhyming slang for years, with years replacing ears once the rhyming origin was forgotten

don't care a fig does not refer to fruit but is from Italian *fico*, a gesture of contempt

the **donut peach** originated in Asia

doom and gloom is an expression that arose during or soon after World War II

door furniture are the handles, lock, and other fixtures on a door

doo-wop (1969) is so called from the nonsense harmony phrases sung under the vocal lead

the **Dorian mode** is the scale represented by the white keys on a piano

Doric order is the biggest column, then Ionic, then Corinthian

a **Dorothy bag** is a woman's handbag gathered at the top by a drawstring whose loops are used as a handle; traditionally used by bridesmaids to carry confetti, etc.

the part sticking up from a dolphin's back is the **dorsal fin**

do-si-do (1929) is from French *dos-à-dos*, "back to back"

a **dotted note** is a musical note followed by a dot to indicate an increase of length equal to one half of its simple value

to **double a part** is to act two different roles in the same piece

a **double adapter** is any of several devices that allows two electrical items to be plugged into a single power outlet

a **double bass** is also called the **bass fiddle**, bass viol, contrabass, string bass, bull fiddle, or bass

a **double bed** is the same as a **full bed**

a **double bind** is being faced with two irreconcilable demands or a choice between two undesirable courses of action

a **double bobble** occurs when somebody reaches for a word which is the wrong word and then mistakes another word for that wrong word, e.g., Hobbesian choice when misused for a difficult choice

double bogey is two strokes over par on a golf hole

when two brothers marry two sisters, the children are known as **double cousins**

double Dutch is a jump-rope game using two ropes

a **double eagle** is three strokes under par on a golf hole

double entendre means "double understanding"

double header comes from railroading a train with two engines on it

double jeopardy is the prosecution of a person twice for the same offense

a **double negative** is two negative elements to make a negative or positive statement (examples)

to **double O** is to examine or spy

double pneumonia affects both lungs

double take dates from the 1930s

double time is a rate of military marching approximate to twice as fast as **quick time**; **quick time** is 120 steps of 30 inches per minute, and double time is 180 steps of 36 inches per minute

whammy is from "wham" and became associated in the 1950s with the cartoon *Li'l Abner*, in which Evil-Eye Fleegle could "shoot a whammy," meaning "put a curse on somebody" by pointing a finger with one eye open and a **double whammy** with both eyes open

a **double-barreled name** is a hyphenated surname

a **double-blind test** is a form of scientific testing in which neither the tester nor the subjects tested know which are the control items and which are the test items

double-cross (1834) is from double and cross in the sense of "pre-arranged swindle or fix" and originally meant to win a race after promising to lose it

a margarita glass has what is called a **double-domed bowl**

a **double-hung window** has a top section that can slide down and a bottom section that can slide up

double-quick or **double time** is the quickest step next to a run

{ a **double-wide** is two connected mobile homes }

doubting Thomas alludes to one of Jesus's apostles, Thomas, who refused to believe in Jesus's resurrection until he saw and touched the body

a **doughnut hole** is a small ball-shaped pastry made in the same manner as a doughnut and roughly the size of a hole in a doughnut; originally, they were not the dough from the center of a ring-shaped cake but "nuts" of dough formed by hand, deep-fried, and enjoyed in the 17th century

the **Douglas fir**, discovered in 1825 by Scottish botanist David Douglas, is botanically in the pine family; it yields more lumber than any other American species

douse the glim is a synonym for **put out the light**

dove gray is a medium gray color with a slight tint of pink or blue, like that of a dove

Dow Jones, short for Dow Jones Industrial Average, was first published in 1884 by Charles Henry Dow (d.1902) and Edward D. Jones (d.1920), later publishers of *The Wall Street Journal*

Down East is a term for northeastern New England, derived from sailing downwind, to the east

dump in **down in the dumps** is from the 16th century meaning "a dazed or absent-minded state"

to be **down on one's marrow bones** is to be in an abject condition

to be **down on your uppers** (referring to shoes) is to be scuffing along, in poor circumstances

down the hatch is a drinking toast of nautical origin

down to the ground means "thoroughly, entirely, completely" as in, "that suits me down to the ground"

the allusion in **down to the wire** is the imaginary wire at the finish line in a horse race

down under is Australia, New Zealand, and adjacent Pacific Islands as viewed from the northern hemisphere, the antipodes

the allusion behind **down-and-out** is to boxing

Down's syndrome is named after English physician L.H. Down

downward-facing dog (or downward dog) is a yoga pose in which the hands and feet are on the floor and one's rear end is pointed up so that the body is in an upside-down V

the **Dr. Pepper** soft drink was patented in 1906 by the Dr. Pepper Co. of Dallas, Texas, and was named for U.S. physician Dr. Charles Pepper

in **draft horse**, draft is used in the sense "pull or draw"

a **drag bunt** is hit down the first baseline, usually by a left-handed batter

drag queen dates to 1941, though drag as feminine attire worn by a man dates to 1870

in **drag race**, drag is derived from "a kind of vehicle as opposed to a break (carriage frame)" or "sledge," or drag as slang meaning "automobile"

dramatis personae are the characters of a play

dramatic poetry relates to a story, such as Samuel Taylor Coleridge's "The Rime of the Ancient Mariner"

Downing Street, a short street in London, was named for British diplomat Sir George Downing (c.1624–1684) and has the residence of the prime minister (at Number 10), hence its metonymic use for "the British government," attested from 1781

drawing paper started out being generally a thick-sized paper for draftspersons and for watercolor painting

drawing pin is the British term for thumbtack

drawing room is a shortening of *withdrawing room*, the room to which the ladies withdrew, leaving the men to smoking and drinking

drawing the nail means absolving oneself of a vow

drawn butter is melted, clarified, and seasoned

{ a **dream catcher** is a decorative Native American object in the form of a hoop and net with attachments such as feathers }

dress circle is so called because it is a circular row of seats at an entertainment, the spectators of which were expected to be in dress clothes

dress parade is a military parade in full uniform for review

dress in **dress rehearsal** refers to the cast being dressed in appropriate costume

dressed to thy'n eyes—spiffed up head to toe—was changed over time to **dressed to the nines**

dribs and drabs is first recorded in the nineteenth century and each of the words means "small quantity or amount," making this an emphatic phrase

dried plum is another name for a prune

ice floating in small, harmless pieces in the sea is **drift ice**

drink like a fish refers to the fact that fish swim with their mouths open most of the time, presumably continually drinking

drive a point home is an allusion to hammering a nail

drive time is the part(s) of the day when many people commute to work

a **drop cap** is a large initial that sits within the margins and runs several lines deep into the paragraph, pushing some normal-sized text off these lines; the large letter at the beginning of the first word of a chapter is also called a dropped initial or set-in cap

a **drop cookie** is one formed by dropping a spoonful of dough onto the baking sheet

drop in the bucket (or ocean) originated in Isaiah in the Bible

a **drop kick** is a kick given to the ball as it rebounds after having been dropped from the hands

to **drop one's candy** is to make a big blunder

a **drop shipment** is an instance of sending purchased goods directly from the manufacturer to a customer or retailer without an intermediate distributor, billed through a third party

a **drop shot** in tennis is so called because after a hit, it drops abruptly to the ground

a **drop waist** has the seam at the hips rather than the waist

a **drop-leaf table** has one or more hinges that allow part of the tabletop to fold down

dropping the food, in restaurant-speak, is delivering it to the table

drop-stitch is a pattern in knitted garments made by dropping a made stitch at intervals

a **drugstore cowboy** is a person who dresses like a cowboy but has never worked as one

druidical circles is a popular name for certain ancient enclosures formed by rude stones circularly arranged, as at Stonehenge

a **drum kit** basically has a foot-operated bass drum, snare drum, suspended cymbal, and one or more tom-toms

before advertising in media came about, traveling hawkers of various wares would enter a village in their wagons and attract an audience by beating a drum in an attempt to **drum up** trade

a **drumly flosh** is a muddy swamp or stagnant pool overgrown with weeds

a traveling salesman in early times may have beat a drum or rung a bell to stir up business, giving us **drumming up trade**

the **Drummond light**, a torch that burns calcium oxide (lime) and gives off intense white light, 1854, was named for Scottish engineer Capt. Thomas Drummond, R.E., (1797–1840), who invented it around 1825

drunk driving is an example of hypallage because it is the driver, not the driving, that is drunk; the British version is drink-driving

dry beer is a beer from which the sugar is extracted and fermentation is longer, making it light and crisp, with less aftertaste

a **dry dock** can be drained to allow inspection and repair of ship hulls

{ a **dry drunk** is a sober person who behaves as if drunk }

dry goods are differentiated from groceries and hardware

when you smile a nervous or feeble little smile out of embarrassment or not knowing what to do, you have the **dry grins**

dry ice is solid carbon dioxide or the cold dense white mist produced by this in air

to rent an aircraft without a crew is a **dry lease**; a **wet lease** is to hire an aircraft with a crew

the higher the gin ratio, the more a martini is entitled to be called a **dry martini**

dry mounting is a process of bonding a print to a mount using a layer of adhesive and a hot press

dry pastels are a mixture of pigment powder agglutinated using a gum-based binder, then shaped into sticks and dried

to **dry roast** is to roast without oils

a **dry run** is dry, "unproductive," and this was first a World War II term for simulated bombing runs

a **dry sink** is an antique kitchen cabinet with an inset basin, now mainly a decorative furnishing

a **dry slope** is an artificial ski slope for practice and training

dry steering is the act of turning the wheels of a car that is not moving

dry stone fruits are the almond, walnut, hazelnut, coconut, chestnut, cashew, pine nut, pistachio, peanut, Brazil nut, and pecan

dry wilts is a phrase describing a "state of advanced decrepitude"

in **dry wine**, all the sugar has been converted into alcohol

dry-aged beef is hung in climate-controlled rooms for weeks so the texture becomes gelatinous and the flavor concentrated

dry-roasted means roasted without fat or oil

du jour is from French *plat du jour*, "dish of the day," and by the early twentieth century it appeared on restaurant menus, then was abstracted as an all-purpose modifier around 1989

a **dual edition** is the publication of a book simultaneously in hardcover and paperback

a **dub-dub** is a restaurant server or waiter, a clipped pronunciation of the first letter of waiter and waitress

duchess potatoes are mashed potatoes, butter, egg yolks, and seasoning used as a garnish or fried in small cakes; also called duchesse potatoes, pommes duchesse

duck sauce is a sweet-and-sour sauce of apricots, plums, sugar, and seasonings—to be served as a condiment with cooked duck or pork

duck soup appeared in a Tad Dorgan cartoon in 1902, in reference to a man juggling a set of miscellaneous items, and it means some action that was easy or presented no challenge, a cinch to complete

duck's quack is equivalent to cat's meow

duct tape got its name from its original use for repairing leaks in ducted ventilation and heating systems

a dude is a city-dweller, especially one vacationing on a ranch—hence, **dude ranch**

use **due to** only if you mean "caused by" or "resulting from"

a **duffle coat** (or **duffel coat**) is heavy, often hooded, and generally knee-length for bad weather

dulce de leche (from Latin *dulcis*, "sweet") is a Latin-American (literally "milk candy") concoction of caramel and sweet cream, as a spread or flavoring for something like ice cream

dumb down (1933) was first a U.S. term

a **dumb waiter** is a small elevator for delivering food, etc., the dumb meaning "missing a quality normally belonging to an item"—meaning the waiter is not animate

the **dumdum bullet** (1897) was named for the Dum-Dum arsenal in Bengal, where the British made them to use against fanatical charges by tribesmen

> **dunk a basketball** is based on the act of dipping a doughnut in a cup of coffee with one hand

the tough fibrous lining of the cranial cavity and spinal canal, the **dura mater**, is Latin for "hard mother"

durable goods are those not for immediate consumption and able to be kept for a period of time

durum wheat gets its name from Latin *durus*, "hard," as it is a type of hard wheat

a hardcover book's paper cover is a **dust jacket** or dust wrapper

a **dust ruffle** is a decorative fabric around the bottom of a piece of furniture

{ a **Dutch auction** is one in which the auctioneer starts with a high price, which is gradually lowered till met with a bidder }

Dutch cheese is a synonym for **cottage cheese**

a door divided horizontally for separate opening is a **Dutch door**

a **Dutch oven**, a large pot with a tight-fitting lid or cover that was heated in a fire by heaping coals around it, is most often produced in Holland where the casting process for these ovens originated

originally, **Dutch treat** referred to an invitation by a host who, instead of paying for his guests, made everyone pay for himself

a **dwarf planet** is a celestial body that is in orbit around the sun, has a nearly round shape, is not a satellite, and has not cleared objects from its orbit

dwell time is the time spent in the same position, area, stage of a process, etc.

dyed in the wool refers to the discovery that yarn dyed before being woven (in the wool) retained its color better than yarn dyed after being woven (in the piece)

{ E }

E. coli stands for *Escherichia coli*, a motile Gram-negative bacillus

use **each other** for two, **one another** for three or more people

eager beaver is a metaphor that probably became popular because it is a near-rhyme

ear candy (1977) is music which has an instant and direct appeal, but probably without lasting impact or significance, patterned on eye candy and arm candy

your little finger is called your **ear finger**

it was early Native Americans who taught us to, literally, keep an **ear to the ground** to listen for horses' hooves as cowboys approached

ear training in music is the teaching of pitch and rhythm recognition

Earl Grey tea, a blend of Indian and Sri Lankan black teas flavored by oil of bergamot, was probably named for the 2nd Earl Grey (1764–1845) said to have been given the recipe by a Chinese mandarin

an **early adopter** is a person who starts using a technology or product as soon as it becomes available

TV time before prime time is **early fringe**

early innings refers to the first, second, and third innings of a baseball game

an **earned run** is a baseball run scored without the aid of errors by the opposing team's fielders

earnest money is that paid to confirm a contract

to give someone an **ear-settin'** is to give a scolding or reprimand

the potato was once called an **earth apple**

earth colors are paint pigments made by refining naturally colored clays, rocks, and earths

Earth Day (April 22) was created in 1970 as a global day of observance of the need to protect the earth

earth light is the light reflected by the earth, as upon the moon, and corresponding to moonlight; it is also called **earth shine**

earth pig is another term for the aardvark

Earth Shoes are so called as they were first imported to the United States from Denmark on April 22, 1970, the first Earth Day

an **earth tone** is any rich, warm brownish hue

earth-based religion is the worship of all aspects of nature; nature as a whole considered to be the source of universal consciousness and energy; various forms and traditions involve this

earth-mother (1904), the folkloric spirit of the earth, was conceived as sensual, maternal, and is a translation of German *Erdmutter*

earthquake lights are the mysterious flickering glow seen over the ground during an earthquake—perhaps a reaction of rocks when stressed to the breaking point

an **easel** or **cabinet picture** in the Renaissance was a small one meant to be displayed on an easel

East Indies is still loosely applied to India, Indochina, and the Malay Archipelago of Southeast Asia

Easter Island was named for the day of its discovery

Easter Sunday is technically redundant

easy chair, a chair adapted for sitting or half reclining in an easy posture, dates to 1707

an **easy rider** is a sexually satisfying lover

eat crow probably refers to the fact that crow meat tastes terrible

to **eat the wind** is to take a walk

to **eat up the camera** is to be appealing or engaging on the silver screen

eat your heart out goes back as far as Diogenes Laertius who credited Pythagoras with saying "Do not eat your heart"—meaning "Don't waste your life worrying about something," 2,500 years ago

eating house is a synonym for restaurant

eau de cologne is 3–5 percent aromatic essence; eau de toilette is 4–8 percent; eau de parfum is 8–15 percent and perfume is 15–30 percent

in parts of New England and the Great Lakes, gutters are often referred to as **eaves troughs** or **eaves spouts**

an **echo sounder** measures the depth of a seabed or detects objects in water by the time taken for sound echoes to return to the device

an **ecological footprint** is the sum of an entity's impact on the environment, especially involving consumption and pollution

{ ectopic, as in **ectopic pregnancy**, is from Greek *ektopos*, "out of place" }

an **edge city** is a highly urbanized, yet officially unincorporated community adjacent to a major established city, with residences, varied businesses, entertainment districts, and large shopping areas

the **edge effect** is the effect of an abrupt transition between two quite different adjoining ecological communities on the numbers and kinds of organisms in the marginal habitat

an **edge tool** is any tool with a sharp cutting edge

the **editio princeps** is the first printed edition of a work

the difference between an **educated guess** and an estimate is that an estimate pretends to be true within certain limits, and an educated guess merely claims that it is a guess based on expertise within a field and on currently available knowledge

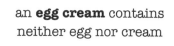

{ an **egg cream** contains neither egg nor cream }

egg on has the root sense "to urge on by poking with a sharp instrument" and comes from Old Norse *eggja*, "to incite, urge"

egg on your face may go back to slapstick in Victorian theaters, where the fall guy would get eggs broken on his forehead—like the custard pie thrown in the face that we are more familiar with

an **egg ring** is an open ring, often with a handle, used to keep an egg perfectly round during poaching or frying

an **egg roll** is a Chinese roll made of diced meat or prawns, and shredded cabbage with other vegetables, fried in a casing of thin egg-dough, hence the name; it is also called a spring roll. Over the years, spring rolls and egg rolls have become the same item in many countries. However, the traditional spring rolls are typically encased in a lighter, more delicate pastry wrap and are smaller than egg rolls, but the size of spring rolls has also changed over the years, becoming larger and more like egg rolls in size.

egg tempera is the traditional form of tempera paint consisting of pigments ground with pure egg yolk

the **egg tooth** is a special tooth that chicks have to break out of an egg—but which they lose after birth

an **egg wash** is a mix of egg yolk with water or milk and brushed over bread or pie before baking to enrich the color and gloss

eggs Benedict was named for a woman who requested the combination at New York's Delmonico's restaurant and consists of poached eggs and grilled ham on toasted English muffins, topped with hollandaise sauce

eggy bread, bread that has been dipped in an egg mixture and fried, is the same as French toast

in **egoistic hedonism**, the goal is one's own happiness; **universalistic hedonism** is the greatest happiness for the greatest number

Egyptian reed is papyrus

an **Egyptian Sphinx** has a man's head and lion's body; a **Greek Sphinx** has the head and chest of a woman, body of a lion, and wings

the **Eiffel Tower** was erected in the Champ-de-Mars for the Paris Universal Exposition of 1889 and at 984.25 feet was the world's tallest structure at the time—named for its designer, Alexandre Gustave Eiffel (1832–1923)

the **Eightfold Path** is the Middle Way and part of the Four Noble Truths that the Buddha taught as the path to nirvana or enlightenment and consists of Right View/ Understanding, Right Thought, Right Speech, Right Action, Right Livelihood, Right Effort, Right Mindfulness, Right Concentration; also called Noble Eightfold Path

an **eight-point cap** has an octagon-shaped crown and is worn by policemen

{ **eighty-six** means a restaurant kitchen has temporarily run out of a dish }

an **El Dorado** is a place offering fabulous wealth or opportunity (after the legendary place in South America, "the gilded one")

El Niño is "the Christmas child," referring to its beginning in late December

Èlan vital is the force of creative evolution underlying all activity in the universe

elbow grease is a humorous Americanism dating to 1672

elbow-lifting is a euphemism for a fondness for drinking

the card player who is dealt to first is the elder, **elder hand**, or forehand

electronic mail debuted in 1977, not long after the **floppy disk** (1972) and just before the **hard disk** (1978)

an **elephant in the room** is a big issue or obvious truth that no one wants to discuss or acknowledge; a problem or issue that

is present but which everyone avoids or ignores; also called eight-hundred-pound gorilla in the room

elevator music is soft background music

eleventh hour is an allusion to the parable of the laborers in the Bible's Matthew

the **Elgin Marbles** (1809) are sculptures and marbles (especially from the frieze of the Parthenon) brought to England and sold to the British government by Thomas Bruce, 7th Earl of Elgin (1766–1841)

the **elite eight** are the eight regional finalists of the NCAA Division I basketball tournament

em dash is the long dash used in punctuation; the **en dash** is shorter, and the **hyphen** is even shorter

embarrassment of riches does not usually refer to money—but to a profusion of anything that would be desirable, even in smaller quantities

ember days are twelve days of the year (divided into four seasonal periods, hence the Latin name *quatuor tempora*) set aside by the Church of England for fasting and prayers; from Old English *ymbren*, "recurring"

a poem typographically arranged into a recognizable shape is **emblem poetry**

emerald cut is a square-shaped gem with stepped facets

the **emergent year** is the nonexistent year between 1 BC and AD 1 or the epoch or date from which any people begin to compute their time or dates

emery boards are made with emery, a polishing powder from corundum and magnetite

the small kidney-shaped basin in hospital rooms is an **emesis basin**

en masse (1802) is French, literally, "in mass"

en passant (1665) is from French, meaning "in passing"; in reference to chess, first attested in 1818

{ an **éminence grise** wields power away from public view; derived from the Capuchin monk who was secretary to French statesman Cardinal Richelieu (1585-1642) }

eminent domain dates to 1625 and originally referred to ultimate or supreme lordship

an **emotional quotient** is an index of emotional intelligence; also called emotional intelligence quotient

an **emperor moth** has eyespots on all four wings

the **emperor penguin** is the largest species and it has a yellow patch on each side of the head

empty calories are those obtained from foods with no nutrients

an **empty word** is one that only has a grammatical function and no meaning in itself, like the infinitive "to"

en bloc and **en masse** both have a sense of "all together"—but en masse is applied to people and en bloc to things

en chinga is colloquial Spanish for "fast, hurriedly, quickly"

en croute literally means "in a crust"

en route is French for "on the way"

a bathroom that is **en suite** is immediately adjoining a bedroom

encaustic painting is painting by means of wax with which the colors are combined, and which is afterwards fused with hot irons, thus fixing the colors

encyclopedic fiction is any work of fiction employing a variety of forms to explore its subject exhaustively, such as *Moby Dick*

an end-of-aisle display in a supermarket is an **end cap**

the **end grain** is the grain in a piece of wood that shows at the end of a cut-off length

the mark or marks at the end of an article, chapter, or book is simply the **end mark**

end product and **end result** are redundancies for product and result

enfant terrible actually applies to young adults (generally male) who go out of their way to shock or embarrass but at the same time are considered talented

technically, **England** is not a country and neither are **Scotland** or **Wales**; England and Scotland are kingdoms and Wales is a principality. All occupy **Great Britain**, the largest island of Europe. Add **Northern Ireland** and you've got the **United Kingdom**, which is a country.

English billiards (also carom) is played on a table with no pockets

English breakfast is a relatively hearty breakfast of eggs, meat, baked goods or cereal, fruit or juice, and tea or coffee, eaten in the United Kingdom

English breakfast tea is a traditional blend of Ceylon, Kenyan, and Indian teas—served for English breakfast

English muffins (an Americanism) were not invented in England, nor **French fries** in France, or **Danish pastries** in Denmark

English mustard is a variety of bright-yellow pungent mustard from ground white and brown mustard seeds and colored with turmeric

English sunbathing is sitting fully clothed in the sunshine

entre nous, "between us," can be employed seriously for a confidence or secret

entry words in dictionaries are usually boldface; they are also called headwords or lemmas

epic poetry tells a story but has a specific style and form, such as Homer's *Iliad* and *Odyssey*

an **epicene pronoun** is a gender-neutral pronoun

Epsom salts were originally obtained by the evaporation of the water of a mineral spring at Epsom Downs in Surrey, UK

Epstein-Barr virus (1968) was named for British virologist Michael Anthony Epstein and Irish-born virologist Yvonne M. Barr

an **equilateral triangle** has all three sides the same length; a scalene triangle has all three in different lengths; and an isosceles triangle has two sides of the same length

an **equinox day** means it is a twelve hour day almost everywhere on the planet

equity capital is that portion of the capital of a business provided by the sale of stock

an **ergative verb** is a verb which, when used with no object, automatically changes the subject into the object; break is ergative because when we say "the window broke," the window is the thing getting broken, it is not the vandal

Erin go bragh means "Ireland for ever"

the **Erlenmeyer flask** is the one used in chemistry class with a wide flat-bottomed flask and narrow neck (named for a German chemist)

words used in place of those that might be considered sacrilegious or obscene ("golly," "gosh") are **escape words** or **Deconic swearing**

Eskimo Pies date to 1921

Eskimo roll is a complete rollover in kayaking, from upright to upside-down to upright

the snappy comeback that comes to mind too late to do any good is an **esprit de l'escalier**

an **essential fatty acid** is a fatty acid required for human metabolism that cannot be synthesized by the body and must be present in the diet

an **essential nutrient** is any substance that must be obtained from food for good health because the body cannot produce enough of it on its own

an **essential oil** tends to have the characteristic fragrance of the plant, fruit, or flowers from which it is extracted

estate tax is a federal tax levied on a deceased person's gross estate before that estate is divided

et al. (*et alia*) means "and others" (plural is **et alii**, "and other people") — which are both more specific than **et cetera**, "and the rest;" only et al. and et alii can refer to people, whereas et cetera refers to things

eternal camping ground is a phrase meaning "future state of existence"

ethnic cleansing (1991) is a translation of Serbo-Croat *etnicko ciscenje*

European plan is a rate that includes no meals (except maybe a light or Continental breakfast); **American plan** includes at least breakfast and an evening meal

eustatic change is a worldwide change of sea level produced by an increase or decrease in the amount of seawater

evaporated milk is concentrated and unsweetened; **condensed milk** is reduced thick milk with sugar added

Eve with a lid on is apple pie in diner slang

even-aged describes a woodland with trees of approximately the same age

even-toed ungulates include the ruminants, camels, pigs, and hippotamuses

every dog has its day is a proverb (mid-1500s) alluding to the lowly status dogs once held

every so often means "occasionally" while **ever so often** means "frequently"

everyday is an adjective; the time expression is every day

{ **Evian water** is from Evian-les-Bains in France }

ex cathedra means "from the throne" or "authoritatively"

ex gratia "(done) out of grace, as a favor" is generally followed by payments for reasons of goodwill or settlement of some grievance

ex libris — found on bookplates — means "out of the library (or books) of"

ex nihilo (1573) is Latin for "out of nothing"

ex officio (1532) is Latin, meaning "in discharge of one's duties," and can be loosely used to mean "comes with the job"

ex post facto (1632) is from Middle Latin, meaning "from what is done afterwards"

exact same is a lazy shortening of "exactly the same"

exact sciences are physics, chemistry, astronomy, etc.; **pure science** is regarded as essentially theoretical (in contrast to **applied science**, which is practical), **social sciences** include anthropology and sociology; **physical sciences** are geology, meteorology, etc.; and **natural sciences** are botany and zoology, as well as chemistry and physics

an **exclamation mark** or point is also known as a screamer, a gasper, a startler—and it was once called a note of admiration; it comes from Latin *io*, "exclamation of joy," and was created by stacking the *i* above the *o*

traditionally, **excuse me** was used for minor offenses, and **pardon me** was reserved for more serious situations requiring a more explicit apology

expletive deleted became a popular term during the time of Richard Nixon's White House tapes

an **exploded view** is a picture that shows all the separate parts of something and indicates how they fit together

an **explosive volcano** erupts rocks, lava, gas, and pyroclastic surges; an **effusive volcano** is characterized by streams of fluid lava flowing over large areas

{ an **express wish** is one that is distinctly presented }

expression marks is the collective term for musical directives, including tempo, volume, technique, phrasing, and mood

extended family is a group of relatives by blood, marriage, or adoption—living in close proximity or together

an **extended metaphor** is a metaphor that is extended through a stanza or entire poem, often by multiple comparisons of unlike objects or ideas

the eyes of a potato are also known as **external buds**

external combustion examples are the steam engine and steam turbine; **internal combustion** engines include gasoline and diesel engines

extravehicular activity is a fancy term for astronauts' activity in space outside the spacecraft

extreme sports include snowboarding, sky-surfing, free climbing, barefoot water skiing, bungee jumping, zorbing, and parkour

eye dialect is any unusual or nonstandard spelling that depicts either an uneducated or youthful speaker (examples: wuz, enuff)

an **eye pillow** is a small pillow, usually with an herbal or scented filling, placed over the eyes for reducing stress and for soothing

an **eye rhyme** is a similarity between words in spelling but not pronunciation—like dove and move

to **eye-bite** is to bewitch with a malign influence whatever the eye glances upon

an **eyebrow flash** is an unconscious upward movement of the eyebrows when people approach each other and are ready to make social contact

an **eye-waiter** is one who performs duties diligently only while his/her master is looking

{ F }

the **F number** for a camera stands for "focal length"—indicating the ratio between the focal lengths of a camera lens and the diameter of the aperture

fabric sculpture is an art form of soft sculpture made from textiles, espcially dolls and figures

a **face brick** is one suitable for exposure to view in a finished building

face the music refers to "Rogue's March" played when a U.S. Army member was disgraced and discharged

a synonym for **face value** is **nominal value**

a **fact bite** is a very short piece of information; a piece of trivia

factory farming is a system of large-scale industrialized and intensive agriculture that is focused on profit with animals kept indoors and restricted in mobility

Fair Isle is the name of one of the Shetland islands, used to designate woolen articles knitted in certain designs characteristic of the island

fair use is the right to quote copyright material without securing permission, based on it being brief and clearly attributed

fairney-cloots are small horny substances above the hoofs of horses, sheep, and goats

small colored lights for decorating an outdoor Christmas tree are **fairy lights**

a **fairy ring** is a naturally occurring ground circle usually caused by fungi or other biological agents

fairy tales are seldom about fairies

fait accompli, French for "accomplished fact," is pronounced FAYT-uh-kom-PLEE

Fall Classic is the World Series

fall guy was first a professional wrestling term

{ in **fall in love**, "fall" is the sense of passing suddenly from one state to another }

falling star is another name for meteor or shooting star

rain, snow, or hail is also known as **falling weather**

Fallopian tubes are named for Gabriello Fallopio, an Italian anatomist

a card played in order to mislead opponents into thinking that it is one's strong suit is a **false card**

false dawn is the transient light that precedes the sun's rising by about an hour

a **false friend** is a word or phrase of one language that resembles one in another language but has a different meaning

a **false fruit** is one formed from other plant parts besides the ovary, examples being the strawberry and the fig

a **false pond** is a mirage

the term **family values** was in use by 1916

a **fan brush** is a fan-shaped bristle brush used for subtle blending of wet paint

a **fan light** is a window over a door, so called from the semicircular form and radiating sash bars of those windows, which are set in the circular heads of arched doorways

Fannie Mae (1948) gets its name from FNMA, the acronym of Federal National Mortgage Association, established 1938

in **far from the madding crowd**, madding means "acting madly"

1950s jazz players used the expression **far out** to describe experimental music, which was far out of the mainstream

the **Farm Belt** is the north-central plains and within it is the Corn Belt and part of the Grain Belt

at first, a **fashion plate** literally meant "a picture showing a fashion," and then it gained the figurative meaning of a person who dresses in current fashion

fashion roadkill is any person who tries to dress fashionably, but looks ridiculous

fashion victim is a person who follows every clothing trend

fast and loose was originally an old fairground game

the term **fast food** was first used in 1951

fat cat (1928) first meant "a rich backer of a political party"

Fata Morgana (1818), literally Fairy Morgana, is a mirage especially common in the Strait of Messina, Italy, named for Morgana, the "Morgan le Fay" of Anglo-French poetry, sister of King Arthur

father confessor is the Roman Catholic priest who hears confessions and gives advice

faux pas is literally "false step"; the plural of faux pas is faux pas

fava bean is a pleonasm (redundancy) like free gift—because *fava* in Latin means "bean"; it is also called the broad bean, horse bean, or Windsor bean

the **feed dog** is the part of a sewing machine that feeds the material under the needle

to **feel pale** is to feel sick

feeling all mops and brooms means "out of sorts"

feet of clay, a real weakness in someone or something otherwise considered strong and infallible, is from the book of Daniel in the Bible (a great statue with feet of clay)

the **female side** of the family is the distaff side (a spinning term), the opposite of the spear side

femme fatale is a relatively recent phrase from the early twentieth century

fence-jumpin' is another word for adultery

{ **feng shui** is literally "wind water" in Chinese }

a **feral cat** is a domesticated cat that has returned to the wild, or the offspring of such a cat

the original **Ferris Wheel** carried people 250 feet high in the air and was first installed in 1893; the engineer was George W. G. Ferris (1859–1896)

feu de joie is a way of saying bonfire

few in number is a common redundancy

Fibber McGee's closet refers to household clutter, especially a messy area or room

fiber plants are plants capable of yielding fiber useful in the arts, as hemp, flax, ramie, agave, etc.

fickle finger is a capricious quasi-supernatural agency that controls events

fictive kin refers to someone who, though unrelated by birth or marriage, has such a close emotional relationship with another that they may be considered part of the family

fiddler's green is the place where sailors expect to go when they die

field day is an extraordinarily good time, while heyday is prime time

field officers in the U.S. Army are above captain and below brigadier general

in its earliest sense, **field trial** referred to a test of young hunting dogs to gauge how well they would point and retrieve

fife and drum was once a metaphor for military life

fifteen minutes of fame is a commentary on the amount of time anyone is really in the spotlight, from Andy Warhol's "in the future, everybody will be world famous for fifteen minutes"

the term **fifth column** is from the Spanish Civil War, when a general stated he had four columns encircling Madrid and a fifth column (traitors) working for him in the city

in coaching days, the **fifth wheel** was a cumbersome object carried at the rear of a carriage

fifty-first state is an epithet for Puerto Rico, a commonwealth whose citizens have U.S. citizenship

fig or **full fig** is the complete set of clothes for an occasion

fig leaf can refer to anything intended to hide something indecorous or indecent

Fig Newtons were named after Newton, Massachusetts

figgy pudding is from the dialect term fig, which meant "raisin"

the fixed chair on a boat for a person trying to catch large fish is called the **fighting chair**

early American settlers had to put out great prairie fires and learned that setting a circle or strip of land on fire could stop the path or lessen the impact of a big fire—giving us the phrase **fighting fire with fire**

figment of the imagination is something which exists only as an arbitrarily framed notion of the mind, and this phrase dates to 1847

the **figure of eight** (or **figure eight**) is the symbol for infinity in mathematics

figure of speech is any expressive use of language, as a metaphor, simile, personification, or antithesis, in which words are used in other than their literal sense, or in other than their ordinary locutions, in order to suggest a picture or image or for other special effect

the **file extension** is the group of letters after the period in a filename, such as .doc or .txt, indicating the purpose or contents of the file

filet mignon is French, literally "dainty fillet"; filet mignon (plural filet mignons or filets mignons) means a slice cut from the small end of beef tenderloin

to **fill one's shirt** is to eat heartily

fill the bill was first a reference to a theatrical poster or bill

film noir, French for "black film," was a term coined in 1946 for a genre depicting urban anxiety and world-weary anti-heroes

film star is dated to 1914 and the preferred American term, **movie star**, 1919

the **filter lane** is a lane of traffic reserved for those making a specific turn at the next junction

filthy stuff is a euphemism for good pitching (baseball) or money

fin de siècle is an adjective from French, meaning "end of century"

final outcome and **final results** are redundant

final solution (1947) is a literal translation of German *Endlšung*

final straw (and the camel's back) became a feather (and a horse's back) until Charles Dickens revived the old Biblical proverb in 1848

a **financial planner** helps clients plan and prepare some or all of their personal or business finances—usually the management of assets and liabilities but also insurance and taxes

fine art is any art created for its own sake as opposed to **commercial artwork**

an object's, substance's, or energy's **fine structure** is its composition on a small scale and in considerable detail

fines herbes is a mixture of equal parts chopped parsley, chervil, chives, and tarragon

fine-toothed comb reflects the literal meaning better than fine-tooth comb

the **finger board** is the part of a stringed instrument against which the fingers press the strings to vary the tone—as well as the keyboard of a piano, organ, etc.

a **finger buffet** is a whole series of finger food

each finger has a **finger pad**

finger painting is a Chinese watercolor technique using a finger instead of a brush

finger trouble is a term for an error caused by operating a control wrongly or pressing the wrong key on electronic equipment

fingers crossed is an allusion to the superstition that making the sign of the cross will avert bad luck

a **finishing trowel** is the flat, rectangular tool used to smooth plaster or concrete work

a **Finnegan pin** is a nonexistent part or tool, or a thing whose name is forgotten or unknown (1938)

a **fipple flute** is the same as a recorder or flageolet—a flute blown from one end like a whistle

fire and brimstone is eternal punishment in hell (Genesis 19:24, Revelation 19:20)

the **fire-back** is the back wall of a fireplace

fire-dogs is another term for andirons

fireflies glow for a while but die down; lightning bugs flash their taillights for only a few seconds and never in the same place twice

fire-new is a synonym for brand-new

in early use, **firing squad** was synonymous with firing party, a "squad detailed to fire over the grave of someone buried with military honors"; during World War I it took on the meaning of "squad detailed to shoot someone sentenced to death by court-martial"

first chair is a premier musicians playing a particular instrument in an orchestra—seated closest to the audience, taking the lead for that instrument's movements, and playing any solos

a child of your first cousin is your **first cousin once removed**

the offspring of a pair of differing purebred animals is the **first cross**

a **first edition** is the entire original run of copies of a book; the **first issue** is the first printing or original press run

the **first finger** is also the forefinger or index finger

first light, the time when light first appears in the morning, started as a term in the armed forces for the time when light was sufficient for military operations to begin

a woodsman once had three meals: **first lunch** at 5 p.m., second lunch at 9 p.m., and third lunch at 1 p.m.

United States and communist nations, **Third World** refers to countries that do not align themselves with either democratic countries or communist countries, **Fourth World** is the very poorest nations

> **first magnitude** constitutes the brightest stars; the naked eye can make out stars of the sixth magnitude

your **first name** is also your **forename, given name**, or **Christian name**

a civic celebration on New Year's Eve with cultural events and family-oriented entertainment is called **first night**

a **first occurrence** cannot be called first annual because it did not happen the previous year

first position in ballet is the feet turned outward with the heels touching

first principles are the fundamental concepts on which a theory, system, or method is based

a **first responder** is a certified, often volunteer, emergency, medical, or law enforcement officer who is the first to arrive at an accident or disaster scene

first violin leads the orchestra

of the **first water** means of the first excellence, as a diamond

First World refers to industrialized capitalist countries (North America, Europe, Japan, Australia, New Zealand), **Second World** refers to industrialized nations except the

the phrase is **first-come**; first-served has a "d" on the end

a **fiscal year** is any twelve-month period between settlements of financial accounts, as in the U.S. government's October 1—September 30 fiscal year

a **fish cake** contains shredded fish and mashed potato

a **fish stick** in the United States is a **fish finger** in Britain

fish story is a term based on fishermen traditionally exaggerating the size of their catch

fishing expedition is a metaphor that may have its origins in the older expression "fishing voyage" and referred to any extended sea voyage

a **fishing vest** is a sleeveless jacket with many pockets for carrying small objects

fit as a fiddle lost a letter along the way; originally, it was fit as a fiddler—someone who danced and scampered while playing music

fit to be tied is mid-nineteenth century in origin, and the phrase evokes someone so hysterically furious that they need to be tied down

a **fitted cap** is a baseball cap that is not elasticized or adjustable at the back

five by five is a saying meaning "a good clear signal"

the **five elements** of feng shui are fire, water, wood, earth, and metal

five fingers is a fisherman's name for a starfish

five o'clock shadow dates from the 1930s, when it was first used in an advertising campaign for Gem razor blades

the **five sacraments** are confirmation, penance, orders, matrimony, and extreme unction

the **five Ws** are who, what, when, where, and why

the **five-second rule** is the belief that if one picks up a dropped food item very quickly, it is safe to eat it

> **five-spice powder** is typically fennel seed, cinnamon, clove, star anise, and peppercorn

the **five star system** originated in grading hotels

a **fixed asset** is any long-term asset, as a building, tract of land, or patent

fixed oils are natural animal or vegetable oils that are nonvolatile, different from essential oils

a **fixed star** is one whose relative position to other stars stays the same, as distinguished from a planet which shifts its relative position

a **fixed-wing aircraft** is traditional, compared to **rotating-wing aircraft**

flag-fallen means unemployed, from the sixteenth- to seventeenth-century custom of lowering a playhouse flag when no performance was held and actors were out of work

the term **flash flood** only dates to 1940

flash in the pan originally referred to muskets whose pans emitted a flash but did not cause the weapons to discharge

flash memory is the computer memory that retains data in the absence of a power supply

a **flash mob** is a group of people who organize on the Internet and then quickly assemble in a public place, do something bizarre, and disperse

flashbulb memory is a memory for a significant and extremely emotional moment or event

to be in a **flat spin** is to be panicked (from an airplane position involving loss of control when flying)

to **flat-hat** is to fly recklessly low in an airplane

flavor of the month first referred to ice cream

flea market comes from Dutch colonial days from the Vallie (Valley) Market in Manhattan, which was abbreviated Vlie Market and later pronounced flea market

the **Flehmen reaction** is the look a cat has when it savors an unusual or evocative scent—the head is raised and the mouth is held slightly open

flesh color is an oil paint color achieved by mixing white and yellow ocher

to **flesh out** is to elaborate, add nuance and detail

a fingernail was once called a **flesh-spade**

fleur-de-lis is from French "flower of the lily," used much as a heraldic device on the royal arms of France

flight ceiling describes the highest altitude at which an aircraft may fly due to lack of air density and craft velocity

flim-flam (1538) is a contemptuous echoic construction

flint implements are tools, employed by men before the use of metals, such as axes, arrows, spears, knives, wedges, etc., which were commonly made of flint, but also of granite, jade, jasper, and other hard stones

to **flip one's lid** is an allusion to a pot boiling over

> **flip side** was first a term referring to the less important side of a phonograph record

flip-flop, the thong sandal (1960s), is named as imitative of the sound of walking in them (flip-flap had been used in various echoic senses since 1529); the sense of "complete reversal of direction" dates from 1900

floating debt is that which is repayable in the short term

a **floating island** is a meringue (or a few) floated on a sea of custard

floating ribs or **false ribs** and **lower ribs** are not attached directly to the breastbone

a **floor plan** is a diagram of a room or story that is drawn to scale

a **floor-through apartment** is one that occupies an entire floor of a building

a **Florida room** is simply a sunroom

in **flotsam and jetsam**, the former is floating relics from a wreck and the latter is freight purposely thrown overboard in a time of distress

flower children were hippies who typically wore flowers in their hair

broccoli is a **flower cluster**, the Brussels sprout is a bud

flower girl was originally a girl or woman who sold flowers in the streets

flue gas is a technical term for the gaseous combustion product (smoke) that comes out of a stove or a furnace

fly agaric is a mushroom with a narcotic juice which, in sufficient quantities, is poisonous

fly by the seat of your pants refers to an experienced pilot's ability to sense changes in vibrations in the seat, meaning the airplane may be going into a stall

fly in the face of is an allusion to a dog that flies in the face of its enemy

the earliest reference to **fly in the ointment** was in the Bible's Ecclesiastes, "dead flies cause the ointment of the apothecary to send forth a stinking savour"

fly nut is a nut with wings

fly off the handle refers to a hammer or ax losing its head when loose after a blow has been struck

fly-by-night is said to be an old term of reproach to a woman, signifying that she was a witch, and was extended to "anyone who departs hastily from a recent activity," especially while owing money

a **flying buttress** is a contrivance for taking up the thrust of a roof or vault which cannot be supported by ordinary buttresses and consists of a straight bar of masonry, usually sloping, carried on an arch, and a solid pier or buttress sufficient to receive the thrust

with **flying colors** is an allusion to a victorious fleet sailing into port with flags still flying at the mastheads

fruit bats or megabats are sometimes called **flying foxes**

some pre-20th century phrase coinages that may be surprising include: **flying machine** (1736), **acid rain** (1859), **old-age pension** (1879), **department store** (1887), **contact lens** (1888), **Mother's Day** (1890), **modern art** (1895), **motor car** (1895), **motion picture** (1896)

right after World War II we needed a name for the phenomenon **flying saucer** (1947)

focaccia bread is Italian for "bread baked in the hearth"

the **focal plane** is the place at the back of the camera where the image is focused on the film

the term **focus group** was first used around 1965

{ **Foggy Bottom** is a term for political routine and government bureaucracy }

foie gras is literally "fat liver" in French

a **foliage leaf** is a normal leaf as opposed to petals or modified leaves

folic acid (from Latin *folium*, "leaf") is a vitamin found in leafy vegetables; folic is pronounced FOE-lik

folk etymology is a term for words and phrases that have resulted from changes based on "folk" or "popular" notions; a folk etymology arises when a word is assumed to derive from another because of some association of form or meaning, but in fact the word has a different derivation

follow suit is originally from cards, to play a card of the same suit as that which led

a **foo fighter** is any unidentified flying object described as a ball of fire or light, from the World War II comic strip "Smokey Stover"

foo yong is a Chinese dish or sauce with egg as the main ingredient

food for worms is a dead human being and **food for fishes** are victims of drowning

food mile is a unit of measurement for every mile over which a foodstuff is transported from producer to consumer

a **food processor** is an electric kitchen tool that is used to chop, grate, mince, slice, puree, and blend food ingredients; a blender is an electric kitchen appliance that consists of a tall container with a removable lid and motor driven blades at the bottom that blend, chop, mix, or liquefy foods depending on the speed setting selected; in general, blenders are better suited to working with liquids (they are also called liquidizers or liquefiers), and food processors work wonders with more solid foods, and of the two, the food processor is the more versatile

a **food web** is made up of food chains; a **food chain** is a series of organisms, each depending on the next for food

fool's gold was the term for a "gold mineral" brought back from voyages to find a Northwest Passage

to **foot the bill**, "pay," is a reference to signing one's name at the foot of the bill as a guarantee that payment will be made

it's **foot-and-mouth disease** not "foot-in-mouth" as a disease; the latter is a punning metaphorical term

use **for a while**; "for awhile" is wrong because "for" is implicit in "awhile"

you get something free, not **for free**—because it's an adverb, not a noun

for goodness' sake properly has an apostrophe

the fact that many city birds live on next to nothing reinforces the sense of paucity suggested by the expression **for the birds**

> **force field** is a science fiction term for an invisible, strong barrier

force majeure is French "superior strength" for unforeseeable circumstances that prevent someone from fulfilling a contract

examples of **fore-and-aft** clippings are: Amer(ican) Ind(ian) to Amerind, binoc(ular)s, bio(graphical)pic(ture) to biopic, (French) frie(d) (potatoe)s to fries, (in)flu(enza) to flu, op(tical) art, (re)frig(erator) to fridge, sci(ence) fi(ction) to sci-fi, and sit(uation) com(edy) to sitcom

foregone conclusion is from Shakespeare's *Othello*

foreign body is any substance occurring in any part of the body where it does not belong, and usually introduced from without

a **foreign language** is learned mostly for cultural insight while a **second language** is learned mostly for utilitarian purposes

forget-me-nots may have gotten their name from the last words of a knight who drowned while trying to pick these flowers by a riverside

a **fork lunch** or supper is a light meal eaten with a fork

the word fork was thieves' slang for finger, so **forking over** and **forking out** became slang for paying or handing out money

formic acid was coined from Latin *formica* "ant," so called because it was obtained from red ants

the Chinese purportedly introduced the idea of **fortune cookies** in San Francisco's Chinatown in the nineteenth century

forty winks is a short nap, especially after dinner (1567)

the **forty-ninth parallel** is the boundary (basically) of the United States and Canada

the **forward slash** in computing is the /, in contradistinction to a **backslash** \

the **Fosbury flop** high-jumping technique (1968) was created by U.S. athlete Dick Fosbury (b. 1947), who used it to win the 1968 Olympic gold medal

the opposite of clean bill of health is a **foul bill of health**

a **found poem** is a passage within prose that unintentionally reads like poetry

{ the outermost strands of a spider web are the **foundation lines** }

the **four corners** of the earth have been designated as Ireland, just southeast of the Cape of Good Hope, west of the Peruvian coast, and between New Guinea and Japan—each 120 feet above the geodetic mean and with measurably high gravitational pull

the **Four Noble Truths** are the doctrines of Buddha: all life is suffering, the cause of suffering is ignorant desire, this desire can be destroyed, the means to this is the Eightfold Path

a piece of wood that is rectangular, flat, and has all edges (faces, sides, and ends) 90 degrees is called **four square**

four-legged word is a humorous term for any long polysyllabic word, often scholarly and pretentious

the term **four-letter word** (1934) is said to have come from the use of a proliferation of such words during World War I

the **fourth dimension** is a postulated spatial dimension in addition to length, area, and volume

the **fourth estate** is the press or journalism in general

fourth position in ballet is one foot in front of the other turned out parallel

the **Fourth World** are the poorest and most underdeveloped of the Third World

fox and grapes is a term for someone who wants something but cannot obtain it and then tries to pretend that he or she does not really want it

fox marks are brown spots or stains in a book caused by dampness affecting impurities in the paper

a **fox terrier** is a breed originally used to unearth foxes

foxes walk with short steps, alternating walking with trotting; the **fox trot** modern dance mimics this, alternating short and long steps

fraidy-cat, c. 1910 slang, is from a child's pronunciation of afraid

a **frankfurter** is a smoked sausage, **hot dog** describes a frankfurter served in a bun or roll, and **wiener** is actually "wiener-wurst" or Vienna sausage and later became a synonym for frankfurter

fraternal twins do not necessarily resemble each other but are born at the same time from two fertilized ova; identical twins, who resemble each other closely, are of the same sex, born at the same time, and from a single fertilized ovum

Freddie Mac (1992) is the Federal Home Loan Mortgage Corporation

a high diver jumping off a board is a **free fall**, and so is an astronaut in orbit; it is not always an uncontrolled plummet

> originally a **free lance** was a free companion or a person free of occupational or political party obligation or allegiance

free lunch, from the 1800s, alludes to the custom of taverns offering food free of charge to induce customers to buy drinks; it was soon extended to other kinds of gifts but is often used in a negative way, as in the example

free range is supposed to mean that poultry is allowed to roam without being confined and feeds on naturally grown crops, consuming only a vegetarian diet

free rein is the correct spelling as the allusion is to horses

free running is the activity of combining parkour with gymnastics to pass obstacles and demonstrate athletic talent

free verse is poetry that does not rhyme or have a regular meter

free will is the belief that physical causes do not entirely shape the world and that mental processes can act to influence things

freedom lawn is residential land designed to allow a variety of naturally occurring plants to grow without cultivation or cutting

free-floating anxiety refers to vague feelings of fear/anxiety without any observable cause or source

freeze-drying is preserving by rapidly freezing something and then subjecting it to a high vacuum to remove the ice

a **freeze-up** is a period of extreme cold

freezing rain is rain that freezes on impact with the ground or objects

French braid is a hairstyle gathering all the hair into one large braid

French cuffs are folded back and fastened in a double layer and are also called double cuffs

a plastic stencil for making curves is a **French curve**

a **French door** is one composed of glass panes

French dressing has no counterpart in France, and Russian dressing is not Russian; the latter is so named from the inclusion of caviar in early versions

a **French fold** is a sheet of paper printed on one side only and folded over from left and right to form a section with uncut bolts

the French in **French fry** comes from a method called frenching, which is slicing vegetables into long, thin strips; French fries actually came from Belgium, not France (French fried potatoes, 1894)

the **French horn** developed from the simple hunting horn in the seventeenth century

French hours refers to a shorter more efficient workday without breaks or lunch hour

a **French kiss** is known as an English kiss in France

to take a **French leave** comes from the French custom of leaving a ball or dinner without saying goodbye to the host or hostess

the English call a condom a **French letter** and the French call it an **English cap**

French mustard or **Dijon mustard** is a mild mustard that combines brown and black varieties of seed with wine or unripe grape juice (*verjuice*)

a **French pastry** has a filling of fruit or custard

the **French poodle** is not French, and the **Great Dane** is not Danish

French stick is another term for baguette

in England, **French toast** is simply sliced bread fried in bacon fat or butter

a **French twist** is the hair in a vertical roll at the back of the head

French vanilla is a strong vanilla flavor or aroma, possibly from vanilla grains, not a "type" of vanilla but rather a precooked custard loaded with egg yolks and used as a base for the ice cream flavor

French-cut, of food like green beans, means sliced obliquely

a **fresh breeze** is 20–24 miles per hour

the display case for meat that is packaged at the grocery store and the self-service meat counter and the butcher's area the **fresh meat counter**

{ a **freshwater town** or **freshwater college** implies a rustic or provincial setting }

a **Freudian slip** is a slip of the tongue that inadvertently reveals what's on the mind of the speaker

on a pierced earring, the part you put onto the post from the back is called the **friction nut**

a **fried egg** in golf is a buried lie in a sand trap with only the top of the ball showing

fritto misto is a dish of various foods, especially seafood, deep-fried in batter (Italian "mixed fry")

frog hair (also called fringe, apron, collar) is the closely mown grass that surrounds a putting green, between the putting surface and any rough that might also surround the green

a **frog in the throat** is said to allude to medieval times, when there was a fear that drinking water contained frogspawn and a frog could start growing inside the body

frog legs or frogs' legs are the forms to use

from away is used to describe anyone residing in Maine who does not hail from the state

from pillar to post comes from real tennis, a tactic of tiring an opponent by having him pursue the ball from one side (pillar) of the court to the other (post)

get-go in **from the get-go** is a shortening of "get going"

the **front apron** is the wider part of a necktie and the **neck end** is the skinny end

front line was originally used in reference to trench warfare in France in World War I

front matter comprises things in the beginning of a book, like an introduction and table of contents

the **front of the house** includes the areas of a restaurant open to the public or public view, such as the lobby, bar, and dining room

a **frontage road** is a smaller road that runs alongside a highway or major road

the function of **front-line troops** became well established in World War I when for years two armies faced each other across no man's land in two lines of trenches

if a tree trunk cracks during cold weather, that is a **frost crack**; when the wound heals, a ridge called a **frost rib** or **frost ridge** is often left

the **frost line** is the maximum depth of ground below which the soil does not freeze in winter

evidence of severe cold is retained in **frost rings**, lines between the annual growth rings of trees

frou-frou (1870) is from French for "a rustling"

{ beer flavored with fruit or fruit juice for the second fermentation is **fruit beer** }

fruit cocktail (1922) is a mixture of sliced or diced fruits, and it is synonymous with **fruit cup** (1931); **fruit salad** (1861) is a salad composed of fruits

fruit leather is mashed fruit dried to form a thin sheet

fruit salad is two or more rows of military campaign ribbons on a uniform

fruit soup is any soup with a cream and pureed fruit, most often served cold

fruit(s) de mer is seafood or any edible crustacean

fryin' size is said of a young person or a runt in the American West

frying pan (1382) and **fry pan** were once New England terms

fu yung or **foo yong** means "in a sauce made with eggs and other ingredients" and is from Chinese, literally "lotus"

fuddy-duddy dates to 1899, but its origin is unknown

fugitive colors are pigments that gradually fade when exposed to sunlight

full boat is the full price or total amount, or all of something

full boil and **rolling boil** are synonyms

a **full brother** or sister is one born of the same mother and father

in bingo, **full house** is the set of numbers needed to win

full monty may derive from "the full amount"

beans have long been considered an energy food, so to be **full of beans** is to be active and energetic

if someone is **full of ginger**, they have mettle or spirit

full speed ahead derived from full steam ahead, a nautical term

full stop in Britain is the term for a period ending a sentence

full-tilt boogie describes a pizza with everything

a **fun run** is a long race or marathon, usually to raise money for a charity

function words are prepositions, pronouns, conjunctions, articles, etc., that have a predominantly grammatical role

a **functional illiterate** is one whose reading and writing skills are below what is needed to function normally in society

functional shift or conversion is the process by which words change parts of speech without the addition of a prefix or suffix, as in soldier on, the verb, being created from soldier, the noun.

a **funnel cloud** is a cone-shaped storm that appears to be hanging down from a cloud, but unlike a tornado, it does not touch the surface of the earth

funny farm is a slang term dating only to 1963

fusion cuisine is any dish combining ingre-

> the **funny bone** is a nerve, not a bone; the name funny bone is a pun on the humerus, the arm bone that gets strange tingles when it is bumped

full tilt, "full speed," is from the encounter at full gallop of knights in a tilt

full-spectrum light refers to light that covers the entire spectrum, from low infrared to ultraviolet and above

dients or methods of two or more regional or ethnic culinary traditions

fusion food or cuisine is a mixing of elements from regionally different culinary traditions

future history, a narration of imagined future events, is a great oxymoron

{ **future shock** is the disorientation we feel as a result of too much change }

futz around may derive from the Yiddish arumfartzen

{ G }

g force is a unit of inertial force on a body that is subjected to rapid acceleration or gravity, equal to 32 feet per second per second at sea level; also written g-force

Gaelic football is a rough football-like game mainly played in Ireland with fifteen players to each side, and the object of the game is to punch, dribble, or kick the ball into a goal

Gaia hypothesis is the hypothesis that the earth and its atmosphere should be regarded as a living, self-regulating organism

galactic noise is unidentified radio-frequency radiation coming from beyond the solar system

the **Galapagos Islands** are named for the massive tortoises living there, from Old Spanish *galapago* "tortoise"

the **gall bladder** is the membranous sac in which the bile, or gall, is stored up, as secreted by the liver

the **gall of bitterness** is the most bitter grief, an extreme affliction

galley-west is sideways, or askew; to knock galley-west is to bring confusion or knockout completely

Gallup poll, an assessment of public opinion based on a representative sample, was devised by George H. Gallup, a U.S. statistician

gambler's fallacy is an argument that because something has not occurred in the past, it is due or likely to occur

game animal refers to any wild animal that is hunted and suitable for human consumption

one's **game face** is neutral or serious, focused and determined

the term and concept **game show** originated in the United States in 1965

game to the last means "unyielding to the end"

gamma ray was so named (1903) as it was originally regarded as the third and most penetrating kind of radiation emitted by radium (gamma is the third letter in the Greek alphabet); now these are known to be very short X-rays

a **gandy dancer** is a railroad maintenance worker or seasonal itinerant worker

to **gap out** is to space out, become distracted

garam masala ("hot spice") is a mix of spices in Indian cooking—usually cinnamon, cardamom, cloves, cumin, coriander, and pepper

the **garbanzo bean** is also called the chickpea

a **garden burger** is a non-meat patty made of ground vegetables

the **garter snake** is one of several harmless American snakes so called from its conspicuous stripes of color

gas chamber started as a scientific term in the late 19th century for an apparatus used in microscopy for studying gases' action on organisms

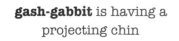

gash-gabbit is having a projecting chin

a **gateleg table** has leaves and hinged legs that swing like gates

a **gateway drug** is habit-forming in that it leads the user to other addictive drugs

the **Gatling gun** (1870) was named for designer Dr. Richard Jordan Gatling (1818–1903) and was first used in late battles of the American Civil War

the **GED** or General Equivalency Degree is fulfilled by passing an examination

gefilte fish (1892) is not a species, but fish loaf made from various kinds of ground fish and other ingredients; the first word is from Yiddish, from German *gefillte*, "stuffed"

Geiger Counter (1924) was named for physicist Hans Geiger (1882–1945), who invented it with W. Müller

a **gel bracelet** is a plastic bracelet worn as a wristband, often embossed with a message of support for a cause

General American is the variety of English spoken by the greater populace with a lack of regional characteristics

general consensus and **consensus of opinion** are redundant

Generation D is the digital-era generation, which is comfortable and expert with computers and other devices; also called digital generation

Generation E is the entitlement generation

generation gap is the term that inspired the name Gap for the clothing store, to attract youth to buy its clothes

generative grammar is a linguistic theory that attempts to describe the tacit knowledge that a native speaker has of a language by establishing a set of explicit, formalized rules that specify or generate all the possible grammatical sentences of a language, while excluding all unacceptable sentences

a **generic word** is one referring to a commercial product, formerly a brand name that is no longer protected by trademark

genetic engineering was first acknowledged in 1969

genetic fingerprinting is the identification of people by their unique DNA

genetically modified pertains to a living organism whose genetic material has been altered, changing one or more of its characteristics; bioengineered

the **Geneva convention** is an agreement made by representatives of the great continental powers at Geneva and signed in 1864, establishing new and more humane regulations regarding the treatment of the sick and wounded and the status of those who minister to them in war; ambulances and military hospitals are made neutral, and this condition affects physicians, chaplains, nurses, and the ambulance corps

Genghis Khan translates to "supreme conqueror" or "universal ruler"

the spirit or character of a place is the **genius loci**

genre painting is that which depicts scenes from ordinary life, especially domestic situations

gentian blue is a purplish blue color

a **gentle breeze** is 8–12 miles per hour

a **gentleman farmer** is one who is well-to-do and farms for pleasure; the plural is gentlemen farmers

an upmarket term for a valet in Victorian times was **gentleman's gentleman**, equivalent in status to the **lady's maid**

a **geodesic (or geodetic) line** is the shortest path between two points on a surface of any shape

geodetic surveying (or engineering) takes the curvature of the earth into account

geological time is divided into four eras and eleven periods

German chocolate cake refers to Baker's German Sweet Chocolate, German being an employee of Baker's who developed the sweet chocolate in the recipe

> **German measles** are not German but rather were discovered by a German doctor

German potato salad is a hot or warm potato salad including bacon, onion, celery, and green pepper mixed with seasonings, sugar, and bacon fat

to **get a wiggle on** is to hurry

get one's ducks in a row probably alludes to lining up target ducks in a shooting gallery

get one's goat may be based on goats being famously irritable creatures

to **get the mitten** is to be rejected or discarded by one's sweetheart

get the short end of the stick may come from getting the end of a stick poked up one's behind by one in command of a situation, who held the other end of the stick

to **get there with both feet** is to be very successful

a **ghost word** is one created by an editor's or printer's error and somehow perpetuating from there

a **Gibson girl** (1901), a woman considered stylish in the late 1890s to early 1900s, was named for Charles Dana Gibson (1867–1944), U.S. artist and illustrator, whose main model was his wife, Irene Langhorne

gift horse started out as given horse; gift horse dates back to 1546

the **Gila monster** is named for a river in Mexico and Arizona

gimlet eye, one with a piercing stare, is from the T-shaped boring tool called a gimlet

gimme caps are the one-size-fits-all hats given away as promotions

gin rummy was created by Elwood T. Baker in 1909 and evolved from eighteenth-century whiskey poker, according to John Scarne

Ginnie Mae (1970) is from GNMA, the acronym for Government National Mortgage Association

to **gird one's loins** literally means "to wrap a belt around one's waist"—as belting loose clothing would allow freer bodily movement, and the saying is now used to mean "to prepare oneself for something requiring strength and endurance"

girl Friday (1940) is patterned after the man Friday in Defoe's *Robinson Crusoe*

to **give someone the large** is to give them their freedom

to **give the horrors** means to terrify

one's **given name** can include the middle name as well as the first name because, unlike the family name, which is inherited, it is given by the parents

glad hand (1895) is used somewhat ironically as the hand of welcome, a cordial handshake or greeting

{ **glad rags** (or glad clothes) dates to 1902 for one's best or fanciest clothes }

glad-warbling is singing or walking joyfully

glare ice (smooth, glassy ice) is probably from the obsolete glare "frost"

glass in **glass ceiling** (1984) describes how such a barrier is "unofficially acknowledged," i.e., it is not visible but understood

glass wall is a barrier to lateral movement within an organization, often due to prejudice

glee club is based on glee as a song in three or more parts and is based on Old English *gleo*, "entertainment, music"

an aircraft's line of descent to land is its **glide path**

global common describes the earth's unowned and shared natural resources: ocean, atmosphere, space

global dimming is the worldwide decline during the last few decades of the intensity of the sunlight reaching the Earth's surface, caused by particulate air pollution

Marshall McLuhan popularized the term **global village** in 1960

a **glory hole** is a place where objects are thrown or lie in confusion

a **glove compartment** or glove box in a car was originally just that, a holder for gloves and other small articles

glutinous rice is a variety of sticky, milky-colored Oriental rice containing amylose and amylopectin; also called pearl rice, sticky rice, sweet rice

G-man, an FBI agent, was a shortening of government man

to **go across lots** is to proceed by the shortest route possible

to **go bare** is to be uninsured

to **go by water** is to follow the sea as a calling

> **go fly a kite** first was the equivalent of saying "ask someone else—not me"

one theory of **go haywire** is that it acquired its sense of "chaotic disorder" from the wild shipping about of baling wire (hay wire) when a bale of hay was opened by cutting the wire with the blow of a hatchet

go off half-cocked goes back to the use of the flintlock of the eighteenth century, in which the flint could snap and ignite the powder before the hammer was fully retracted

go south, "vanish, abscond," came into use in the 1920s, probably from the mid-nineteenth century notion of disappearing south to Mexico or Texas to escape pursuit or responsibility, reinforced by the Native American belief (attested in eighteenth-century colonial writing) that the soul journeys south after death

go the distance started as a boxing term

go to the dogs, from the 1600s, alludes to the traditional view of dogs as inferior creatures

go west was a nineteenth-century British idiom for "die, be killed" and popularized during World War I; probably from thieves' slang, wherein to go west meant to go to Tyburn, hence to be hanged

goat-rope is a messy, disorganized situation

the protective flap on a baseball face mask is a **goat's beard**

go-cart (1676) was originally a "litter, sedan chair" and an "infant's walker" (1689); the modern form go-kart (1959) was coined in reference to a kind of miniature racing car with a frame body and a two-stroke engine

to ensure that no bad spirits move into a body when one sneezes, **God bless you** was said so the body and spirit, which were briefly parted, could reunite

God moves in a mysterious way originated with poet William Cowper—as well as the phrases **the worse for wear** and **variety is the spice of life**

go-go, (1964) "fashionable," came from slang "the go" or "the rage" (1962); first appearance of go-go dancer is from 1965

golden handshake (1960) inspired golden handcuffs (1976) and golden parachute (1981)

golden hour in medicine is the first sixty minutes following a serious accident or injury, when emergency care is most critical

golden raisins are made from white grapes

golden syrup is amber, looks and tastes like honey, and is from extracted and boiled sugar cane juice

goose bumps (or gooseflesh) is derived from skin resembling that of a plucked goose, produced by cold, fear, etc.

Goldilocks planet is a colloquial term used to describe a planet with conditions suitable for life

golf words having to do with birds are albatross (three strokes under, also called double eagle), eagle (two strokes under), birdie (one stroke under), and buzzard (two strokes over)

a **goon coon** or a person beyond all hope is also a **gone goose** or **dead duck**

gone to pot comes from Elizabethan times when leftover meat was thrown into a big pot for another meal

Good Friday is an example of "good" in the sense "holy, observed as a holy day"

a **good landfall** is the sighting of land in conformity with the navigator's reckoning and expectation

someone's **good offices** are kind or helpful acts

the exact phrase **good Samaritan** does not appear in the Bible

goo-goo, "amorous," was perhaps connected with goggle, since the earliest reference is goo-goo eyes; the sense of "baby-talk" is from 1863

goony bird is a synonym for **albatross**

goose heaven is the abiding place of late, lamented pets

goose month, especially in Canada, is the month in which spring migration occurs (mid March to mid-April)

goose pimples were named for their similarity to the skin of a plucked goose

a military step in which the legs are swung forward rigidly to an exaggerated height is the **goose step**

a **gopher ball** in baseball is one that is hit for a home run

the **Gordian knot**, a complicated problem, is from a myth involving Gordius, founder of the Phrygian capital, who tied his chariot to the citadel with a knot—which only the conqueror of Asia could cut

Mark Twain coined the term **gossip column**

a **grace note** is an extra note for embellishment, not necessary for the harmony or melody

grace under pressure is a phrase from Ernest Hemingway

graham cracker was named for Sylvester Graham (1794–1851) who developed the whole-grain cracker out of concern for health and nutrition

with a **grain of salt** is a translation of the Latin phrase *cum grano salis*, possibly an antidote to poison that had to be taken with a grain of salt to be effective

grammar folk are educated people

at one time, **grammar schools** were those set up for teaching Latin and/or Greek

the sixty-third or eighty-first year of one's life is the **grand** (or **great**) **climacteric**

grand cru is the French classification for the most superior wine

grand écart is another term for the gymnastic feat "the splits"

grand mal, "convulsive epilepsy," (1842) is French for "great sickness"

Grand Marnier, cognac-based liqueur (1905), is French for "great" plus Marnier-Lapostolle, the name of the manufacturer

grand opera has a plot that is generally serious, even tragic, and sung throughout

grand prix (1863) is from French for "great prize," originally in reference to the **Grand Prix de Paris**, international horse race for three-year-olds, run every June at Longchamps since 1863

grand slam originated in winning all thirteen tricks in the game of bridge (not related to slam "hit" or "loud bang")

grande dame, "great lady," is often used in an ironic or semi-ironic context

grandfather clause (1900) is a clause in the constitutions of some Southern states, exempting from suffrage restrictions the descendants of men who voted before the Civil War

grandfather clock derives from a song "My Grandfather's Clock" by Henry Clay Work (1832–84) of Connecticut

Granny Smith (as in apples) was Australian gardener Maria Ann Smith

granulated sugar is so called because the last step in processing white table sugar is sending it through a granulator where it is dried and formed into tiny grains

Grape Nuts cereal was introduced in 1898 by Charles W. Post

the **grapefruit league** denotes major league baseball teams that spring-train in Florida

grapes of wrath are first found in the Book of Revelation, and John Steinbeck adapted it as the title of his 1939 novel

the **grapevine telegraph** is gossip or news conveyed in a mysterious way

graphic arts include engraving, etching, lithography, seriography, drypoint, and offset, and the result is a "print"

grass roots (1912) is a U.S. political usage stemming from a general metaphor "the fundamental level" recorded by 1901

grass widow (1528) originally meant "an unmarried woman who has lived with one or more men" or an "abandoned mistress"

grasshopper mind is that of one unable to concentrate on any single subject for long

grasshopper pie is custardlike, flavored and colored with green crème de menthe, and served in a graham-cracker crust

to be **grave as a mustard pot** is to be serious and solemn

Graves' disease was named for Irish physician Robert James Graves (1796–1853), who first recognized the disease in 1835

to ride the **gravy train** (late nineteenth century) means to secure an ongoing situation that provides good pay or other benefits with little labor or trouble, the equivalent of "living on Easy Street," and it may have originated among hoboes and other vagabonds who hopped trains as a way of life

gray goods is a collective term for computer equipment

gray water is relatively clean waste water from baths, sinks, washing machines, and other kitchen appliances

the **gray whale** is actually black

gray-collar worker describes mechanics or maintenance people

{ one with a **greasy tongue** uses soft, unflattering words }

your **great aunt** or **great uncle** is the aunt or uncle of your mother or father

a **great circle** is any circle on the surface of a sphere which lies on a plane through its center—or a circle which divides into two equal parts—as the equator

a **great coat** is a large, loose calf-length overcoat with capelike collars for shedding rain

Great Danes originated in Germany, not Denmark

the **Great Divide** is the boundary between life and death

a **great room** is a large open room usually serving several functions, as a dining room, living room, and family room

Great Scott! refers to Winfield Scott, commander of the Mexican War and the Whig candidate for president in 1852, who was quite pompous

great shakes is a term that comes from shooting dice

Great War, used to describe World War I by 1914, was previously used of the Napoleonic Wars; this term was used for the 1914–1918 war by the generation that lived through it, but it went out of use after World War II ended

Broadway was nicknamed the **Great White Way** in 1901 after a snowstorm, when it adopted the title of the novel *The Great White Way*

sliced bread went on the market in 1958; the **greatest thing since sliced bread** dates to 1969

Greek coffee is very strong and served with fine grounds in it

Greek salad in Greece is a word that translates to "country Attic salad"

green beans are also called string beans and snap beans

green belt is just below the brown belt in martial arts

green corn is the tender ears of young sweet corn, suitable for eating

green flash is a green coloration of the upper portion of the sun, caused by atmospheric refraction and occasionally seen as the sun rises above or sinks below the horizon

the salad dressing name **Green Goddess** was given to a dressing created for actor George Arliss when he performed in a play called *The Green Goddess*; it is a mayonnaise-based dressing with tarragon vinegar, anchovy, parsley, chives, scallions, garlic, and tarragon

green jumper is a horse that has just been taught to jump; **green horse** is an untrained horse

green manure is fertilizer consisting of growing plants that are plowed back into the soil

green onions are also called bunching onions; scallions were originally specific green bunching onions from Ascalon in Palestine; shallots resemble these but have grayish bulbs

a **green pepper** is the unripe fruit of a sweet pepper

green plants were put in dressing rooms of Elizabethan theaters to relax the actors, hence, **green room**; now so painted that color because it is restful to the eyes

green sea is a wave that breaks in a solid mass on a vessel's deck

green tea is from unfermented leaves and **black tea** from fermented leaves

green-eyed monster comes from Shakespeare's *Othello*

greengrocers' apostrophe is any apostrophe mistakenly placed before the final "s" in a plural word ending in "s"; also written greengrocer's apostrophe

the **greenhouse effect** is natural and indispensable—without it the average temperature would fall from 59° F to 0° F

greenhouse gas that traps heat in the atmosphere is 60 percent carbon dioxide, 15 percent methane, 12 percent CFCs

when plants put out their green shoots, as in the spring or after a drought, they are said to be **greening out**

the **Gregorian calendar** is the one now in general use

Gregorian chant, so called for Pope Gregory I (reigned 590–600), is applied to the ancient system of ritual music, otherwise known as plain-chant or plain-song, which is founded on the Antiphonarium, of which Gregory is presumed to have been the compiler

Grey Poupon mustard is named for Maurice Grey and Antoine Poupon, Dijon mustard makers of the eighteenth-century

grind to a halt goes back to the days of the windmill

a **grinning match** is when two or more people endeavor to exceed the other(s) in the distortion of facial features

grizzly bears are also known as bruins and brown bears

a **grocery store** is smaller; a **supermarket** is big

{ the top layer of a wedding cake is known as the **groom's cake** and was originally made of fruit }

the **gross national product** is the gross domestic product plus income from foreign investments

ground cover is low-lying plants that spread and require little maintenance

the **ground run** is the movement of an aircraft along the ground just before takeoff or just after landing

an aircraft's **ground speed** is its speed relative to the ground, as opposed to airspeed

ground squirrel is another name for the gopher

the **ground state** is the lowest energy state of an atom or other particle

the term **ground zero** began being used in 1946 (after Hiroshima) to describe the devastation left by an atomic bomb

a **groundhog** and **woodchuck** are the same and are also known as a whistle pig; the woodchuck has nothing to do with wood or chuck, but comes from Cree *otchock*

Groundhog Day is always February 2

the phrase trick-or-treat is a **group word**—a phrase that functions as a single word (also: due to, hit or miss, in spite of)

the lines on a snail's shell are the **growth lines**

if you are on **Grub Street**, you are either a needy author or literary hack

grudging praise is praising with envy

a **grundy** or Mrs. Grundy is a person who is prudish and the picture of propriety

g-string was first spelled gee-string, as it is of Native American origin, though not much else is certain about it

gubber-tushed is when teeth stand out, and not in order

guided imagery is words and/or music used to benefit a subject by evoking positive imaginary scenarios

guided missile (1945) became a feared word in the 1950s

guinea pig was so named guinea, "distant country," and pig (imprecise term for) "animal"; it is also called a cavy

the **Gulf Stream** is the warm ocean current of the North Atlantic

a **gull wing** door is that on a vehicle or aircraft that opens upward

a **gum eraser** is a block of gummy, easily crumbled rubber used to erase smudges, pencil marks, and the like especially from artwork

the expression **gun moll** comes from Yiddish *goniff's moll*, meaning "thief's girl"

gunboat diplomacy is foreign policy carried out with the backing of the threat or use of military force

gung-ho, **gizmo**, **task force**, **hit the sack** are expressions that entered English during World War II

gunmetal gray is a dark gray color with a tint of blue

gutta-percha (1845) is from Malay *getah percha*, literally "the gum of percha," the name of the tree

a **guy-wire** is a metal guy rope used to stabilize a tall structure, such as a radio mast

gweek-gwak is the squeaking noise made by someone walking in leather boots or in shoes with rubber soles

{
gyro (pronounced YEE-roh or ZHIR-oh) **sandwiches** are authentically cooked on a spit; the Greek origin *guros* meaning "turning"
}

{ H }

to **habbie-gabbie** is to throw money into a crowd

habeas corpus means literally "you should have the body," the first words of a Latin writ requiring a person to be brought before a court of law

hacking jacket refers to hack in the sense of "ride a horse for pleasure"

the deepest part of the ocean is the **hadal zone** or **ultra abyssal zone**

hag-ridden (1684) is an old term for sleep paralysis, the sensation of being held immobile in bed, often by a heavy weight, and accompanied by a sense of alien presence

a **Hail Columbia** is a severe scolding or punishment

Hail Mary in football is a last-ditch effort to throw a long pass for completion and the term dates to 1972

hair cells are cells with hairlike processes in the sensory epithelium of certain parts of the internal ear

a **hair extension** is a synthetic swatch of hair that is attached to make a longer, fuller, or different hairstyle

hair of the dog (that bit you) is based on the ancient folk treatment for a dog bite of putting a burnt hair of the dog on the wound

a **hair space** is a very thin space between letters or words

a **hairline fracture** often occurs on a flat bone and is a crack without noticeable separation but which moves enough to possibly cause injury to tissues

hair-trigger's underlying meaning is something may be triggered with the pressure of something as slight as a hair

hairy eyeball is a look of disdain or disapproval

the original **halcyon days** were the seven days before or after the winter solstice, December 14–28

half and half in the United States is half milk and half heavy cream

a **half bath** has a toilet and a sink

half blood is relationship through only one parent

half seas over, slang for "drunk" (1736), was said to be from the notion of a ship heavy-laden and so low in the water that small waves (half seas) wash over the deck; half seas over, "halfway across the sea," is recorded from 1551, however, and it was given a figurative extension to "halfway through a matter" by 1697

a broad step between flights of a stairway is a **half space**

the **half title** in a book is a righthand page with the title, just preceding the title page

half-assed, "ineffectual," is perhaps a humorous mispronunciation of haphazard

one's **half-birthday** is the day exactly six months before or after one's real birth date

half-hardy plants like cabbage and lettuce are able to survive temperatures slightly below freezing

half-life first meant "unsatisfactory way of living" until the sense in physics, "amount of time it takes half a given amount of radioactivity to decay," first attested 1907

half-light is dimness, such as at dusk

as a memorial, flags on land fly at **half-staff** and on ships and at naval stations fly at **half-mast**

half-wit (1678) originally was "a would-be wit whose abilities are mediocre"; the sense of "simpleton" (one lacking all his wits) is first attested to 1755

the **halo effect** is the favorable bias in interviews, intelligence tests, and the like generated by an atmosphere of approbation

ham meaning "inexpert" first referred to performers, then was used for amateur telegraph or radio operators (**ham radio**)

a **ham-and-egger** is an ordinary or regular person, from the old days when miners held boxing matches; the winner got money, the loser got a ham and egg meal

hamster care is high-volume health care where patients do not receive specialized attention

back in the eighteenth century, the saying was hand over hand, not **hand over fist**, and was a nautical term meaning "to make fast and steady progress up a rope"—then with **hand over fist**, it became "a flat hand passing over the fist gripping the rope"— eventually any steady progress forward

{ gloves can be called **hand shoes** }

a **handbag situation** is a weak but theatrical confrontation, harmless altercation; also called handbags at dawn

handbags at ten paces is a verbal spat, especially between athletes on the field

a **hand car** is a small car propelled by hand, used by railroad laborers, etc.

hand-cut is a term used to enhance the menu value of French fries and other vegetables

to be **hand-minded** is to prefer and be more adept at manual activities rather than mental ones

a **hands-down victory** occurs when a jockey's win is so assured that he drops his hands and relaxes his grip on the reins when nearing the finish line

handwriting on the wall (or writing on the wall) comes from the Bible (Daniel 5:5-31), in which the prophet interprets some mysterious writing that a disembodied hand has inscribed on the palace wall, telling King Belshazzar that he will be overthrown

handy as a pocket in a shirt is synonymous with "convenient"

to **hang a Louie** is to make a left turn while driving a vehicle

to **hang a Ralph** is to make a right turn while driving a vehicle

hang up one's fiddle means to give up or quit

hang-dog (1677) was first a despicable, degraded fellow, so called either from the notion of being fit only to hang a dog, or to be hanged like one

hanger steak is one that "hangs" between the last rib and the loin, a cut of beef similar to flank or skirt steak in texture and rib-eye in flavor and from the diaphragm that hangs between the last rib and the loin; also called hanging tender, butcher's steak, butcher's tenderloin, onglet

doors have a **hanging side** and a **shutting side**

> **hanky panky** seems to be a variation of the much older expression hocus pocus

hansom cabs are named for J.A. Hansom, who registered the Patent Safety Cab in 1834

a **hapax legomenon** is Greek for "a thing said only once"—and it is a word that occurs once in corpus or a language

happy as a clam was originally happy-as-a-clam-at-full-tide and may refer to the fact that when the tide is full, nobody is digging clams

happy bunny is synonymous with **happy camper**

happy hunting ground is, among some Native American peoples, a place of peace and abundance to which people are believed to go after death

happy-clappy refers to any Christian congregation that is extremely enthusiastic, loud, and musical

hara-kiri, suicide by disembowelment, is from Japanese "belly-cutting" and is pronounced HA-RA KEERY

hard and fast means being so completely aground as to be immovable

hard cheddar or **hard cheese** is British slang for "tough luck"; it expresses sympathy about a petty matter

fermented apple cider becomes **hard cider** and fully fermented turns into cider vinegar

hard drugs are considered addictive; soft drugs are not considered addictive or causing dependence

hard g is the term for the "g" sound in "get" and "give," as distinct from the **soft g** in "gem," "giraffe," and "generation"

a hyphen always part of a word is a **hard hyphen**; a hyphen used only when a word is split is a **soft hyphen**

> **hard sauce** contains butter and sugar, with brandy, rum, or vanilla

hard sell implies an aggressive approach toward a potential buyer; soft sell is a more subtle, suggestive approach

hard water is that which contains large amounts of minerals

to **harden off** is to gently acclimate a plant to cold, wind, or sun

quahog is another name for **hard-shell clam**

Hare Krishna (1968) is from the title of a Hindu chant or mantra, from Hindi *hare*, "O God!" and Krishna, name of an incarnation of the god Vishnu

hark back was an early hunting term for a hound retracing tracks to find a lost scent

a **harp seal** has a harp-shaped mark on its gray back

Harris tweed is a trademarked fabric made in Scotland, especially on the island of Lewis and Harris

harum-scarum is a reduplication based on hare and scare

Harvard beets are cut-up beets cooked in vinegar, sugar, butter, and cornstarch, said to have been created by a Harvard student or so-named because of the beets' color being the Harvard color, or could be a corruption of the name of a tavern in England named Harwood

the term **Harvard death** refers to a death that happens though all symptoms were successfully treated or all medical tests came out normal

harvest home is a festival held at the completion of the harvest

has-been, "one who has outlived his fame," is first attested in 1606

the original name of **hash browns** was hashed brown potatoes (1900); hash, from French *hacher*, "chop up," is a dish of cut-up bits

the **hash mark** is #

Hasidic Jews and **Orthodox Jews** both believe Old Testament laws and other sacred Jewish writings; Hasidism started in the 18th century and emphasizes close communion with an omnipresent God and a Kabbalah-influenced mysticism

hasta la vista, a rivederci, auf Wiedersehen, and **au revoir** mean "until we meet again" or "farewell"

hasty pudding was an ancient dish of flour boiled in water to thick consistency, with milk or beer added afterward

hat head is hair that is flattened out, disarranged, or full of static electricity from the wearing of a hat; also called hat hair

hat in the ring refers to the Ringstrasse (Ring Street) of Vienna, Austria—where those seeking office solicited support, hat in hand

hat trick is originally from cricket, "taking three wickets on three bowls," and extended to other sports (especially ice hockey) around 1909; allegedly because in cricket this feat entitled the bowler to receive a hat from his club or to pass the hat for a cash collection

hatha yoga is derived from Sanskrit *hatha*, "force"

hat-honor is respect shown by taking off the hat

a **haul road** is an unpaved road used to truck goods and supplies to remote areas

{ in the Middle Ages, being **hauled over the coals** was the test for someone accused of heresy }

haut monde in French is "high world" as in "the fashionable world"

haute couture is French, literally, "high dressmaking"

haute cuisine translates to "high-class cooking"

to **have seen the elephant** means to have undergone a disappointment of high-raised expectations

having a screw loose originally referred to the cotton gin

Hawaiian guitar is the lap-held metal string guitar notable for its nasal, vibrato effects

Hawaiian pizza is a pizza topped with pineapple and ham or prosciutto

hay fever was once known as hay asthma, summer catarrh, rose catarrh, rose fever, and rose cold

Hear! Hear! is a shortening of Hear him! Hear him!

heart failure is when the heart is unable to pump enough blood

on the hand, the **heart line** is closest to the fingers, then the **head line**, then the **lifeline**

heart on one's sleeve comes from chivalry, when a knight wore a scarf or other item from his lady tied to his sleeve

heat exhaustion is caused by excessive loss of salt and water, causing dizziness, nausea, cramps, fainting, etc.

heat haze is an obscured atmosphere in hot weather, with shimmering near the ground distorting views in the distance

the **heat index** is the discomfort level of combined heat and humidity

the air-tight sheet on top of a yogurt, pudding, etc. container is **heat-sealed film**

it is **heaven's sake** (not heavens' sake, heaven's sakes, etc.)

the **Heaviside layer** (E Layer) of the atmosphere was named for Oliver Heaviside, the English physicist who predicted its existence

heavy cream is that which contains a lot of butterfat; **light cream** is sweet, with less butterfat than heavy cream

the term **hell on wheels** originally applied to the Union Pacific Railroad's saloon railcars

an **heirloom plant** is one that has survived more than fifty years and may be passed down from generation to generation

heavy going is a person or situation that is difficult or tedious; **heavy lifting** is hard or difficult work

heavy metal was coined by William Burroughs in his book *Naked Lunch*

a **hedge word** is one used to protect the writer, e.g., alleged, reportedly, reputed

the **hedonic treadmill** describes humans' capacity for continual adaptation to emotional circumstances, resulting in an ongoing return to a point of relative neutrality

the originator of the Barney Google cartoon came up with the phrase **heebie jeebies**

hee-haw was first recorded in 1815 as Hiu Haw, probably imitative of the sound of a donkey's bray

heel-taps is the liquor left in the bottoms of glasses after drinking

Henry **Heinz** mass-produced ketchup and expanded to make other projects; he saw an ad for "21 Styles of Shoes" which spurred him to come up with his "57 Varieties"

heirloom seed is any seed handed down generation to generation and generally passed among individuals, rather than sold in catalogs

the **Hellenic culture** falls between the Helladic and Hellenistic—the Iron Age and Classical Greek culture

Hell's Angels, the motorcycle club, was first attested 1957; they were called Black Rebels in the 1954 film *The Wild One*, and earlier the phrase had been used as the title of a film about World War I air combat (1930)

a **helping verb** is an informal term for an auxiliary verb, which combines with a main verb to help it express tense, mood, and voice

helter-skelter first appeared in Shakespeare's 1597 drama *King Henry IV*

hen party dates back to 1887

hens' teeth means anything very rare or impossible to obtain

herb tea is any tea made from leaves of plants other than the tea plant

herbes de Provence is a blend of herbs used for seasoning, such as basil, bay leaf, chervil, fennel, lavender, marjoram, oregano, rosemary, sage, summer savory, tarragon, and thyme

chemists were once called Hermes, after the legendary inventor of chemistry, so

hermetically sealed means "sealed by chemists' methods"

the **hero sandwich** is also a submarine, hoagie/hoagy, torpedo, garibaldi, or poor boy (etc.)

shingles and zoster are other names for **herpes zoster**, caused by the virus of chickenpox

hesitation forms or embolalia are terms like: like, well, uh, you know

hic jacet is Latin for "here lies," commonly the first words of Latin epitaphs

hi-fi (1950) is an abbreviation of high fidelity (1934)

higgledy-piggledy (1598) was probably formed from pig and the animal's suggestions of mess and disorder

high and dry is a nautical metaphor; it can also refer to a sandwich with no condiments (diner slang)

to have **high color** is to have flushed cheeks/complexion

a **high court** is a supreme court of justice

high fidelity is sound reproduction on electronic equipment that gives faithful reproduction

High German refers to the language of inland Germany (the mountains), and **Low German** was that of the northern lowland areas; High German gave way to things like Yiddish, and Low German to English, Flemish, Dutch, etc.

high hurdles are 42 inches high

high jinks is a variant of high pranks

high life is the life of high society

high muck-a-muck may come from Chinook *hiyu*, "plenty," and *muckamuck* "food," from a Nootka phrase meaning "choice wheat meal"

high noon is exactly 12:00 noon

> **high on the hog**—choice selections from the sides and back of the animal—give us this term

a sculpture in which figures project from the background by half or more than half their depth is **high relief**

the **high road** is the easiest way or the best way, either literally or figuratively

high seas are like highway, the part of the ocean not in the territorial waters of any particular sovereignty, usually a distant three miles or more from the coastline

the British equivalent of Main Street is **High Street**

high tea is a light cooked dish along with tea at the usual teatime, also called meat tea; it is generally served between 5 to 6 p.m.

there are two **high**, or **flood, tides** and two **low**, or **ebb**, tides each lunar day—which is shorter than the solar day

high words is an archaic term for "angry words"

a **highball glass** is around 13.9 fluid ounces, **old-fashioned glass** around 9.6, **short glass** 7.7, and **port glass** 3–5.75;

a highball glass is large and straight, broader than a **Collins glass** and slightly narrower than an old-fashioned glass

to be **high-colored** is to have a strong, deep, or glaring color

higher animals include mammals and other vertebrates; **higher plants** include vascular plants and the flowering plants

higher mathematics is more advanced and abstract than standard arithmetic, algebra, geometry, and trigonometry

high-five, originally U.S. basketball slang, dates to 1980 as a noun, 1981 as a verb

the instrument in a drum set with two cymbals together is the **high-hat cymbal** (with a superior and an inferior cymbal); also called choke cymbals

the Scottish dance the **Highland fling** originally celebrated victory

hightail it refers to animals, such as mustangs and rabbits, which raise their tails high when fleeing danger

hill of beans refers to the planting practice of placing the seeds in clumps in a little mound (hill) of soil

the **Hippocratic oath** (1747) was created in the spirit of Hippocrates (c.460–377 B.C.E.), but not written by him

{ in **hissy fit**, hissy may come from hysterical }

in **hit the hay**, the image is of a weary wanderer in a barn of hay

to **hit the maples** is to bowl

hive mind is a type of collective consciousness where individuality is stifled; a state of conformity; also written hivemind

a **hobo bag** is a style of handbag or purse that is typically large and characterized by a crescent shape, a slouchy posture, and a long strap designed to wear over the shoulder

Hobson-Jobson (1634) is British soldiers' mangled Anglicization of the cry they heard at Muharram processions in India, *Ya Hasan! Ya Husayn!* (O Hassan! O Husain!), mourning two grandsons of the Prophet who died fighting for the faith—leading to the linguists' law of **Hobson-Jobson**, describing the effort to bring a new and strange word into harmony with the language by fitting it to the sound and spelling patterns of the borrowing language

Hobson's choice is the option of taking the one thing offered or nothing (after Thomas Hobson [1544–1630], an English livery stableman, from his requirement that customers take either the horse nearest the stable door or none)

on a ham, the **hock end** is also called the **Maryland end**, while the thick end is the **Virginia end**

hocus pocus is first attested in the 1600s with the meaning "juggler" and "a conjuror's trick"

ho-de-ho is defined in the *Oxford English Dictionary* as "an exclamation, used as the appropriate response to hi-de-hi"

Hodgkin's disease (1877) was named for Dr. Thomas Hodgkin (1798–1866) who first described it

hog heaven (1884) is a place or state of foolish or idle bliss

to many Americans, the expression **hog on ice** is known only from the title of the book by Charles Earle Funk (1948); it is from the expression "as independent as a hog on ice," where hog refers to the stone in the game of curling when it comes to rest

hog washers is another name for overalls

{ **ho-hum**, an expression of boredom, was first attested in 1924 }

hoi polloi means "the many," so you need not add the determiner "the," which makes it redundant

hoisin sauce ("seafood sauce") is made from soya beans, vinegar, sugar, garlic, and various spices

hoity-toity is a reduplicative phrase based on the obsolete hoit, "to romp"

hokey-pokey was an early form of cheap ice cream, the name derived from hocus-pocus; hokey-pokey once meant "something meaningless or pointless"

the expression (not) **hold a candle to** seems to have come from the practice of a servant holding a candle for a master who was walking or working and became the literal origin of the idiom meaning "be in a menial position to someone"

to **hold one's potato** is to be quiet

hold the fort derives from an order given by Union General William Tecumseh Sherman in 1864 near the end of the Civil War, "Hold the fort at all costs, for I am coming"

hollandaise sauce originated in Holland and is also called Dutch sauce

in ceramics, etc., **hollowware** is any piece that is either hollow or deeply concave, as opposed to flatware

a **Hollywood bed** is a low bed with a headboard but no footboard

a **Hollywood no** is a lack of response to an email, phone call, proposal, etc.

holus bolus is energy or violence, as in "He goes at it holus bolus"

the **Holy Ark** is the closet where the Torah is kept in a synagogue

Palestine and **Holy Land** are used interchangeably for parts of modern Israel, Jordan, and Egypt

holy mackerel is a euphemism for Holy Mary

home economics is a term dating to 1899

the term **home fries** is dated to around 1950

the **home key** is either of two keys on a keyboard acting as the base position for one's fingers in touch-typing (left F, right J)

home page (1993) actually entered the language before website (1994)

a **home truth** is an unpleasant fact about oneself

Homo sapiens is Latin, literally "rational, wise man"

Homo sapiens sapiens is fully modern man

homogenized milk is whole and processed so the cream will not separate from the milk

when you write "your," but you really meant "you're," that is a **homonym slip** ("too" for "two," etc.)

if you use "there" instead of "their," that is a **homophone slip**

honeydew melon was developed around 1915 and so named for its sweetness

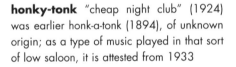

{ **Hong Kong** means "fragrant harbor" in Chinese }

honky-tonk "cheap night club" (1924) was earlier honk-a-tonk (1894), of unknown origin; as a type of music played in that sort of low saloon, it is attested from 1933

hoochy koochy was an erotic, suggestive women's dance (1898) and was associated by some with the Chicago world's fair of 1893 and belly-dancer Little Egypt

every piece of Velcro has two parts: **hook tape** and **loop tape**

Boulder Dam (1936) became **Hoover Dam** in 1947

a **horizontal symmetry letter** is an uppercase letter that has top-bottom symmetry (B, C, D, E, H, I, K, O, X)

the **horned toad** is not a toad; it is a lizard

hors de combat means "out of action"

hors d'oeuvres means "outside the work(s)" because appetizers are outside the principal task of preparing the meal; hors d'oeuvres when capitalized is Hors d'Oeuvres

horse and horse is the equivalent of **neck and neck**

horse chestnut (1597) is a tree probably native to Asia, introduced in England c.1550, and the name also was extended to similar North American species such as the buckeye and said to have been so called because it was food for horses

the origin is unknown for **horse latitudes**, the belt of calm and light airs which borders the northern edge of the northeast tradewinds

horse opera is a slang term for a western (movie, usually)

horses tended to be viewed more positively in the American West, where the term **horse sense** originated; others regard horses as rather stupid

horse whisperer is a person who tames and trains horses by gentle methods and speech

a **horseback opinion** is one given hastily and without consulting authorities

from the **horse's mouth** alludes to examining a horse's teeth to determine its age and hence its worth

horse's neck is an old term for ginger ale with vanilla ice cream

hospital corners are professional bed-making, with neat and secure folding of sheets and other bedding under the mattress corners, typical of hospitals

having the **hot coppers** means having a parched throat and mouth from excess drinking

hot cross buns, a traditional Good Friday food called cross buns until the early nineteenth-century, became hot cross buns because of a popular vendors' rhyme

to **hot desk** is to share a desk or work space with others on different shifts/schedules

while Tad Dorgan did feature hot dogs in a few of his cartoons, he was not the originator of the term **hot dog**; hot dog (dating to at least 1900) is simply an extension of the older use of "dog" to mean a sausage, as "hot" describes its temperature and sometimes its spicy content

hot pants, "short-shorts," is from 1970, probably influenced by earlier sense of "sexual arousal" (1927)

hot pepper is fast turning in jump rope (also bullets, hot peas, vinegar, pepper, whipping)

hot-and-hot (of individual dishes of food) are those served one at a time as soon as cooked

hotel journalism or **hotel reporting** is secondhand reports from a sheltered location or perspective in an otherwise unsafe place

originally, in the eighteenth-century, the term **hot-pot** denoted a type of hot punch (ale and spirits, spiced and heated)

measurement of time by the height of the sun is still common; **hour by sun** means an hour after sunrise or before sunset (others were suncoming, sun-an-hour, sun-two-hours, midday, sun-four-hours-up (etc.), sunset, sober light (twilight), first-hour-night, (etc.)

an **hourglass** has sand for an hour, a **sandglass** for any amount of time, and an egg-timer for six minutes or less

a **house church** is a group meeting for Christian worship at a private home

house organ uses the word organ to mean a means or medium of communication, or of expression of opinion; especially a periodical which serves as the mouthpiece of a particular business or company (the "house")

household gods are the gods presiding over the house and family, the Lares and Penates

HOV lane is the High Occupancy Vehicle lane, a highway lane marked with painted diamonds which indicate that it is for multi-passenger vehicles, created to alleviate traffic congestion and improve air quality; also called diamond lane

how come is a casualism for why

hubba-hubba, a cry of excitement or enthusiasm, was first recorded in 1944

the **Hubble Space Telescope** (HST) is in orbit above Earth's atmosphere (370 miles)

huckleberry chowder is extreme eccentricity

Huckleberry Finn first appeared in *The Adventures of Tom Sawyer* (1875) and then *The Adventures of Huckleberry Finn* (1884)

hue and cry is from a French legal phrase "outcry and cry"

a **hugger-mugger** is a lead sentence in a newspaper article that is crammed with details

the **hula hoop** was the brainchild of Wham-O

human ecology is the study of interaction between people and their environment

human geography (or anthropogeography) is a political/cultural branch of geography concerned with the social science aspects of how the world is physically arranged

umble pie (now **humble pie**) was meat pie made with tongue and entrails and served to umbles (women and children) as men were served the best meat

hump day is the middle of the workweek, usually Wednesday

Humpty Dumpty was a French nursery rhyme hero (1810), probably a reduplication of Humpty, a pet form of Humphrey; in English there was first a humpty-dumpty drink (1698), "ale boiled with brandy"

a **hundred-year egg** is any egg (usually chicken) that has been preserved by being covered with a coating of lime, ashes, and salt before being shallowly buried for one hundred days and which then has a pungent cheeselike flavor

Hungarian goulash is from *gulyas* "handyman or herdsman's stew"

hunger march came into the vocabulary by 1908 and was very important in the 1920s and 1930s

hungry ghost is a type of supernatural being, condemned to desire more than it can consume—often depicted with large belly and tiny mouth

hunky-dory (1866) was perhaps a reduplication of hunkey, "all right, satisfactory" (1861), from hunk, "in a safe position" (1847)

hurdy-gurdy (1749) was perhaps imitative of its sound and influenced by (c.1500) *hirdy-girdy*, "uproar, confusion"

hurley-hacket is the sport of tobogganing

hurly-burly is a reduplicative phrase based on the obsolete *url*, "to make a commotion"

hurrah's nest is a term for hubbub, mess, disorder

a **hurricane lamp** is so called because it is designed to stay lit even in high winds

there is a special tape for protecting windows called **hurricane tape**

a **hush puppy** is deep-fried cornmeal dough

{ **hurry sickness** is a behavior pattern characterized by continual rushing and anxiousness; an overwhelming and continual sense of urgency }

a **hybrid car** has more than one power source, such as an electric motor and internal combustion engine or an electric motor with battery and fuel cells for energy storage

the term **hydrogen bomb** existed in 1947, years before it was actually made (1952)

hydrogenated fat is a bland white semi-solid saturated fat made from unsaturated liquid oil

hydrogenated oil is an oil with trans-fatty acids that has been chemically changed from a room-temperature liquid state into a solid

the **hyoid bone** is the bone in the base of the tongue, the middle part of the hyoid arch

a **hyphenated American** is any citizen who can trace his order ancestry to a specific part of the world, e.g., African-American, Italian-American

hypnogogic jerks are the spasms that happen right when you fall asleep, and **hypnopompic jerks** happen right when you are waking up

after an archaeology dig, you will have **hyponychial dirt** (under the nails)

hysteron proteron (1565) is from Greek, meaning "the latter (put as) the former" for a figure of speech in which what should come last is put first

{ **I** }

iambic pentameter is the most common meter in English verse and consists of a line ten syllables long that is accented on every second beat

ice beer is brewed at sub-zero temperatures and then the ice crystals are strained off to remove excess water and any impurities

an **ice candle** is an icicle

ice cider is an alcoholic beverage made from sweeter varieties of frozen apples

ice cream is an alteration of iced cream, "cream cooled by means of ice," but the "d" was dropped around 1744; ice cream is reputed to have been made in China as long ago as 3000 BC but did not arrive in Europe (via Italy) until the thirteenth century

the waffle-type (or wafer) **ice cream cone** (usually light brown, conical, with a flat bottom—though authentic ones can be huge, look like a real waffle, and have a pointed tip) is baked in a round shape and rolled (first by hand, later mechanically) as soon as it came off the griddle; the sugar-type ice cream cone (darker brown, thicker and crunchier, and conical in shape, coming to a point) can be made the same way; a second way of making these is by pouring batter into a mold, then baking it. There are cake cones, too, that look just like waffle cones, but the difference is that sugar cones use more sugar than the cake cones.

the medical term for an **ice cream headache** is spheno pulatine ganglio neuralgia

ice cream pants are men's white summer pants, especially when worn with a blazer

an **ice cream shot** is an easy hunting shot

ice dancing is a style of ice skating, usually by couples, involving choreographed dance moves

the **ice front** is the lower edge of a glacier

an **ice nucleus** is a small atmospheric particle around which an ice crystal grows

{ an **ICE number** is any In Case of Emergency number(s), especially programmed into a cell phone under the name ICE }

ice wine is made from grapes that froze on the vine

iceberg lettuce got its name from the fact that California growers started shipping it covered with heaps of crushed ice in the 1920s; it had previously been called crisphead lettuce

icebergs break apart to form bergs, bergy bits, or bitty bergs—or growlers

an icebox cookie is a type of cookie with the dough formed and chilled before being sliced for baking; also called **refrigerator cookie**

iced tea is the correct form and will probably not change form the way iced cream and iced water did

idea hamster is any person who is creative and constantly thinking up new ideas

idée fixe (from French "fixed idea") is an idea that dominates the mind

the **ideo locator** on a map is the "You Are Here"

the **Ides of March** refers to March 15 on the Roman calendar, the date of Julius Caesar's assassination in 44 BC; also the eighth day after the nones in the ancient Roman calendar (the fifteenth day of March, May, July, October, the thirteenth of other months)

an **idiopathic disease** is an illness of unknown cause

idiot box referred to televisions from 1959

idiot card is another name for a cue card

an **idiot light** (dating to 1968) is any colored warning light on a vehicle's instrument panel (as for low oil pressure)

the plural of **idiot savant** is idiot savants or idiots savants; the origin is French, literally "learned idiot"

idiot strings refers to the string that attaches mittens to prevent a child from losing one

if I were is the correct phrase when one is referring to a conditional future event

Latin *ignis,* "fire," gives us **igneous rock,** which is formed from the cooling of molten lava

ignis fatuus, "will o' the wisp, jack-o'-lantern," is from Latin, literally "foolish fire"

ill wind is from the longer expression ill wind that blows nobody good"

an example of **imitative magic** is a voodoo doll, where an action is performed that imitates the desired event; a rain dance is also imitative magic

the **immaculate conception** was of Mary; the immaculate (or virgin) birth was of Jesus

immovable feasts are feasts which occur on a certain day of the year and do not depend on the date of Easter; as, Christmas

what you are **immune from** cannot touch you (free of some duty, liability, restriction) and what you are **immune to** may touch you but has no effect, i.e. you are impervious to it; so use "immune to" for a disease or persuasion and use "immune from" for other things, like punishment

the pronoun "it" is an **impersonal pronoun** when used without definite reference or antecedent, as in "it was sleeting"

an **impersonal verb** is a verb used with an indeterminate subject, commonly, in English, with the impersonal pronoun "it" as, "it rains; it snows"

an **improper fraction** is one in which the numerator is greater than the denominator, such as 6/5

in a jam dates to the early 1800s when Appalachian frontiersmen discovered that, like bait, homemade jam attracted animals to be trapped

in a pig's whistle is "quickly," "in no time"

thieves in medieval Germany's Black Forest often shared cabins known as *kajuetes*, which gave rise to the phrase **in cahoots**

in esse means "in actual existence"

in flagrante delicto in Latin is "in blazing crime"

in fourteen languages means "to a great extent, to a very high degree" as in "I was sick in fourteen languages"

in hock can be traced to the card game faro, in which the last card in the box was called the hocketty card; when a player bet on a card that ended up **in hock,** he was at a disadvantage and was himself **in hock** and at risk of losing his bets

the phrase "**in like Flynn**" referred to Errol Flynn's prowess in seducing women

in loco parentis (1710) is Latin for "in the place of a parent"

in media res (1786) is Latin, meaning "in the midst of things"

in memoriam is the correct spelling

in **one fell swoop**, fell refers not to failing but to cruel or mean

in **over a barrel**, the allusion is to the practice of draping a rescued person (from near drowning) over a barrel to eject water

archaeological finds are mainly described **in situ**, Latin for "in its (original) place; in position"

{ **in spots** is "here and there" as in "She is clever in spots" }

if someone is **in still water**, they are free from strife

in the bag comes from hunting lingo or cockfighting

on the first slave ships, there were small cubicles referred to as "doghouses"—and slaves were in them, giving us **in the doghouse**

in the groove is an allusion to the reproduction of music by a needle on a gramophone record

in the hole also means "having a score below zero"

in the money is racetrack jargon for a horse that comes in first, second, or third and refers to a bettor whose horse finishes in one of those places

in the 1500s, pink meant "the embodiment of perfection;" **in the pink** dates only from about 1900

the allusion is to a shipwreck in, **in the same boat**

in the suds means to be in trouble or distress, as on washing day

in the wings and **wing it** are expressions from the theater

in vino veritas, Latin for "truth in wine," describes how a person tells the truth under the influence of alcohol

in vitro is Latin, literally "in glass" or "in a test tube"

the background music for entertainment is **incidental music**; the background music in public places is elevator music

income tax has been around since 1799 and the Napoleonic Wars

an **incomplete protein** is any protein lacking one or more essential amino acids in correct proportions as necessary for good nutrition and health, true of many plant foods; also called partial protein

an **indefinite adjective** is a pronoun used as an adjective, e.g., all, any, each, every, few, many, and some

indefinite articles are "a" and "an"; indefinite pronouns are (e.g.) anything, anyone, everyone, something

the schwa is also called the **indeterminate vowel**

an **index fossil** is one useful for dating and demonstrating the relation between strata in which it is found

index learning is superficial knowledge as that gained by perusing the index of a book

{ **India ink** was actually invented in China }

Indian or **Indian corn** means "native to the Americas"

early Native Americans took back a gift when another of equal value was not given in exchange, hence the term **Indian giver**

Indian summer can describe a period of happiness or success occurring late in life

Indian yellow is a yellow-orange pigment obtained from the urine of cows that have eaten mango leaves

indirect labor is work that is not considered in determining costs per unit in producing or manufacturing something, e.g., work done by clerical or maintenance staff

Indo-European was coined in 1814 by physician, physicist, and Egyptologist Thomas Young (1773–1829) and first used in an article in the *Quarterly Review* specifically in reference to the group of related languages and to the race or races characterized by their use

induction cooking is a method involving heating cookware with magnetic energy, either by a special stove coil or specially designed cookware that uses an alternating magnetic field to generate heat rapidly

the **inductive method** is reasoning from the specific to the general; the **deductive method** is reasoning from the general to the specific

industrial archaeology is the study of former industrial buildings and equipment; the study of the period and the work sites of the Industrial Revolution and thereafter

the term **industrial relations** existed by 1904 but did not become established until after World War II

an **infectious disease** is caused by bacteria, protozoa, viruses, or other parasites; if it can pass or be carried to others, then it is a contagious disease (or communicable, transmittable, or transmissible)

the **inferior planets** are Mercury and Venus, whose orbits are closer to the Sun than the Earth's

in-fighting is derived from pugilism as the practice of getting at close quarters with an opponent (1812)

an **infinity pool** is a swimming pool set up to produce a visual effect of the water extending to the horizon (infinity) or into the sea

information technology was a term by 1958, but the abbreviation IT showed up in 1982 and information superhighway came in 1985

infra dig (or **infradig**) is short for Latin *infra dignitatem* "beneath one's dignity"

infra-angelic means "human"

inheritance tax is a state tax on individual shares of a deceased person's estate after the estate has been divided

an **inkhorn term** (1597) or inkhornism is a learned or pedantic word or expression, from a small portable vessel for holding writing ink (1382)

an **inlay card** is a pamphlet accompanying a CD, film, etc., giving an introduction

innate ideas are those which exist, preformed, in the mind at birth—ideas, as of God, immortality, right and wrong, supposed by some to be inherent in the mind, as a priori principles of knowledge

the eye junction nearest the nose, where deposits may form at night, is the **inner canthus**

the central, and often troubled, area of a city is the **inner city** (1968)

the **inner sanctum** is the most sacred place in a church or temple

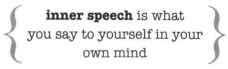

inner speech is what you say to yourself in your own mind

an **inner tube** is so called as it is a separate tube inside a pneumatic core

the box on a Web page where you type in what you want to look up or search for is generically called an **input element**, and more specifically it's called a text input; less formal terms include text field or search box

insalata verde is Italian for mixed green salad

inside of is redundant; just say inside

the protected sea route along the western coast of North America from Seattle to the northern part of Alaska is known as the **Inside Passage** or **Inland Passage**

insight meditation (or *vipassana*) is a type of Buddhist meditation that aims to develop insight into the nature of phenomena through focused attention

{ an **instant book** is one rushed into print following an event of great public interest }

instrument landing is an aircraft landing made entirely by means of instruments

intaglio printing is a printing process that uses an etched or engraved plate; the plate is smeared with ink and wiped clean, then the ink left in the recesses makes the print

intellectual property is anything created for which one may apply for a copyright, patent, trademark, etc.

intelligent design is a theory that nature and complex biological structures were designed by intelligent beings and were not created by chance; abbreviation ID

the German term *Intelligenz-quotient* (1912) gave us **intelligent quotient** (1921)

an **intention tremor** is a trembling of a body part when attempting a precise movement

intents and purposes means "under usual or normal circumstances"

inter alia, "among other things," is used to give more emphasis to the writer's pronouncements

at the base of each finger is an **interdigital pad**

the concept of an **interest rate** forms the basis of capitalism

interior decorating is the decoration of the interior of a building or room, especially the artistic effects; interior design is the art or process of designing the interior decorating/decoration of a room or building

one's **internal clock** is a person's innate sense of time

to the east of the **International Date Line**, it is a day earlier than it is to the west

interrogation point is another term for question mark

Interrogatory astrology answers a client's question by studying the positions of astronomical bodies at the time

an **interrupted projection** is a map that is not continuous and looks like a fruit peel

the **intertragic notch** is the small groove or notch between your tragus (the bump of cartilage between your ear and temple) and your earlobe

interval training is alternating two activities, such as jogging and walking

into is for entering something, for changing the form of something, or for making contact; otherwise use "**in to**" (if you can drop the "in" without losing the meaning, you want in "to")

a person's **intonation pattern** is the rise and fall in the pitch of his or her voice according to the sense of what is being said

intrinsic motivation is the undertaking of activities because of their own appeal and not because of external research or punishments

the zoological term for the male copulatory organ of an animal is the **intromittent organ**

intrusive rocks are rocks which have been forced, while in a plastic or melted state, into the cavities or between the cracks or layers of other rocks

inverse proportion is when an increase (or decrease) in one valve is related to or results in a decrease (or increase) in the other

an **inverted sentence** is any sentence in which the normal word order is reversed, with the verb coming before the subject or the complete subject and predicate coming after another clause

iodized salt is common table salt with iodine added for nutritional reasons

ipse dixit (1477) is Latin for "he (the master) said it," a translation of Greek *autos epha*, a phrase used by disciples of Pythagoras when quoting their master

ipso faco is Latin for "by the very fact of" or "thereby"

an **Irish bull** is an expression that contains a ludicrous self-contradiction: "I will give my last dollar to be a millionaire."

Irish coffee is coffee with Irish whiskey and cream

{ an **Irishman's hurricane** is a dead calm }

Iron Age, attested in 1592, is from Greek and Roman mythology and originally meant "the last and worst age of the world"; the archaeological sense of "period in which humans used iron tools and weapons" is from 1879

iron crow is another way of saying crowbar

the year 1920 had the first recorded use of **iron curtain**

an **iron ride** is a rollercoaster or track-based amusement ride

an **ironic event** is an incongruous event, one at odds with what we might have expected

an **irrational number** is one that cannot be expressed exactly as the ratio between two numbers—as the ratio between the circumference of a circle and its radius or pi

an **irregular verb** is any whose past tense and past participle are not formed by adding -ed, -d, or -t to the present tense, or a verb that does not follow the general rules of inflection

irritable bowel syndrome is a stress-associated abdominal pain with diarrhea or constipation

IS-A describes a relationship within a hierarchy showing that an entity is a type of another entity, e.g., a cat IS-A mammal

ish kabbible (1921), "I should worry," is of unknown origin, but perhaps derived from Yiddish **nisht gefidlt** and popularized (perhaps coined) by comedienne Fanny Brice

the **isthmus of fauces** is the orifice by which the mouth connects with the pharynx, the respiratory and digestive tracts

Italian sausage is a type of coarse pork sausage seasoned with garlic, fennel seed, and possibly anise seed and made two ways, hot (with chile peppers) or sweet (without chile peppers)

> **itsy-bitsy** (1938), "charmingly small," is from itty (1798, in a letter of Jane Austen), baby-talk form of little

ivory tower suggests elegant detachment in a cool, white aerie where a poet or philosopher might retreat to think and write

Ivy League is originally a sportswriter's term, but it has nothing to do with the number four. The term was first used in 1937 by the New York *Herald-Tribune* sportswriter Caswell Adams. He used it in reference to the unofficial conference of teams also known as the Old Ten. The teams were Army, Brown, Columbia, Cornell, Dartmouth, Harvard, Navy, Pennsylvania, Princeton, and Yale. In 1940, Army and Navy dropped out of the association, and the membership has remained the same ever since. The league was formalized in 1954 and played its first games as a formal organization in 1956. The term Ivy Colleges is a few years older, first appearing in the *Herald-Tribune* in 1933 by sportswriter S. Woodward. The name derives from the ivy that supposedly climbs the walls at these venerable institutions. Some attribute the name to the Roman numerals for four (IV), asserting that there was such a sports league originally with four members. The Morris *Dictionary of Word and Phrase Origins* helped to perpetuate this belief. The supposed "IV League" was

formed over a century ago and consisted of Harvard, Yale, Princeton, and a fourth school that varies depending on who is telling the story.

Iyengar yoga is a form of hatha yoga created by B.K.S. Iyengar, based on Patanjali's Yoga Sutras

{ J }

Jack cheese is another name for Monterey Jack cheese

Jack Frost is a personification of winter dating to 1847

jack o' lantern (1663) was a local name for a will-o-the-wisp (Latin *ignis fatuus*), mainly attested in East Anglia but also in southwestern England; the extension to carved pumpkins occurred around 1837

a **jack o' the clock** is any of the mechanical figures that come out regularly to strike the bell of a clock

a **jack plug** is the type found on some audio equipment, with a single shaft plug making the connection that transmits a signal

the **jack rabbit**, which is classified as a hare, received its common name from the fact that its long, large ears were thought to resemble those of a jackass

Jack Russell is a type of terrier (not recognized as a distinct breed) named for the Rev. John Russell (1795–1883) of Devonshire

a **jack-at-a-pinch** is a man whose services are used only in an emergency

a **jacket potato** is a baked potato served with the skin on

jack-in-the-box (1570) was originally a name for a sharp or cheat who deceived tradesmen by substituting empty boxes for others full of money; as a type of toy, it is attested from 1702

SS Car Company was the original name of the **Jaguar Car Company**

jai alai is Basque for "merry" (*alai*) "festival" (*jai*)

jam session is first recorded as a term in 1933

Jane Doe started as a name in legal proceedings to designate an unknown or unidentified woman or girl

a **janus word** is one having opposite or contradictory meanings, as "cleave" the **Japanese beetle** is a pest of fruit and foliage as an adult and a pest of grass roots when it is larva

a **Japanese garden** often uses bamboo, mondo grasses, pine, and small pools of water containing koi

Japanese paper is made of vegetable fibers (mulberry bark) and is not sized; it is used for arts and crafts

Japanese thermal reconditioning (or Japanese hair straightening) is a method of permanently straightening human hair using a solution to break disulfide bonds in hair, then ironing, then applying a solution to rebuild the disulfide bonds

jaw breaker is a word that is hard to pronounce

the **Jazz Age** was the 1920s—a carefree and prosperous time as reflected in novels like those of F. Scott Fitzgerald

je ne sais quoi is a term for a quality that cannot be described or easily named

Jekyll and Hyde, in reference to opposite aspects of a person's character, is from Robert Louis Stevenson's story, *The Strange Case of Dr. Jekyll and Mr. Hyde,* published in 1886

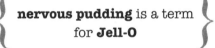

nervous pudding is a term for **Jell-O**

jelly bean is a bean-shaped candy with a jellylike center

before **jelly rolls** got their name, they were called **jelly cakes** and in England they are **Swiss rolls**

jerry-built (1869) is either from English dialect *jerry*, "bad, defective," a pejorative use of the male nickname Jerry, or from nautical slang *jury*, "temporary," which came to be used for all sorts of makeshift and inferior objects

Jerusalem artichoke is not from Jerusalem nor is it an artichoke; it is an edible tuber from North America, *girasole articiocco*, "sunflower artichoke," mistranslated to English as **Jerusalem artichoke**

circadian dysrhythmia is the technical term for **jet lag** (1969)

jet propulsion was a concept recorded in 1867, but **jet engine** did not come to be until 1943

jet ski is a trademark

there are typically two or three **jet streams** in each of the northern and southern hemispheres at any given time, moving generally west to east from 30,000–45,000 feet up

a **jetted pocket** is one without a flap

the rough spots intentionally created on the sides of roads to alert drivers are **jiggle-bars** or **rumble strips**

Jim Crow is the term for the former practice of segregating black people (United States)

jim-dandy (1844) may be from an old song, "Dandy Jim of Caroline" (1840s)

jimson weed (1812) is an American English shortening of Jamestown-weed (1687), from the Jamestown, Virginia, colony, where it was discovered by Europeans (1676); British soldiers mistook it for an edible plant and subsequently hallucinated for eleven days a **jitney bus** was one that carried passengers for a nickel, jitney being slang for nickel

job action refers to a temporary action, such as a strike or slowdown, by workers to make demands or protest a company or managerial decision

job lot (1851) is a batch of articles sold or bought at one time, especially at a discount

jock itch is derived from jock as in jockstrap, which is from the slang *jock* meaning "genitals"

joe-pye weed (1818) is said to be so called from the name of an Indian who used it to cure typhus in New England

Johannisberg Riesling is from the name of a castle and village on the Rhine in Germany where it was originally produced

John Bull, the personification of the typical Englishman, is represented as a stout, red-faced farmer in a top hat and high boots—from a character in a 1712 satire

John Doe had its beginnings in legal use—a legal fiction standing for the plaintiff, and **Richard Roe** was the defendant

John McIntosh was the first to cultivate the red apple of that name

johnny-cake is attested in 1739 and of unknown origin, perhaps from Shawnee cake, from the Indian tribe; its folk etymology since 1775, however, connects it to journey cake

joie de vivre is more than exuberance; rather a joy of living that is steadier than simple high spirits

join together is a redundancy

a **joke spelling** is something like "donut" for doughnut

the **Jolly Roger** skull-and-crossbones flag may have derived from the French *jolie rouge*, meaning "pretty red," and refers to a red pennant also known as the *jolie rougere*, flown by seventeenth- and eighteenth-century French buccaneers in the Caribbean

the **Jordan almond** is not related to Jordan but is from Middle English *jardyne almaund*, "garden almond"

another name for a stick of incense is **joss stick**

jow-fair is an old term for a wedding broken off at the last moment, at the church

joy-to-stuff ratio is the amount of time a person has to enjoy one's material goods in comparison to the amount of time one spends accumulating the material goods

a **Judas hole** is a small hole cut in a door or wall to allow one to see in but remain unseen

a **judge advocate** is a staff officer serving as legal adviser to a military commander

the **jugular vein** is actually an artery

the **juice sacs** of an orange are the small pockets that combine to make up the fruit's pulp

juke boxes were once situated in juke joints, disreputable places for indulgence of pleasures

juke joint or juke house was first a road-house or brothel, now a cheap roadside establishment for food, drink, and music

jumbo shrimp include the larger species, like the prawn, and are caught commercially and used for food as in jambalaya, okonomi-yaki, poon choi, bagoong, Kerala, and scampi; shrimp are classified as miniature, small, medium, large, extra large, jumbo, and colossal

> a **jump jet** can take off and land vertically, not needing a runway

a line in a newspaper or magazine article that says "continued on page ___" or "go to page ___," is called the **jump line**

jump seat, a folding seat between the front and back seats of a limousine or similarly large vehicle, or a similar seat for temporary use in an aircraft or train, is also the refer-ence for an off-duty pilot taking a spare seat in an aircraft cockpit to get to a location

jump the gun refers to a runner jumping ahead of the starting shot

jump the shark denotes the point at which a popular television show has gone past its peak and has resorted to stunt programming, after which it is eventually canceled

the middle of a trampoline is the **jumping bed**

jungle gym was formerly a U.S. trademark

a **community college** is a **junior college** established to serve a particular commu-nity and sponsored by local government;

both junior colleges and community colleges award associate degrees

the term **junk food** came into the language around 1973

jury-rig is a nautical term for an emergency replacement for broken equipment

the spelling is **just deserts** and has nothing to do with post-dinner sweets; it is from French *deservir*, "deserve"; remember that just deserts pertains to what you deserve (helps with spelling!)

justice of the peace is a judicial officer or subordinate magistrate appointed for the conservation of the peace in a specified district, with other incidental powers speci-fied in his commission

{ K }

K ration, an emergency food ration of a single meal, was named after U.S. physiologist Ancel B. Keys (1904–2004)

K Street is a major thoroughfare in Washington, DC known for the offices of think tanks, lobbyists, lawyers, and advocacy groups

Kama Sutra (1883) comes from Sanskrit and is an ancient treatise on love and sexual performance

kangaroo court comes from the verb *to kangaroo*, meaning "to convict a person on false evidence"

kangaroo feathers once meant "an impossible thing"

a **kangaroo word** is one that contains within itself another word that is a synonym of itself: evacuate, vacate

karma yoga is described as the discipline of selfless action as a way to perfection

the **Kashmir goat** of the Himalayas yields the wool to make cashmere

to **keep the ball rolling** is an allusion to rugby or bandy

keeping up with the Joneses was coined by cartoonist Arthur Momand in the early twentieth century, based on his own Long Island experience

a **keeping-room** is one used as a sitting room or parlor (1790)

the **Kegel exercise** for the pelvic floor muscles was named for Dr. Arnold Kegel, who advocated such exercise in the late 1940s

kemo sabe was not from a Native American language but was created by the Lone Ranger's inventor to mean "faithful friend"

Kentucky colonel is an honorary title given to individuals noted for their public service for the state of Kentucky, United States.

kettle corn is a sweet-and-salty variety of popcorn that adds granulated sugar, salt, and oil

a **kettle hole** is a geological hollow, usually filled in with a lake due to the melting of a glacier

kettle of fish, "mess, muddle," is from a *pretty kettle of fish,* a corruption of "kiddle of fish" with a kiddle being a basket set in the opening of a weir for catching fish

kettle stitch is a stitch made in sewing at the head and tail of a book

kew-kaw means upside-down

the **kewpie doll**'s name comes from Cupid

the **key grip** on a film crew is in charge of the camera equipment

the long fabric key holders used by many people are called **key lanyards**

a **kick pleat** is the slit in the back of a skirt or coat to allow more freedom of movement

kick the bucket originates from slaughterhouses, where hogs were slashed and hung by a pulley with a weight called a bucket

a **kick turn** in skateboarding is a turn made with the front wheels off the ground

kid gloves are made from kidskin, lambskin, or a similar leather

the **kill zone** is the area of the body where a bullet would likely kill the person—used on targets for shooting practice

king's weather is a term for fine weather

kiss of death is probably of Biblical origin, referring to Judas Iscariot's kiss of Jesus, which facilitated his arrest

kiss of life was a name used in the 1960s for mouth-to-mouth resuscitation

key lime pie takes its name from Key West, Florida

in music, the **key signature** is the group of sharps or flats placed to the right of the clef on a staff to identify the key

a **keyhole saw** is used to cut small holes like keyholes

keynote address dates to 1905

a **kick plate** is the metal piece at the bottom of a door, etc., to protect it from damage

kiss the hare's foot is to be so late as to miss dinner and have to eat leftover scraps

a **kissing cousin** originally was any relative known well enough to be given a kiss in greeting

kissing-comfits are sweets to make the breath pleasant

kit bag (1898) is a chunky bag in which to carry a soldier's or traveler's belongings

a **kitchen midden** is a refuse heap from an ancient dwelling

kitchen pepper, from the seventeenth century on, was a mixture of black or white pepper, allspice, cinnamon, cloves, ginger, and nutmeg

kitchen police is a term that originated during World War I

the phrase **kith and kin** originally denoted one's country and relatives, later one's friends and relatives

a **kitten heel** is a type of low stiletto heel on a woman's shoe

kiwi fruit, originating in China, was renamed Chinese gooseberry when exported to New Zealand and renamed for the New Zealand bird kiwi when imported to the United States

klieg light is named for two brothers, A. T. and J. H. Kliegl, who invented the arc studio light

knick-knack (or knickknack) dates to 1580, a reduplication of *knack*, "stratagem, trick"

a **knob of butter** is equivalent to a lump

knock on wood refers to guardian spirits thought to live in trees and who are summoned by knocking

a **knot garden** is a formal one laid out in an intricate design (not necessarily a "knot")

know like a book goes back to the days when there were so few books they had to be memorized in order to pass the information along

know the ropes was first a nautical expression from the days when a sailor or apprentice had to be knowledgeable of rigging and rope handling

knowledge box is a humorous name for the head

{ **knuckling down** is from the late seventeenth-century game of marbles }

Kobe beef is from a region of Japan famous for Wagyu cattle, known for the meat's rich flavor; American Kobe is created from cattle with Wagyu genetics but raised in North America and often crossbred with Black Angus

Mozart's works were catalogued and assigned numbers called **Kochel numbers**

the **Komodo dragon** (1927) was named for the Indonesian island of Komodo, where it lives

kosher food is a variety of foods that have been prepared, grown, and processed in accordance with Jewish laws; some of the common requirements include: killing animals and processing foods in accordance with Jewish laws; restrictions from eating grapes grown by non-Jewish grape producers; restrictions from eating specified animals or specified parts of certain animals; removing blood by draining away or broiling food from animals containing blood, such as meats; not combining and eating meats of poultry, wild birds, and mammals with dairy foods; and using only utensils that have been used to eat kosher foods

the **Krebs cycle** is named for Sir Hans Adolf Krebs, German-born British biochemist

Kris Kringle may be an alteration of German Christkindl, "Christmas present," or "Christ Child"

the **Ku Klux Klan** (1867) is a made-up name, supposedly from Greek kyklos "circle"; originally an organization of former Confederate officers and soldiers, it was put down by the U.S. military in the 1870s, then revived in 1915 as a national racist Protestant fraternal organization, growing to prominence but fractured in the 1930s

the best-known type of Chinese karate is **kung fu** (from Chinese words translating to "merit master" or "one who is highly skilled") and the most famous Korean karate is **tae kwon do**; **karate** is Japanese

{ **kung pao** is a Szechuan dish of chicken and peanuts, chiles, etc. }

kyrie eleison, c.1225, is a Greek liturgical formula adopted untranslated into Latin Mass, literally "Lord have mercy"

{ L }

La Niña (Spanish "the girl child") is a cooling of the water in the equatorial Pacific

a **lace pillow** is a cushion placed on the lap to provide support when lacemaking

lactic acid is formed in sour milk and is also produced by muscle tissues during strenuous exercise

la-di-da, mocking of affected gentility, is from c.1883, a derisive imitation of an affected way of talking

Lady Luck, "fortune," dates to 1932

lady's fingers is an alternative name for okra

laid paper is made on wire molds that give it a characteristic watermark of close, thin lines

laissez faire is literally "allow people to do as they will" in French

lake-effect snow is created when cold, dry air passes over a large warmer lake, such as one of the Great Lakes, and picks up moisture and heat

the term **la-la land** is a reduplication of LA, Los Angeles

lamb fries are fried lamb's testicles

the original **lame duck** was a member of the British Stock Exchange who couldn't meet his liabilities on settlement date

the glass cylinder over the wick of an oil lamp is the **lamp chimney**

a **lamp room** is the room at the top of a lighthouse in which the signal light is housed

the rank **lance corporal** is based on an analogy with obsolete *lancepesade*, the lowest grade of noncommissioned officer, based on Italian *lancia spezzata*, "broken lance"

a **lancet window** is high and narrow with a pointed head

a **land breeze** is one blowing toward the sea from land, especially at night due to the relative warmth of the sea (compared to sea breeze)

land bridges are prehistoric land connections that allowed colonization, such as the ones that existed across the Bering Strait and English Channel

in the Bible, the **land of milk and honey** is a land of prosperity and plenty promised by God to the Israelites

the **land of Nod** is a pun with biblical allusion to the place name Nod in Genesis

Land's End is England's southwesternmost point, a rocky promontory

to be **land poor** is to be unable to work all the land one owns

a **landscape architect** designs the major components of a garden or yard—such as drainage, grading, walkways, and walls—and also constructs them

don't use **language** when you mean "**writing system**"—Chinese is a spoken language with no characters; the Chinese writing system uses thousands of characters

the **language arts** include grammar, composition, and spelling

language competence is defined as a speaker's subconscious, intuitive knowledge of the rules of his or her language

language engineering is any of a variety of computing procedures to human language, including speech recognition, machine translation, parsers, and other natural language applications

a **language maven** is a self-appointed authority on language usage

the **language of flowers** is the set of meaning attached to different flowers that are given to others singly or as part of arrangements

language police refers to any person or group crusading for a particular usage or omission within a language; also called language cops, tongue troopers

> **language pollution** is the rampant use of nonformal language and slang

lapis lazuli, a sky-blue semiprecious stone, is pronounced lap-us-LAY-zuh-lee

a **lapsus calami** is a slip of the pen; **lapsus memoriae** is a slip of the memory

lapsus linguae is another way of saying slip of the tongue

lares and penates are the sum of one's personal or household effects

what we call calorie to measure the energy value of food is technically the **large calorie**

the **large intestine** is the cecum, colon, and rectum

Las Vegas could have been Des Plaines if the French had beaten the Spanish getting there—as both mean "plain, lowland"

in a **laser printer**, the paper is dusted with a powdery ink and the image codes of characters are projected onto it by a laser, which causes the ink to fuse to the paper, reproducing the images

laser tweezers use light to move individual molecules within cells

last hurrah comes from a 1956 novel about a political boss of an eastern U.S. city

the **last of pea-time** means the end of anything and the attendant sadness of an ending

the **latch bolt** is the one activated by a doorknob, as opposed to a **dead bolt**

latchkey child is from the 1940s United States, when children started letting themselves into their homes after school because the parents were working

late plate is a meal eaten after the regular family-style time

latent heat is that quantity of heat which disappears or becomes concealed in a body while producing some change in it other than rise of temperature, such as fusion, evaporation, or expansion, the quantity being constant for each particular body and for each species of change

vertical thinking is logical; **lateral thinking** is illogical, an unorthodox approach to problem-solving, often looking at a problem from other "sides" rather than head-on; the concept of lateral thinking originated in 1966

a **Latin cross** is a plain cross where the vertical part below is longer than the other three parts

the economics phenomenon whereby many small purchases add up to a significant expenditure over time is the **latte factor**

the Mormons call themselves **Latter-Day Saints**

a **lattice window** is one with small panes set in diagonally crossing strips

laughing gas is the nontechnical term for nitrous oxide

laughing-stock (1519) is formed by analogy with whipping-stock, "whipping post," and later also "object of frequent whipping" (1678)

laughter lines is a newer term for **crow's feet**

dating to 1958, **laundry list** is a long random list of items

the **law of averages** is a law affirming that in the long run, probabilities will determine performance

the **law of the jungle** derives from Rudyard Kipling's *The Jungle Book* (1894)

lawn tennis is the more formal name for the game we play

to **lay an egg** refers to egg as "zero"

the **lay figure** is an artist's jointed dummy of the human body; the word is from Dutch *leeman,* "joint man"

> Bonnie Cashin, a U.S. fashion designer, coined **layering** in 1950, also called **layered look**

Le Creuset, the French cookware manufacturer, is pronounced luh kru-ZAY

lead poisoning is also called plumbism

the **leading edge** is the folded part of the fabric of a collar and the break line is where the collar folds

a **leading question** is one that suggests its own answer

leaf mold is soil consisting of decayed leaves

{ **leaf vegetables** include cabbage and Romaine lettuce, spinach, Swiss chard, endive, and cress }

leap year may have gotten its designation from the fact that in a bissextile year, any fixed festival after February falls on the next weekday to the one it fell on the previous year

a **learner's dictionary** is a monolingual dictionary for foreign learners of a language; the pioneer was A.S. Hornby's *A Learner's Dictionary of Current English* (1948)

a **learning cottage** is a residential trailer used as a temporary or portable classroom

learning curve dates from the 1920s and arose as psychological jargon

learning disability is now the standard accepted term in official contexts

a **leather-ears** is a person of slow comprehension

the top rail of a fence is the **ledger board**

the **Leeward Islands** are more sheltered from the prevailing northeasterly winds than the Windward Islands of the Lesser Antilles

if you are facing downstream, with your back to the river's source, the **left bank** is on your left, and the right bank is on your right

the **left brain** controls the right side of the body and usually the language functions of speech and writing

the **left coast** is the West Coast of the United States or Canada

left wing first referred to the National Assembly in France, where nobles sat to the president's right and the Commons to the left; left wing is often considered radical or socialist, liberal or progressive—while right wing is conservative

left-legged is clumsy in walking or dancing

a **leg drama** is a ballet

leg warmers, tubular knit garments worn from ankle to knee or thigh, date to the 1970s for popularity but were used earlier by rehearsing dancers

legal eagle dates to 1949, and **legal beagle** to 1953

a **legal pad** is 8½ × 14 inches

Lytton Strachey's phrase **legend in one's lifetime** (1918) described the celebrity culture to come

a **leisurable activity** is one carried out without haste or deliberation

lemon sole is actually a type of flounder, not sole, and derives from French *limande* "flatfish"

lèse-majestè is literally "wounded majesty" and means "an affront to the dignity of an important person"

less is more an is an aphorism from Robert Browning

letterbox format is the showing of a movie on TV with its original theater aspect ratio (width to height) in which horizontal bands appear on the top and bottom of the TV screen

level playing field, a state or situation of impartiality and fairness, came into the language around 1979

lexical definition is the meaning of a word in actual usage by speakers of a certain language

a word's **lexical meaning** is its meaning in isolation from any context, the meaning of the base (as the word "play") in a paradigm (as plays, played, playing)

lexical semantics is the study of the meaning of words and phrases and the relationships between them, such as synonymy, antonymy, and hyponymy

ley farming is the alternate growing of crops and grass

Leyden jar (1755) was a vial used for accumulating and storing static electricity, from Leyden (modern Leiden), Holland; it is so called because it was first described in 1746 by physicist Pieter van Musschenbroek of Leyden (1692–1761)

the **Lhasa apso** dog (1935) gets its name from Tibetan "Lhasa terrier,' Lhasa being the capital of Tibet

liberal arts were distinguished from servile or mechanical arts and originally referred to arts and sciences "worthy of a free man"

a **library edition** is a book using higher-quality paper and binding, especially for libraries holding the standard editions of written works

lick and a promise refers to a cat who gives itself a quick lick, with the promise to complete the cleaning later

lickety whittle is very, even recklessly, fast

lickety-split is a fanciful formation dating to 1848 on Nantucket

licorice stick is an informal term for a clarinet

lie detector is an informal name for the polygraph

a **life coach** is an advisor who helps people with problems, decisions, and goal attainment in daily life

life drawing is drawing the human figure from a living model

a list of all the kinds of birds observed by a person is a **life list**

all of the possible etymologies for the phrase **life of Riley** center on popular music—though Eric Partridge also thought the phrase was British and that it was taken up in America only in the 1930s, negating the popular music theories

life sciences include biology, botany, physiology, zoology, and branches like biochemistry and microbiology

a **lifestyle drug** is one used to improve a quality of one's life rather than alleviate pain or cure disease

light beer was once called **Vienna beer**, one in which lightly roasted malt is used

a **light breeze** is 4.5–7 miles per hour

light cream is also called **coffee cream** or **table cream**

a **light globe** is a nearly evacuated glass globe containing ionized gas, which produces lightning-like patterns when touched

light industry is the manufacture of small or light articles

a **light pen** is a small, photosensitive device connected to a computer and moved by hand over an output display in order to manipulate information in the computer

light pollution involves streetlights and other manmade sources that obscure the viewing of stars and planets at night

light rain is up to 0.1 accumulations per hour, **moderate rain** is 0.1–0.3 per hour, and **heavy rain** is 0.3+ per hour

a **light sculpture** is one that uses light bulbs, the sun, and laser beams as the primary medium of expression

light whipping cream is 30–36 percent fat and **heavy cream** has at least 36 percent fat

a **light year** is not a length of time but a distance, the distance a pulse of light travels in one year (about 5.88 trillion miles)

a **light-foot** is one billionth of a second

a **lightning arrester** is a device placed where a wire enters a building, for th purpose of preventing injury by lightning to an operator or instrument; consists of a short circuit to the ground interrupted by a thin nonconductor over which lightning jumps

lightning bug (1778) is another term for firefly (1658)

like a bat out of hell seems to have originated with U.S. fighter pilots in World War I

like a duck in thunder means struck with consternation

lima beans are named for Lima, Peru, and are also called butter beans; succotash, made from them, derives from Narrangaset *msiquatash* "fragments"

the **limbic system** is the network of the brain involving areas near the edge of the cortex (Latin *limbus*, "edge") and controls the basic emotions and drives

> a **limited war** is a war whose objective is of smaller scope than total defeat of the enemy

Lincoln Logs is a construction toy consisting of miniature, notched logs from which log cabins and similar buildings may be made; Lincoln Logs were invented around 1916 by John Lloyd Wright, son of the notable architect Frank Lloyd Wright

the **Lindy Hop**, a popular dance c. 1931, originated in Harlem, New York and was named for U.S. aviator Charles A. Lindbergh (1902–74), who in 1927 made the first solo nonstop trans-Atlantic flight

{ to **line bees** is to track wild bees to their nest by following their line of flight }

a **line cut** is an engraving consisting only of lines or areas that are solid black or white

a **line drawing** is a drawing done exclusively in line, providing gradations in tone entirely through variations in width and density

lines of communication first referred to the connection between an army in the field and its bases

the **line of scrimmage** (1905) is an imaginary line parallel to the goal lines that passes from one sideline to the other through the point of the football closest to the goal line of each team

Linear B was an early form of Mycenaean Greek deciphered by Michael Ventris

a **line-item veto** is the authority of an executive to veto a specific appropriation in a budget passed by a legislature

a **lingua franca** may be both a language with an extensive reach around the world, as well as a set of specialist terms understood by people in a particular field or culture; *lingua franca* is Italian, literally "Frankish tongue," and was first a form of communication used in the Levant, a type of Italian peppered with Spanish, French, Greek, Arabic, and Turkish words and possibly from an old custom of calling Europeans "Franks"

linguistic typology is the classification of languages according to grammatical features rather than common ancestry or geographical contact

linseed oil for artwork is used as a binding agent so that a pigment adheres to a surface—and is also the principal drying oil used in paints

linsey-woolsey (1483) was first a cloth woven from linen and wool; the words were altered for the sake of a jingling sound

a **liquid asset** is one in the form of money or one that can be quickly converted into money

a **liquid lunch** is drinking alcohol at lunchtime instead of eating

liquid smoke is a flavoring made from vinegar and a wood smoke concentrate

the **list price** is the selling price of something as stated in a catalog or price list and often subject to discounts

a **literary executor** is a person entrusted with a dead writer's papers and works

literary piano is a synonym for typewriter

litmus paper comes from Old Norse *litmosi*, from *litr*, "dye," and *mosi*, "moss"

litmus test, "a decisively indicative test," dates from the 1950s

little boys' room is a euphemism for men's lavatory, dating from the 1930s, and **little girls' room** from the 1940s

Little Christmas (or **Women's Christmas**) is January 6th, the Feast of the Epiphany

a **little go** is a public examination given about the middle of the course, which is less strict and important than the final one

{ **little green men** was first recorded in 1961 and derives from cartoons of such creatures emerging from flying saucers }

little neck clams refers to the clamming area of Little Neck, Ipswich, Massachusetts

the **littoral zone** is that part of the shoreline that lies between high and low tides

live load is the weight of cargo or passengers that a vehicle carries; **dead load** is the weight of the vehicle itself

live oak, a very large evergreen of the United States, is so named from its being evergreen

live parking means parking that is permitted only if the driver remains inside the vehicle

a **liver spot** (or **age spot**) was so named because it was supposed to depend on some disorder of the liver; these brownish patches on the skin often occur in old age and most often in people with pale, sun-damaged skin

a **living rock** is one that is not detached but still part of the earth

living room, attested from 1825, is a "room set up for ordinary social use," as opposed to bedroom, dining room, etc.; living room in the United States is sitting room in the United Kingdom or lounge room in Australia

living will, a written request that, if the signatory suffers severe disablement or terminal illness, he or she should not be kept alive by artificial means, dates to 1969

lo and behold is actually redundant, meaning "look and behold"

lo mein are Chinese noodles that look like spaghetti

load lines are waterlines to show the level the water should reach when the ship is properly loaded

a **load of codswallop** is stuff and nonsense

loaded for bear, dating from the mid-1800s, alludes to the heavy charge of powder or lead that hunters use for large animals, like bears

money-lending shark and shark accountant are terms slightly predating **loan shark** (1905)

a **loan translation** is the process whereby a compound word or expression is created by literal translation of each of the elements of a compound word or expression in another language, as marriage of convenience from French *mariage de convenance.*

lobster Wenburg was renamed **lobster Newburg** by Delmonico's after the patron for whom it was named got into a drunken brawl in the establishment

lobster shift (equivalent in meaning to graveyard shift) is likely from the newspaper business; lobster was a popular term of derision, meaning "fool, sucker," and lobster shift may have originally referred to the late-night hours of some slogging journalists

local color is the true color of an object in ordinary daylight as distinguished from its apparent color when influenced by atmospheric conditions, artificial light, etc.

lock, stock, and barrel were the main parts of an old rifle

a **locum tenens** is a person who temporarily fills in for another and undertakes their professional duties

locus classicus is a "defining example"

locust years constitute a period of economic hardship (coined by Winston Churchill)

the poles of a tepee (or tipi) are the **lodge poles**

log tongs are the tool used for grasping and moving logs and embers in a fireplace

the expression **lone wolf** alludes to the tendency of some species of wolf to hunt alone, rather than in packs

a **long row to hoe** was probably a well-established expression years before Davy Crockett first recorded it in 1835

long sauce stands for beets, carrots, and parsnips

long sugar is molasses

long suit is a suit of which one holds originally more than three cards

the **long tail** or **long-tail effect** is a business model in which there is profitability to selling slow-selling items, especially on the Internet; the demand curve of products versus sales, peaking at very high and then tailing away

a **long waist** is a low waist on a person's body or on a dress

long con is a complex confidence trick that requires extensive planning (from 1930s underworld slang)

long in the tooth means "aging" and originally applied to horses, because their gums recede with age

long johns were named for German gymnastics teacher Friedrich Ludwig Jahn, who introduced a full-body exercise suit

the **long list** is the full listing of wines offered by a fine restaurant

long roll is a prolonged roll of the drums to signal an attack by the enemy and to signal troops to arrange themselves in line

longleaf pine is also called **fat pine**

to **look parsnips** means to look displeased or sour

loose cannon (1900) was popularized after a phrase used by U.S. President Theodore Roosevelt, "I don't want to be the old cannon loose on the deck in the storm"

the original reference to **loose ends** was in making of nets

loose sentence is a complex sentence in which the main clause is followed by subordinate clause(s) or modifier(s)

Los Angeles's full name is *El Pueblo de Nuestra Señora la Reina de los Angeles de Poriuncula*

loss leader comes from the 1920s for an article sold below normal price, which leads people to buy other things

lost in the shuffle is a reference to a card missed in a shuffle of the pack (1930s)

lost or **dead metaphors** are words and phrases we still use figuratively, but whose original, literal senses have fallen into obscurity

lost positives are words like *couth, sheveled,* and *kempt* which people think existed as positive forms of *uncouth, disheveled,* and *unkempt*

lost-wax process or *cire perdue* is the method of casting metals in which the desired form was carved in wax, coated with clay, and baked; the wax runs out through vents left in the clay for the purpose, and molten metal is then poured through the same vents into the mold

lottery mentality is the belief that someday one will win a lottery and that one's problems will go away; a desire to become rich by winning a lottery or some other method other than earning it

lotus land (1842) is the fabled land of the lotus-eaters, a land of ease and delight

lotus posture (1880s) and **lotus position** (1962) are translations of Hindi *padmasanam,* sitting with the feet resting on the thighs

love apple is an old-fashioned term for tomato, probably a translation of French *pomme d'amour*—from the former belief in the tomato's aphrodisiacal power

love handles dates from the 1970s

love waves are earthquake waves causing side-to-side shaking similar to the motion of a snake

love-hate relationship dates from 1920s psychoanalysts' jargon

low clouds are those that do not exceed 6,500 feet in altitude; middle clouds are 6,500–20,000 feet

the name **Low German** came from the northern German dialects, and the low area bounded by the North and Baltic Seas; High German came from elevated areas toward the south and the Alps

low-hanging fruit is something easily achieved or obtained; the most readily achievable goal

{ the **low man** on an actual totem pole is really the most important man in the tribe }

low post in basketball is the area under or just to either side of the basket; this offensive position

Lower Ivy refers to any of the Ivy League universities, such as Columbia, Dartmouth, Brown, Cornell, and the University of Pennsylvania, which are generally seen as less prestigious than Harvard, Yale, Stanford, and Princeton

in a typesetter's case, the small letters were originally on a lower level than the others— hence, **lowercase**

{ **lowest common denominator** is the level of the least discriminating audience or consumer group }

lucid dreaming is a form of dreaming in which the conscious mind takes control over the contents of the dream

ludic activity is a psychological term for "play"

lug nuts hold a car wheel onto the axle

to **lump off** is to guess or make an approximation

in a **lunar eclipse**, the earth passes between the sun and moon so that the moon is in the earth's shadow

a **lunar month** is the time between two new moons (twenty-nine days, twelve hours, forty-four minutes)

President Theodore Roosevelt coined the term **lunatic fringe**

lunch pail is another term for lunchbox

lust-dieted means "feeding gluttonously"

Lyme disease had its first outbreak in 1975 in Lyme, Connecticut

lyric poetry is characterized by an expression of the poet's personal feelings—and was originally descriptive of songs accompanied by the lyre (examples are John Keats and Percy Bysshe Shelley)

{ M }

macadamia nuts, which are really seeds, were named for the discoverer, chemist John Macadam

in Britain, **macaroni cheese** is the equivalent of U.S. macaroni and cheese

Mach number is the ratio of flight speed to the speed of sound, i.e., Mach 2 is traveling at twice the speed of sound

macked out means "all dressed up"

a **mackerel sky** is one with rows of white fluffy clouds resembling the pattern on a mackerel's back

hat makers suffered mental illness in the old days when they got mercury poisoning from treating fur, hence **mad as a hatter**

mad as a March hare goes back to Chaucer

mad cow disease became a colloquial term for the disease BSE in 1988

the term **mad money** is for a small sum of money carried by a woman on a date to enable her to reach home alone in case she and her escort quarrel and separate

Madagascar rice was raised in the Carolinas by 1787 and renamed **Carolina rice**

the correct word is "madding" in **madding crowd**, a poetic survival meaning "wild, furious, raving, mad"

Madison Avenue, as a term for the advertising business, was first used in 1944

a **Mae West** is a type of inflatable life jacket (1940), military slang in reference to the screen name of the buxom U.S. film star (1892–1980)

Magellanic clouds were named for Portuguese navigator Ferdinand Magellan (c. 1470–1521, modernized Magellanicus), the first European to round the tip of South America

magic bullet is a quick fix or simple cure for a disease

the **magic hour** is the hour at dawn and again at dusk when the sun produces the most flattering light for photography

magic lantern is a term for the illumination and projection of images first described in A. Kircher *Ars Magna Lucis et Umbra* (1646), and then C. Huygens in 1659 described the projection of images with artificial light rather than sunlight by use of a *lanterne magique* (French "magic lantern")

{ the **Magna Carta**, issued in 1215, is from Latin "great paper" }

magnitude of a star is the rank of a star with respect to brightness, about twenty very bright stars are said to be of first magnitude, the stars of the sixth magnitude being just visible to the naked eye, and telescopic stars are classified down to the twelfth magnitude or lower

magnum opus, "large work," was formerly *opus magnum*, but this is now obsolete

mah-jongg (1922) is from dialectic Chinese (Shanghai) *ma chiang*, "sparrows" — so called from the design of the pieces

a painter's hand rest is a **mahl stick**

mai tai is Tahitian for "the very best"

mail-order catalogs are also called wish books

a **main clause** of a sentence is one that can stand alone as a sentence

the **main guy** is the rope that holds up the center pole in a circus big top

Main Line, the principal line of a railway (1841) also has the meaning "affluent area of residence" (1930s), originally that of Philadelphia, from the main line of the Pennsylvania Railroad, which added local stops to a string of backwater towns west of the city (late nineteenth century) that helped turn them into fashionable suburbs

main squeeze dates to the 1940s, while significant other was coined in the 1970s

Main Street, the principal street of a (U.S.) town was used by 1810 and alluded to "mediocrity, small-town materialism" from the late nineteenth-century, especially since publication of Sinclair Lewis's novel *Main Street* (1920)

maitre d'hotel, or **maitre d'**, is literally French "master of the house"

the **major arcana** consists of the twenty-two trumps of a deck of Tarot cards

a **major piece** in chess is a rook or queen

major-domo (1589) comes from Italian *maggiordomo* or Spanish *mayordomo* from Latin *major domus*, "chief of the household"

we **make a bed** instead of using another verb because beds were once created anew each night from straw on the floor

to **make a long arm** is to reach far, especially in pursuit of food

to **make causey-webs** is to neglect one's work

to **make love** originally meant "to court"

make my day is associated with Clint Eastwood in *Sudden Impact* (1983)

make nice may be imitative of a Yiddish usage and dates to 1957

make one's mark is from the practice of smiths and artisans to mark their wares with a symbol or logo

make one's point, "establish one's argument," comes from crapshooting

make soft is the Hawaiian way of saying "be careful"

the allusion in to **make the grade** is to climbing a hill or gradient

make-work, "busy-work, activity of no value," is attested by 1937

making (both) ends meet is from bookkeeping—originally make both ends mete, "equal," a balance of assets and liabilities

making a virtue of necessity first was in Shakespeare's *Pericles*

mal de raquette is pain caused by excessive use of snowshoes

male chauvinism (1936) and **male chauvinist** (1940) originated in the United States

the cartoonists' term for typographical swears is a **maledicta balloon**

malice aforethought (1581) is premeditated wrongful intention

{ the term **mall rat** dates to the early 1980s }

malt vinegar is made from barley juice

Robinson Crusoe (1719) is the origin of the term **man Friday**

a **man of straw** is a person without money

man of the cloth originally applied to anyone who wore a uniform or livery for work

managed news is a government news release in its own interest

man-browed is the same as unibrow

below each side of the mouth is the **mandarin crease**, and the muscle that pulls the corners up to smile is the **risorius of Santorini**

the **mandarin orange** is either named for the flowing orange robes of Chinese mandarin officials or the superiority implied by "mandarin"

manger scene and **nativity scene** are synonyms

manic depressive (1902) preceded the term **manic depression** (1950s) by a number of years and it has been replaced by the term **bipolar disorder**

a **Manila folder** is a folding cover for loose papers, made from thick Manila paper, a paper of a light yellow-brown color made from Manila hemp or (now) other material

mano a mano (1970s from Spanish, "hand-to-hand") is used figuratively to describe rivalry or confrontation in business

man-of-war (c.1390) in its meaning "vessel equipped for warfare" is from 1484;

the sea creature known as the Portuguese man-of-war (1707) is so called for its sail-like crest

the **mansard roof** is named for French architect Francois Mansard

the **manual alphabet** is different finger configurations corresponding to letters of the alphabet

Manx cats, a breed of domestic cats having a rudimentary tail, containing only about three vertebrae, originated on the Isle of Man

the numbers and letters you use to find a location on a map are called **map reference**

maple butter is the last stage that maple syrup goes through before it becomes maple sugar; the preceding stages are **maple honey** and **maple cream**

maple cream is pure maple syrup boiled down and rapidly cooled until it has a creamy spreadable consistency

a **maquiladora city** is any Mexican border town that offers cheap labor and lax environmental and working standards

maraschino cherries are marinated or preserved in a strong sweet liqueur made from a variety of small bitter cherries

a **March hare** is a brown hare in time of breeding—which causes leaping, boxing, and chasing in circles

Marcus Gunn's syndrome is a condition in which chewing or lateral movement of the jaw causes elevation of the eyelid

Mardi Gras means Fat Tuesday, the last day to get fat before seven weeks of Lent and abstaining

mare's nest came from a phrase, "to find a **mare's nest**," and it means "something that does not exist;" so the sense of the phrase was "to find something amazing"

a **Margherita pizza** honors Margherita di Savoia, a queen of Italy

marine snow is a continuous shower of mostly organic detritus descending from the upper layers of the ocean and resembling snowfall

Mark 1 eyeball is a phrase describing the human eye as a means of visual perception as opposed to radar, telescope, etc.

Mark Twain took his pen name from the idiom *mark twain*, which was a captain's request to mark the river's depth as a boat traveled through uncharted waters

market value is the amount something is worth if offered for sale; book value is the value placed on a company asset by the company itself

{ **market-confirm** means exhilarated by drink, but not intoxicated }

the degree of greenness at which a fruit or vegetable is picked is described as **market-ripe**

married all overs refers to a woman who, once married, does not attend to her appearance

married names go back to ancient Rome; when Octavia married Cicero

the **Mars bar**'s name was inspired by the family name of the confectionery manufacturer that makes it

{ the rotating light on a police or fire vehicle (etc.) is called a **Mars light** }

march gas is methane gas produced when vegetation decomposes in water

the **Marshall plan** (1947) was named for its initiator, George C. Marshall (1880–1959), U.S. Secretary of State 1947–49

the **Marshalltown trowel** is the triangular trowel made in Iowa that is used by many archaeologists

martial art (1920) is so named after either Japanese *bu-gei* (*bu*, "military affairs" + *gei*, "art, craft" or "accomplishment") or Japanese *bu-jutsu*; *bu* + *jutsu*, "art, technique, skill, craft"

martial law (1533) was originally measures taken within a country for the defeat of rebels or invaders or (more generally) for the maintenance of public order

Mary Janes (shoes) are characterized by a strap across the top of the foot

a **masculine rhyme** is one of final stressed syllables, as blow/flow, confess/repress

in **mash note**, mash means "infatuation"

creamed potato and **whipped potato** are synonyms for **mashed potato**; mashed potatoes used to be called Dutch potatoes or German potatoes; mashed potato may also refer to a variation on the dance the "Twist," or mashed potatoes may refer to heavy, wet snow to skiers

masking tape is so called because it "masks" areas that are not to be painted

mason jar can be lowercase or uppercase; it was named for U.S. inventor John L. Mason

Charles Mason and Jeremiah Dixon were the surveyors of the **Mason-Dixon line**

the term **mass medium** dates from the early 1920s

mass murder was first a term in 1917

nouns like sugar, toast, coffee, and rice are **mass nouns**, and nouns like pencil, stone, tree, and biscuit are **count nouns**; mass nouns refer to things that occur as collected or undifferentiated compositions

the term **massage parlor** popped up by 1906

a **mast year** occurs when the number of nuts that trees produce in a given year is exponentially higher than the average

the term **master bedroom** dates from the 1920s

a **master class** is one given by an expert to highly talented students

a **master key** is designed to open a number of slightly different locks

master lode is the principal vein of ore

Mata Hari was the stage name taken by Margaretha Gertruida Zelle (1876–1917), from Malay *mata*, "eye," and *hari*, "day, dawn"

match play in golf is keeping score by counting the holes won by each side, rather than the strokes of individual players

matzo balls are dumplings often served in chicken broth

Maundy Thursday is literally "Mandate Thursday," from Jesus's command to love one another

maw-wallop is a badly cooked mess of food

mechanical energy examples are dynamo and turbine; **electrical energy** examples are motor and lightbulb; **nuclear energy** would be a power station or bomb; a **heat energy** example is a hot air balloon; **radiant energy** examples are solar heating panels and photosynthesis; and **chemical energy** examples are batteries or a gas or oil furnace

a **mechanical pencil** pushes lead out by a mechanism, such as a spring or a screw

May Day (1438) and accounts of merrymaking on this date are attested from c. 1240

the salutation **mazel tov!** comes from Hebrew *mazzal tòb*, "good luck!" and contains *mazzal*, "constellation," and *tòb*, "good"

an admission of guilt is **mea culpa** (Latin "[through]) my own fault" or **peccavi** (Latin "I have sinned")

mealy-mouthed is probably from Old English *milisc*, "sweet," or the first element is from meal on the notion of the softness of ground flour

mean solar day is the time it takes the Earth to make a complete rotation on its axis

the **meat hand** in baseball is the one without a glove

mebby-scales is wavering between two opinions

a **mechanical drawing** is one made with scales, rulers, and compasses

media mail is a U.S. postal class for sending books, recordings, and computer media

words like CinemaScope or WordNet use something called a **medial capital** letter; this is mainly used in names of products, processes, etc.

the line down the center of the tongue is the **median lingual sulcus**

median strip has several regional variants: medial strip, neutral strip, neutral ground, meridian, and boulevard

the **medicinal days** were the 6th, 8th, 10th, 12th, 16th, 18th, etc. of a disease, so called because according to Hippocrates, no crisis occurs on these days and medicine should be administered

a **Mediterranean diet** is one typical of that eaten by people in the Mediterranean region and thought to increase life expectancy and protect against heart disease and cancer—plenty of fruits and vegetables, grains, beans, nuts, olive oil, fish, and poultry

Mediterranean Sea is literally sea "in the middle of land"

meeting of minds is a expression dating to at least the 1960s

meeting seeds were small fruits or aromatic seeds used by parishioners to keep awake in church back in the day

French chef Auguste Escoffier named both **Melba toast** and **peach Melba** for opera singer Dame Nellie Melba; **Melba sauce** is made from puréed raspberries

mellow yellow is another term for LSD

melting pot is an expression that began circulating in the twentieth century after Israel Zangwill's play *The Melting Pot*

Memorial Day focuses on all soldiers who died in or as a result of any war; **Veterans Day** honors all, living or dead, who have served in the armed forces

a hypothetical permanent change in the nervous system brought about by memorizing something is a **memory trace** or **engram**

a **ménage à trois** is literally a "household for three" and describes three people living together—not necessarily with sex involved

mental age is the level of native mental ability or capacity of an individual, usually as determined by an intelligence test, in relation to the chronological age of the average individual at this level

the **Mercalli scale** for earthquakes is different from the Richter scale in that it is based on observed structural damage and people's descriptions

Gerhard Mercator called map collections "atlases" and donated his own name to the **Mercator projection**

Mercedes-Benz (1886) was named by its Austrian manufacturer Emil Jellinik for his daughter, Mercedes

merchant marine first meant the crew of a merchant vessel, now the trading fleet of a nation

the **mercurial finger** is the little finger

the **mercy rule** in sporting parlance is a rule that ends a one-sided contest prior to its natural conclusion

mere exposure effect describes the tendency to like objects to which we are frequently exposed, even if this exposure takes place subliminally

the **meritic zone** is the shallow waters of the ocean from the littoral zone to the edge of the continental shelf—and the shallow waters of a lake that border the land

a **merry-andrew,** "buffoon, zany," originally meant "mountebank's assistant"

merry-gall is a sore produced by chafing

merry-go-sorry is the simultaneous experience of both happiness and sadness

the **Mesolithic Age** was literally the Middle Stone Age

a **mesoscale convective system** is a huge complex of thunderstorms that can sometimes reach the size of Texas

a **meta key** is a keyboard button that functions differently when held simultaneously with the Alt or Control keys

meta-information is information about information, especially information about a document or a web page

the creases across fingers are the **metacarpophalangeal creases**

metallic tinking is a sound heard in the chest when a cavity communicating with the air passages contains both air and liquid

meteoric rise is a very odd term, since meteors always fall

method acting is based on a system by Konstantin Stanislavsky, c. 1926

Mexican jumping beans are seeds containing moth larva that move

Mexican standoff came into usage during the last decade of the nineteenth century, most likely originating in the American Southwest, although one dictionary claims that the term is of Australian origin; one possibility is that it may relate to the difficult and paradoxical social and economic conditions of nineteenth-century and early twentieth-century Mexico

Mexican stud is not Don Juan—it is a variety of poker

a **Mexican tiger** is the jaguar

a **Mexican wave** is a coordinated sequence of waving, standing-up, and sitting-down actions by spectators at a sporting (or other) event to create a wavelike effect

Mexican wedding cakes are small, round butter cookies containing finely ground nuts and rolled in confectioners' sugar after baking; also called Russian tea cakes and Mexican wedding cookies

Michelin guides were founded in 1888 and launched in 1900

{ **Mickey D's, McD's, McDuck's** are nicknames for McDonald's, a fast-food restaurant }

Mickey Finn was a notorious Chicago bartender who allegedly drugged and robbed his customers on a regular basis; hence the name for a drink containing a surreptitiously administered drug

Mickey Mouse was created in 1928 by Walt Disney (1901–66); as an adjective meaning "small and worthless," it dates from 1936, originally used especially of mediocre dance-band music, a put-down based on the type of tunes played as background in cartoon films

a **Microsoft moment** describes a time when one encounters a flaw in Microsoft software or feature and then it crashes, doesn't do something it should, or does something you did not ask it to do and you didn't want

microwave background is the weak radiation detectable from all over the sky, thought to be evidence of the big bang

microwave oven (1955) was not widely used until the 1970s (microwave, 1972)

the **Middle Ages** were from the final fall of the Roman Empire until the Italian Renaissance; the Dark Ages is what Renaissance people called the Middle Ages

Middle America refers to the conservative middle classes of the United States, characterized as inhabiting the Midwest

the **Middle Atlantic** states are New York, New Jersey, Pennsylvania, Delaware, and Maryland

the **middle eight** is a short section of usually eight bars, in the middle of a conventional popular song

Middle English is a term coined in 1819 by the German linguist Jacob Grimm

the **middle game** in chess is after the opening, when all or most of the pieces and pawns are still on the board

the **Middle West** or **Midwest** is made up of Missouri, Kansas, Indiana, Illinois, Iowa, Nebraska, Colorado, and sometimes Ohio

midlife crisis is a term that dates only to 1965

midnight blue is a dark blue color, almost black

something that **might happen** is iffier than something that "**may happen**"

a **migrant worker** moves from place to place to get work, and the term dates to 1923, from the earlier (1899) **migrant laborer**

a **military step** in which the legs are swung forward rigidly to an exaggerated height is the **goose step**

military time is a means of representing time sequentially using twenty-four hours, counting from 0100 (12:01 a.m.) to 2400 (12 midnight); also called **universal time**, and the opposite is **civilian time**

milk chocolate is chocolate enriched with milk powder

single-serving cream or milk for coffee is a **milk/cream cup**

milk glass is also called opaline

milk of magnesia (1880) is a proprietary name for a white suspension of magnesium hydroxide in water taken as an antacid and invented by U.S. chemist Charles Henry Phillips

a **milk run** is a routine, uneventful trip

the **milk shake** seems to have originated in the United States in the 1880s

milk toast is buttered toast usually served in warm milk with sugar and seasonings

in the term **milk tooth**, milk's meaning is one of "infancy," as it refers to the first set of teeth in mammals

{ a cat's kneading of paws on a human's stomach is **milk treading** }

milk-and-water means "weak and vacillating; ineffective"

the **Milky Way bar** is a pun on the bar spiral structure of the Milky Way

a **mincing word** is a coyly euphemistic word used in place of a cruder word

mind game is a term that originated in the United States in the early 1970s

a **mind map** is a diagram used to represent words, ideas, tasks, or other items linked to and arranged radially around a central key word or idea—used to generate, visualize, structure, and classify ideas, and as an aid in study, organization, problem solving, decision making, and writing

mind your p's and q's may have originated from an admonishment by teachers who wanted students to use good handwriting

minimally invasive surgery is also called **keyhole surgery**

the **minor arts** are all art forms other than architecture, painting, sculpture, drawing, and printmaking (which are ordinarily called fine arts)

a very short sentence that does not follow the grammatical structure of a sentence is called a **minor sentence**, e.g., "Wow!", "as if!," or "absolutely not"

philatelists adopted **mint condition** from numismatists

minute detail is redundant

minute steak is so thin that it takes a minute to cook each side on high heat

mirabile dictu translates to "strange to say" or "wonderful to relate"

{ the main difference between **Miracle Whip** and mayonnaise is the sweetener: high-fructose corn syrup and sugar are in **Miracle Whip** }

Miranda Rights resulted from four cases in 1966 collectively known as *Miranda v. State of Arizona*

mirror image is an emphatic way of describing an exact equivalent

mise en place in professional cooking is proper planning of equipment and ingredients for a food preparation and assembly station

mise-en-scene refers to the framing of an event in a film or play

a **miser's dream** is any magic trick that produces money from thin air

miso soup is Japanese and contains fermented soya beans, onions, and seaweed

miss a trick is an allusion to a card game like whist or bridge

the **missionary position** was said to have been recommended by early missionaries to the Polynesian people

mixed media refers to the use of two or more media in a single work of art, such as combining watercolor and gouache

a **mixed number** is an integer with a fraction

mixed voices are voices of both males and females united in the same performance

mixum-gatherum is a mixed or confused collection

mobile phone (1945) was first applied to radio telephones installed in cars

a **mobile sculpture** is one with moving parts

the **Mobius Strip** (1904) was named for the German mathematician August Ferdinand Möbius (1790–1868), who invented it

a **modal verb** is an auxiliary verb that expresses necessity or possibility—must, shall, will, should, would, can, could, may, might

{ a **moderate breeze** is defined as 13–18 miles per hour }

modus vivendi can refer to a compromise or arrangement between two people or groups that allows them to get along

Mogen Davie, "star of David," is the six-pointed star, symbol of Judaism or Zionism, from Hebrew *maghen Dawidh*, "shield of David"

the **Mohs' scale** is describes from one to ten the hardness of minerals, talc being one and diamond being ten—devised in 1812 by the German mineralogist Friedrich Mohs (1773–1839)

molecular biology deals with the cellular process and how molecules interact

a **molecular cloud** is a large and relatively dense cloud of cold gas and dust in interstellar space from which new stars are formed

molecular gastronomy is the study and application of chemistry, physics, and other scientific principles on cooking processes, preparation, and materials

Molly Maguire was a secret society in the mining districts of Pennsylvania (1867–76), named for an earlier secret society formed in Ireland (1843) to resist payment of rents

the **Molotov cocktail** was named for a Russian foreign minister and staunch supporter of Stalin, who had that nickname

mom food is home-cooked food or dishes or those associated with one's childhood; also called comfort food

mom-and-pop store was first recorded in 1951

moment of truth is a translation of a Spanish expression referring to the time of the final sword thrust in a bullfight

Monday morning quarterback derives from American football and originated in the 1930s

a **money clip** is a clip used to hold folded dollar bills, sometimes magnetic

the edible pulp of the baobab is **monkey bread**

monkey business (late 1800s) is a transfer of the tricks of monkeys to human behavior

in Britain, peanuts are often called **monkey nuts**

in **monkey shines**, shines comes from an earlier use of "shine," meaning "brilliant display"

monkey suit comes from the fact that organ grinders dressed their companions in little coats

the monkey in **monkey wrench** is supposedly a corruption of the proper name Moncke, from the London blacksmith who first made the implements

the **Monroe Doctrine** refers to principles outlined by United States President James Monroe in a speech to Congress, December 2, 1823

a **Monte Cristo** sandwich is ham, turkey, and Swiss cheese between batter-dipped grilled or fried bread and served with jelly, mustard sauce, syrup, or powdered sugar

Monterey Jack and **Jack cheese** are synonyms

diarrhea has many euphemistic phrasal terms: **Montezuma's revenge**, **Curse of Montezuma**, **Mexican two-step**, **Mexican fox trot**, **Aztec hop**, **Mexican toothache**, **Tokyo trots**, **Rangoon runs**, **Delhi belly**; Montezuma II (1466–1520) was the Aztec emperor imprisoned by the Spanish conquistadors and then killed by his own subjects

moo goo goi pan, literally "mushroom chicken slice," is a Cantonese dish of sauteed chicken, vegetables, and spices

moo shu pork is a Chinese dish of stir-fried pork strips with vegetables rolled in a thin pancake, and moo shu is literally "dish containing scrambled egg"

a difficult or expensive task that would have a significant outcome is sometimes called a **moon shot**

moonlight requisition is a nighttime foray to steal something

moose milk is a humorous Canadian term for strong liquor

a **moose test** is a test on how a certain vehicle, usually an automobile, acts when avoiding a sudden danger, such as a moose—and, figuratively, any stringent test of the quality of a product

moot point actually means "a point or question to be debated; a doubtful question"

moral turpitude is evil character or lack of integrity

the phrase **more possible** should really be either "**more feasible**" or "**more practicable**"

more than refers to countable items (there are more than fifty pies); **over** refers to general or unspecified amounts (over half the church is full)

more than one way to skin a cat has to do with catfish, not cats

the **Morgan horse** is named for the American owner of the stallion from which the breed descends

mornay sauce is cheese-flavored white sauce (named after a French cook)

{ **morning dress** is formal daytime apparel for men, including striped pants, a cutaway, and a silk hat }

morning goods are any baked goods typically baked and sold fresh in the morning, including muffins, pastries, etc.

Venus is often called the **evening star** or **morning star** and is brighter than any object in the sky except the sun and the moon

the **morris dance** was actually Moorish dance, imported from Spain or elsewhere from the Moors

Samuel Morse (1791–1872) devised the basis of the **Morse code**, perfected by Alfred Vail, son of Morse's benefactor

a **mortal sin** or **deadly sin** is said to deserve everlasting punishment

a **Moses basket** is a UK term for a portable wicker or straw cot for a baby, because Moses was placed in such a basket (Exodus 2)

the **Mosquito Coast**'s (or Mosquitia) name is derived from the Miskito, the indigenous inhabitants and remnants of the Choroteg

mot juste conveys that it is precisely the right word

Mother Goose was probably a translation of mid-Seventeenth century French *contes de ma mére l'oye*, "fairy tales"; the phrase appeared on the frontispiece of Charles Perrault's 1697 collection of eight fairy tales, *Contes du Temps Passé*, which was translated in 1729 as *Mother Goose's Tales*

in British slang (c. 1884), **mother-in-law** was "a mixture of ales old and bitter"

motive power is the energy used to drive machinery

mound builders are tribes of Native Americans who built, in former times, extensive mounds of earth, especially in the valleys of the Mississippi and Ohio Rivers

Mount Everest was named for Sir George Everest (1790–1866), a surveyor-general of India

the **mountain bike** was developed in the 1970s in California

the lingonberry is also called the **mountain cranberry**

illegally made spirits from the Scottish highlands were the original **mountain dew**

mountain goats are not goats but small antelopes

a **mouse potato** is a person who spends too much time on the computer, patterned on couch potato

mouth feel is a product's physical and chemical interaction in the mouth; this concept is used in many areas related to the testing and evaluating of foodstuffs, such as wine-tasting and rheology

mouth organ is another name for the harmonica

mouton enragé, literally mad sheep, is a term for an angry person who is usually calm

a **movable letter** is a letter that is pronounced, as opposed to one that is quiescent

to **move the deck chairs on the Titanic** is to do something pointless or insignificant that contributes nothing to the solution of a current problem

mover(s) and shaker(s) originated in an 1874 poem by Arthur O'Shaughnessy

moving picture was first a reference to flip-books or other pictures representing objects in various stages of motion

moving stairway or **moving staircase** are other ways of saying escalator

Mr. Fixit may have come from a (carpenter) character in short religious films of the 1950s

Mr. Hyde is the bad half of the split personality in *The Strange Case of Dr Jekyll and Mr Hyde*

much of a muchness indicates something is very similar to something else

mud flap and **splash guard** are synonymous

mud pie is a rich chocolate-based dessert similar to a mud pie in appearance; it is also called **Mississippi mud pie**

muffin top is flesh that falls over the waistband of a garment

mug shot dates to 1950, from mug, "face" (1708)

mulberry-faced is very red in the face

a **mulching mower** cuts grass into small pieces and redistributes them uniformly back into the lawn

mulled wine is heated and infused or flavored with a spice or spices; beer, brandy, and cider may also be mulled, and the practice was first recorded in 1607

mulligan stew, made with whatever's available, was hobo slang, probably from a proper name

the pineapple is termed a **multiple fruit** because it forms from the individual ovaries of several flowers; each raised button on its surface is called a fruitlet

mumblety-peg was a boys' knife-throwing game (1627) originally called mumble-the-peg but of unknown origin

mumbo jumbo was originally a representation of a grotesque idol worshipped by some West African people in English explorer Francis Moore's memoir *Travels into the Inland Parts of Africa* (1738)

in **mum's the word**, mum refers to a sound made with closed lips

mung beans, from Tamil *munga*, "the same," take only three days to sprout

a bed that closes into a wall is a **Murphy bed**

Murphy's Law started to be used in 1949 at the Edwards Air Force Base by Captain Edward A. Murphy, an engineer; over the years, aerospace manufacturers and others picked up the phrase

the **muscat grape** is so named because of its musky taste/smell

Muscovy duck is an alteration of musk duck, an allusion to its musky odor

{ a person thought of as old-fashioned or irrelevant is sometimes called a **museum piece** }

a **musk ox** is actually a sheep

mutatis mutandis is literally "things being changed that have to be changed"

Mutt and Jeff, comic strip characters Augustus Mutt and Jim Jeffries, in United States cartoonist Henry Conway Fisher's strip, debuted in 1907

my bad is said to have originated in pickup basketball

{ **my eye** is said to have
first been nautical slang
expressing surprise
or disbelief }

when you are just dropping off to sleep and
you experience that sudden sensation of
falling, that's the **myoclonic jerk**

mystery meat is any type of processed
meat whose source is indistinguishable,
especially that served in a cafeteria

{ N }

nab the rust means "be angry or sulky"

naff off means "go away"

the broad flat part of a fingernail or toenail is the **nail bed**

on a Swiss Army knife, the part where a fingernail can be inserted to deploy a tool is a **nail nick**

Naismith's formula (or rule) is a rule of thumb that helps in the planning of a walking or hiking expedition by calculating how long it will take to walk the route, including ascents: allow one hour for every three miles forward, plus ½ hour for every 1,000 feet of ascent and calculate for the speed of the slowest person in a group

Naked Chef refers to the simplicity of Jamie Oliver's recipes, not his attire

naked flooring is the timberwork which supports a floor

a **naked light** or **naked flame** is one that is unprotected or unenclosed

naked truth, dated to the late 1500s, supposedly alludes to a fable in which Truth and Falsehood went bathing; Falsehood then dressed in Truth's clothes, and Truth, refusing to take another's clothes, went naked

namby-pamby (1726) was a satiric nickname of the English poet Ambrose Philips (1674–1749) mocking his sentimental pastorals addressed to infant members of the nobility; in the sense of "weakly sentimental, insipidly pretty," it is attested from 1745

one's **name day** is either the feast day of the saint after whom one is named or the day on which one is baptized

we may say correctly that a person is **named** either **after** or **for** another person

naming of parts is "becoming familiar with or familiarizing others with the basics of an unfamiliar topic or object"

Napoleonic code is a legal code established by Napoleon I and based on Roman law, that was introduced in 1804 and still constitutes the French civil law code; any of a number of other legal systems are derived from this, such as the civil codes of Louisiana and Québec

narrow at the equator is an American West term for "very hungry"

nasal consonants are those in which pronunciation involves a hum through the nose: m, n, ng

native bear is another term for the koala

natural child is a euphemism for illegitimate child

natural fats are the group of oily substances of natural occurrence, such as butter, lard, tallow, etc., such as distinguished from certain fatlike substances of artificial production, such as paraffin

natural flavors come from the chemical extracts of natural sources (animals, plants, etc.), while artificial flavors come from synthetic sources—but artificial is actually safer and less costly than the chemically prepared "natural" flavors

natural history is the study of animals and plants by observation and presented in popular (not academic) form

natural language (1774) is one that has evolved naturally, as distinguished from an artificial language devised for international communications or for formal logical or mathematical purposes

natural sciences, such as biology, botany, chemistry, geology, and physics, are distinguished from mathematics, logic, mental and moral sciences

a **nature strip** is an area of grass beside a roadway, possibly with a few trees or shrubs, lying in between the footpath part and the roadway proper

the **nautical mile** (1/21,600 of the circumference of the earth) is also called a geographical mile, sea mile, air mile, and international nautical mile; a nautical mile is also a geological mile or Admiralty mile; a knot is the unit for measuring nautical miles

the **navel** is also the **umbilicus**, **belly button**, or **omphalodium**; navel and umbilicus share the same Indo-European root

{ the **navel orange** got its name from having one end that resembles a belly button }

navel-gazing is excessive introspection, self-absorption, or concentration on a single issue

Navy beans got their name because of their extensive use by the Navy

a **Navy SEAL** is a member of the special forces unit for the U.S. Navy who is trained for unconventional warfare on sea, air, and land

ne plus ultra, "utmost limit to which one can go" is from Latin, "no more beyond," traditionally inscribed on the Pillars of Hercules

when the moon and sun are not in alignment, the lowest tides result, called **neap tides**

Neapolitan ice cream's name came from its layers resembling the Italian flag

say **near future** instead of "foreseeable future"

near miss is first recorded in World War II in reference to a bomb exploding in the water near enough to a ship to cause damage but not sink it

neck of the woods was a term used in colonial times by the British to describe a narrow strip of land surrounded by water

neck-bang is the short hair of a woman's neck where the line of hair growth begins

ne'er-do-well is one who is good for nothing, from contraction of the phrase never do well

many biological systems only exist because they have set up **negative feedback loops** that preserve their stability

neo-classical is a style of art, architecture, etc., influenced by classical patterns, especially in reference to eighteenth century English literature

a **nonce word** is one that has been coined or borrowed for a particular occasion and is unlikely to become standard in the language; a **neologism** is a "new word" in the language

something may be **nerve-racking** (from Anglo-Saxon *raxan,* "to stretch"), but you **rack your brains**

Nesselrode pie and pudding were named for Russian statesman Karl-Robert Nesselrode

poultry farmers formerly placed a porcelain or other fake egg in a hen's nest to encourage it to lay more eggs—from this came **nest egg**, money saved to encourage the making of more

Never Land was the place in *Peter Pan*, originally a term for the remote unpopulated northern part of the Northern Territory and Queensland in Australia

a **never-smoker** is a person who has never been a cigarette smoker or cigar smoker and, more precisely, a person who has smoked fewer than 100 cigarettes and cigars during the course of his or her life

New Age is a term used first in the 1840s, becoming truly a movement by 1971

new black is a term for the new rage; the latest fad or trend, especially in fashion

New England's states are Maine, New Hampshire, Vermont, Massachusetts, Rhode Island, and Connecticut; the **Northeast** is all of these states plus the Middle Atlantic states

{ Minnesota is the **New England of the West** }

New Hampshire is named for Hampshire, England

New Jersey is named for the island of Jersey in the United Kingdom

a **new moon** is in the first phase and cannot be seen at all

new potatoes are young potatoes of any variety, especially small early red potatoes

New Wave (1960) first described a type of cinema (from French, *nouvelle vague,* late 1950s)

New World (1555) refers to the western hemisphere or the continents of America, as distinguished from the Old World

{ **new world order** is a term that dates back to 1848 }

New Year's Eve is a term from around 1300; New Year's was the main midwinter festival in Scotland in the seventeenth century, when Protestant authorities banned Christmas, and continued so after England reverted to Christmas, hence the Scottish flavor ("Auld Lang Syne," etc.), and New Year's gathering in public places began in 1878 in London, after new bells were installed in St. Paul's

New York was renamed from New Netherland for the Duke of York

New Zealand was named for Abel Tasman's home of Zeeland, Netherlands

the major beam where a staircase starts is the **newel post**, and it is topped with a **newel cap**

new-fledged means having just acquired feathers

news flash (1904) originally applied to telegraphic news dispatches

niche product is a product that is made and marketed for use in a small and specialized but profitable market

in the Middle Ages, a tally person put nicks in a piece of wood when teams played, and if the winning nick was added during the last minute, it was known as the **nick in time** (later, **nick of time**)

nictitating membrane or **third eyelid** is a thin membrane found in many animals at the inner angle, or beneath the lower lid, of the eye, and capable of being drawn across the eyeball

night owl first meant "owl which flies at night" (1593) and has been applied since 1846 to persons who are up or out late at night; similarly, **night hawk** in the figurative sense of "one who seeks prey at night, one who stays up late" is from 1818

a **night vision** can describe a dream that comes during the night

to be **nimble as a squirrel** is to be quick-footed

a **nimbostratus cloud** can drop precipitation but has no lightning or thunder

nine days' wonder is an old term (c. 1325) for an event or phenomenon that attracts enthusiastic interest for a short while, but is then ignored or forgotten

nine lives is the number of lives proverbially allotted to a cat (since at least c. 1562) and extended to lions, tigers, etc. (1607) and then as a term of contempt for a woman from c. 1225

ninny-broth once referred to coffee

ninth island is a colloquial term for any place outside Hawaii with a large number of Hawaiians, such as Las Vegas

nip and tuck was a nineteenth-century phrase of United States origin, first meaning "neck and neck" as in a close-run race

nip in the bud comes from horticultural pruning

nitrous oxide is also known as **laughing gas**

nitty-gritty was first knitty-gritty, said to have been chiefly used by black jazz musicians, perhaps ultimately from nit and grits, "finely ground corn"

no can do is a pidgin-English-style phrase of United States origin, c. 1945

no comment dates from the 1950s

no dice, from the 1920s, alludes to an unlucky throw in gambling

no great shakes is said to derive from gambling with dice

no holds barred comes from wrestling

no skin off one's nose may be an allusion to fighting (1920s)

noble science is a euphemism for self-defense or fisticuffs

Noble Truth is one of the four main precepts of Buddhism and Buddhist philosophy, specifically that life is suffering, that the cause of suffering is desire, that there can be an end to suffering, and the way to achieve this is following the Noble Eightfold Path

in **noblesse oblige,** birth and social position confer on the person the duty to use their advantages to benefit others

> from the ninth to the eighteenth centuries, no man (or noman) was a common synonym for no one or nobody, so **no man's land** meant "land belonging to nobody"

no stone unturned may be our oldest idiom; termed "old" in 410 BC, it had to do with moving every stone, as advised by the oracle at Delphi, to find a treasure after the Greeks defeated the Persians in 477 BC

no sweat and **not to worry** date to the 1950s

no way became current in the late 1960s

another name for the biblical flood is **Noachian deluge**

a part of a name like "de" or "von" is called the **nobiliary particle**

noble metals are silver, gold, and platinum, so called from their freedom from oxidation and permanence in air; copper, mercury, aluminum, palladium, rhodium, iridium, and osmium are sometimes included

a **noctilucent cloud** is one that appears to "glow" at night, caused by reflected sunlight below the horizon

the **nodding donkey** is a type of pump for pumping oil from land-based oil wells

if something is **nodding to its fall**, it has its top bent down

no-fault insurance as a type of United States motor vehicle insurance is attested from 1967

no-go as a phrase for an impracticable situation was first attested in 1870

no-good (1908) came from the phrase no good, "good for nothing"; **no-goodnik** was first attested in 1960

no-hitter, the baseball term for a game in which one side fails to make a hit, was first attested in 1948

noises off are sounds created offstage to be heard during a play's production—but the term is extended to mean distracting or intrusive background noise

nolo contendere is Latin, literally "I do not wish to contend"

nolens volens is an adverbial phrase meaning "whether a person wants or likes something or not"

a **nom de guerre**, literally French "war name," is an assumed name under which a person engages in combat or some other activity

nom de plume is literally "name of the pen," meaning "pseudonym"

no-man's-land originally referred to plots of waste ground that belonged to no one

non compos mentis (1607) is from Latin, "not master of one's mind"

a **non sequitur** is an inference or conclusion not logically following from a premise

non-aggression, "absence of warlike intentions among nations," is from around 1903

no-name (1979) was originally American English sporting jargon

A **nonce word** is any word with a special meaning used for a special occasion, like catastrophize; the term was coined by the editors of the *Oxford English Dictionary* for words that they found that were "apparently used only for the nonce"

non-compete is a provision that bars an employee, upon dismissal or resignation, from working for or establishing a business that may compete with his or her former employer—or an author from creating a work that competes with something he or she has already written

{ **nonfiction** was first attested in 1903 }

no-nonsense, "not tolerating foolishness, businesslike," came into use in 1928 from the phrase "to stand no nonsense," which is attested from 1821

a **nonpattern word** is one in which each letter is used only once

nonsense word is any word with no determinable or accepted meaning

the phrase **no parking** has been used since 1946

normally aspirated describes an engine that is not turbocharged or supercharged

north light is good natural light without direct sun, especially desired by artists

the **North Star** is Polaris, Ursae Minoris

Northwest or Pacific Northwest of the United States is Washington and Oregon; Idaho and Montana are sometimes included in Northwest

the **nose leaf** on bats is the fleshy leaf-shaped nose part used for echolocation

the **nose leather** of a cat is the part that feels damp; the tip of a dog's nose is also the nose leather a **nose of wax** is a person who is pliant and easily influenced

a **nose pad** is either of the little plastic pieces on many eyeglasses, which rest on the wearer's nose, or the small leathery part of a cat's nose

a **nose ring** is put on an animal for leading it

no-show, "someone who fails to keep an appointment," was originally airline jargon (1941)

a **nosocomial infection** is an illness caused by germs in a hospital

the parker in **nosy parker** originally was a word for a park keeper

not a happy bunny means "displeased"

not dry behind the ears comes from the farm—on a newborn animal the last spots to dry after birth are the little depressions behind the ears

the expression **not know beans about** (something) comes from a rural American saying "not know beans when the poke bag is open"—or "not be able to identify something as ordinary as beans when looking right at them"

not up means when the tennis ball bounces twice before being returned

in **not what it's cracked up to be**, crack is a verb meaning "to brag or boast"—so, "not what it is believed or boasted to be"

not worth one's salt refers to the salary earned by Roman soldiers, who were paid in the valuable commodity salt

nota bene, "mark well, observe particularly," is from around 1721, from Latin

note to self is inserted before a phrase to imply that the reader or listener should take heed

not-for-profit or **nonprofit** refers to an organization or company established for charitable, educational, or humanitarian purposes, and not for making money

a noun or pronoun and all its modifiers is a **noun phrase**; a verb and all its auxiliaries and modifiers is a verb phrase

nouveau pauvre was formed by analogy with **nouveau riche**

nouveau riche, "new rich," came around 1813 and the opposite, nouveau pauvre, is attested from 1965

nouvelle cuisine is a new style of French cooking that avoids rich sauces and emphasizes freshness and presentation

Nova Scotia means "New Scotland"

no-win is attested to 1962

nuclear bomb encompasses both **atomic bomb** and **hydrogen bomb**

nuclear family refers to the parents and children living in one household

the **nuclear option** in politics is an action of last resort

nucleic acid (1892) is a translation of German *Nukleinsure* (1889), from *Nuklein*, "substance obtained from a cell nucleus"

{ **nuisance value** is the significance of a person or thing arising from his or her capacity to cause annoyance or inconvenience }

null and void dates to 1651 and as both words mean the same thing, it is emphatic

numero uno is Italian/Spanish

the **nuptial pad** is a swelling on the inside of the hand of some male frogs and toads that assists grip during copulation

nut meat is the usually edible kernel of a nut

Connecticut was derisively nicknamed the **Nutmeg State** from the reputed skill of Connecticut traders at such deceptions as selling wooden nutmegs

nutty as a fruitcake dates to the 1930s

{ O }

O'Brien potatoes are diced potatoes fried with chopped onions and pimentos or red and green sweet peppers

an **obiter dictum** is an incidental remark

an **object ball** in billiards is any ball other than the cue ball

an **object lesson** is a striking example of an ideal or principle

an **object pronoun** is used as the object of a sentence, such as "me," "him," or "us"

objective art is art whose subject matter consists of recognizable objects

the **objective lens** in a microscope or telescope is the one nearest to the object observed

objet trouvé often describes something which has been found and then turned into an art object, such as a piece of driftwood

an **oblique muscle** is a muscle acting in a direction oblique to the mesial plane of the body, or to the associated muscles, applied especially to muscles of the eyeball and along the abdomen

an **observation deck** is an area of a tall building, often open to the sky, from which the public may look at the surrounding panorama

Occam's razor, "when two competing hypotheses explain the data equally well, choose the simpler," was named for English philosopher William of Ockham (c. 1285–1349)

an **occasional cause** is a phenomenon or circumstance that triggers an action without being its root cause

an **occasional table** is any small table, such as a coffee table, having no particular function

when cooler air forces warmer air upward and the atmospheric pressure is low, the entire system may stall, creating an **occluded front**

an **occulting light** is one in a lighthouse or buoy that is cut off briefly at regular intervals

an **occupational name** is a name, especially a surname like Smith or Taylor, that is derived from an occupation—presumably the occupation of a distant ancestor

occupational therapy is rehabilitation through performing activities required in daily life

an **ocean liner** is a vessel belonging to a "line" of packets ("boat for carrying mail and cargo")

an **October surprise** is an unexpected, but popular, political act made just prior to a November election in an attempt to win votes

ocular dominance is the preference or priority of one eye over the other in use or acuity

the first official **odds and ends** were found in lumberyards—odds were pieces of board split irregularly by the sawmill, and ends were pieces trimmed from boards that were cut to specific lengths

Freud's term **Oedipus Complex** (1910) was based on the plot of Sophocles's play *Oedipus Tyrannus*, in which Oedipus unknowingly kills his father and marries his mother

of one accord means unanimous

off book in theatre is "in rehearsal" or "rehearsing without the script"

off of is redundant

off the cuff is from the use of impromptu notes made on one's shirt cuffs

{ **off the grid** originally meant only a disconnection from the electricity supply }

off the hook was originally a reference to telephony, that one was not in danger of receiving a call if it was off the hook

off the wall alludes to squash or handball when a shot comes **off the wall** at an unexpected or erratic angle

off-base, "unawares," is from 1936 as a figurative extension from the baseball sense of "not in the right position" (1907)

offbeat, "unusual," (1938) is from an earlier sense referring to music rhythm (1927)

off-Broadway is from 1953, and off-off-Broadway is attested from 1967

off-color first meant a color that deviated from the standard/normal, and now it indicates something that deviates from standards of good taste

off-hand (1694), "at once, straightaway," probably originally referred to shooting without a rest or support; as "unpremeditated" attested to 1719

the OED says **off-limits** is first attested in 1952 in a U.S. military (Korean War) sense, but probably was used earlier

the railroad sense of **off-line** was 1926; in 1950, computers

off-message means "departing from an expected or regular theme or issue"

off-peak (1920) originally referred to electrical systems

off-piste (French *piste*, "trail left by a person or animal") refers to skiing on an unprepared, trackless area away from regular ski runs

off-putting first meant (1578) "procrastinating"; "creating an unfavorable impression" was first recorded 1894

white with a tinge of gray or yellow is **off-white** (1927)

oh dark thirty is some unspecified hour in the early morning (implying an unpleasant time to be awake)

oh snap or snap is an exclamation of dismay or disbelief, surprise, or joy; a euphemism for "oh, shit"

on an **oil/hurricane lamp**, the glass cylinder protecting the wick is called the lamp chimney

oil paint is made of ground pigment and a drying oil, such as linseed

oil pastels are a mixture of pigments, wax, and sometimes oily substances in stick form

an **oilseed cake** is any of various varieties of animal feed manufactured from the meal remaining after vegetable oil has been extracted from seeds, such as cottonseed and groundnut

ok by me is a Yiddish expression, with the last part coming from Yiddish *bei mir*

okey-dokey and its variants were not in use until around 1930

old chestnut comes from the ninteenth century play *The Broken Sword*

old crumpet is used as a familiar form of address

English is divided into **Old English** or Anglo-Saxon from the invasion in the fifth century to 1060, **Middle English** from 1060 to c. 1450, and then Modern English

old hat was first recorded in 1911; as a noun phrase, however, it had a different sense in the eighteenth century—"a woman's privates"

old lace is an off-white color, like that of old lace

unpopped kernels are referred to in the industry as **old maids**

Old Nick is the devil

an **old school tie** is a necktie that has the colors of a British public school

Old Town turkey is a Nantucketer's name for any resident of Martha's Vineyard

Old World, pertaining to Eurasia and Africa as opposed to the Americas, is attested to 1877

> **old-fashioned** dates to 1596 in writing; as a type of cocktail, attested from 1901

an **old-growth forest** is one which has never been logged

old-school, in reference to a group of people noted for conservative views or principles on some professional or political matter, dates to 1749

olla podrida (Spanish, "rotten pot") or olio is any dish containing a great variety of ingredients

an **omnium gatherum** is a gathering or collection of all sorts of people or things, a catch-all, and an inclusive group or category

an **on dit** is an item of gossip

someone **on form** is playing or performing well

on one's beam ends, "in a precarious situation," is nautical in origin, as a ship on its beam ends is careened over far enough to founder from water pouring in

on the dot probably is a reference to the minute hand of the clock being exactly over the dot marking the given minute on the dial

on the half shell refers to raw shellfish served in the bottom shell, chilled, and with condiments (c. 1860)

on the house first referred to a British inn or tavern

on the lam is an allusion to a wrongdoer beating (lamming) the road

on the nose is from the early days of radio—cueing out on time was signaled by a finger to the nose

at one time, knights, kings, and other VIPs rode on chargers, while ladies and others rode on smaller saddle horses, begetting the phrase **on one's high horse**

on tenterhooks was derived from the now-obsolete technology of manufacturing woolen cloth—the fabric was stretched on a wooden frame called a tenter and secured by metal hooks (tenterhooks); now it means to be figuratively stretched on the hooks of anxiety or suspense

on the anvil means "in a state of formation"

on the beach is a term for being retired from naval service

originally, only the boss's office had a carpet, so to be called **on the carpet** was to be called to the boss's office, possibly for a reprimand

qui vive translated to "who goes there?" so one who is **on the qui vive** is one who is very alert

on the tapis means "under consideration"

before paved roads, horse-drawn water wagons sprayed the streets to settle the dust, and anyone who had sworn abstinence from alcohol was said to have "climbed aboard the water wagon," later shortened to **on the wagon**

on toast is a common phrase for anything nicely served

once in a blue moon originally meant "never"

one that got away is from fishing mythology

stand means each of the stops made on a tour to give performances or the performance itself and this meaning was transferred to **one-night stand**, first a theatrical term

{ a **one-off** is an unusual or unique person }

a **one-percenter** is a member of the top one percent of a population by wealth, ability, etc.

one's hash is one's own business

one-shot, from 1907, meant "achieved in a single attempt," referring to golf; the meaning "happening or of use only once" is from 1937

one-track mind is a reference to the railway

the term **one-upmanship** (1952) is from the noun phrase one up, "scoring one more point than one's opponent"

one-way came into English in 1906 in reference to travel tickets, in 1914 in reference to streets, and in 1940 in reference to windows, mirrors, etc.

onion blossom is an onion that is cut into a flowering shape and deep-fried in batter

in football, an **onside kick** is one deliberately kicked a short distance in an attempt by the kicking team to regain possession of the ball by recovering it after it has traveled forward the legally required distance of 10 yards, beyond the 50-yard line—with onside meaning "position on the field where the ball may lawfully be played"

onto is used where two elements function as a compound preposition, and **on to** is used when on is an adverb; onto is when you mean "on top of, aware of"—otherwise, use "on to"

oolong tea is a type of partially fermented tea with a taste in between green tea and black tea, from Chinese for "black dragon"

oose is the furry stuff that gathers under beds—also called **dust bunnies**, **trilbies**, or **kittens**

the term **op art** was patterned on **pop art**

op. cit. (1883) is an abbreviation of Latin *opus citatum*, literally "the work quoted"

op-ed is from 1970 for the page of a newspaper opposite the editorial page, usually devoted to personal opinion columns, pioneered by the Pulitzers of the *New York World*

an **open compound** is a compound word with spaces in it, e.g., school bus, science fiction

open content is freely distributable and/or able to be edited, added to, and/or repaired, as in Wikipedia

to **open daylight** (or **open up daylight**) in horse racing is to outdistance a competitor

open sesame is from French *sesame, ouvre-toi*, the magic words by which, in the tale of "Ali Baba and the Forty Thieves," the door of the robbers' cave was made to fly open

an **open shop** hires both labor union and non-union workers; a **closed shop** hires only union members

to **open the kimono** means to expose or reveal secrets or proprietary information

opera window is a small fixed window on each side of the rear passenger compartment of an automobile

opponent muscles are ones that enable the thumb to be moved toward a finger of the same hand (hence, **opposable thumb**)

optical brightener is a fluorescent substance added to detergents in order to produce a whitening effect on laundry

optical mixing is when the eye visually mixes colors from a distance, e.g., seeing blue and yellow and getting the sensation of green

an **oral agreement** is spoken, but a **verbal agreement** can be spoken or written

orange pekoe (black leaf) tea has a number of theories regarding the origin of the epithet orange: perhaps the color of the leaf buds or of the infusion; or originally there might have been some orange bush in the mixture; or it was named for the Dutch House of Orange, which first imported the tea in the seventeenth century; orange pekoe is now simply a grade based on the size and age of the leaves used

an **orange stick** is made of orange wood and is different from an emery board

an **orb web** is circular, formed of threads radiating in a vertical plane from a central point crossed by others spiraling out

an **orbiculate leaf** is a leaf whose outline is nearly circular

if a microscope enlarges an object ten times, then there will be an **order of magnitude** increase in the visual size of the object; if the enlargement is one hundred times, then the increase will be two orders of magnitude and one thousand times will be three orders of magnitude (10X10X10)

an **ordinal adjective** is a ordinal number used as an adjective, e.g., "first" in "first attempt"

organic chemistry is the chemistry of carbon compounds other than simple salts

an **orthographic "word"** is an uninterrupted string of letters preceded by a blank space and followed by a blank space or punctuation mark

osso bucco (braised veal shanks or veal stew) is Italian, literally "bone with a hole; marrow bone"

a definition by example is an **ostensive definition**

{ **ought to** is always right (as opposed to ought) }

the translation of **Ouija board** is French *oui*, "yes," and German *ja*, "yes"

out of hand, meaning "out of control," refers to a failure to keep a firm grip on a horse's reins

out of sorts originated in card-playing, as the deck is out of sorts if it is not fit for play

out of the mouths of babes came from the Bible's book of Psalms

out to lunch arose as U.S. campus slang in the 1950s

the **outer planets** are those outside the asteroid belt: Jupiter, Saturn, Uranus, and Neptune

an **outlet pass** in basketball is made by the player taking a defensive rebound to a teammate to start a fast break

out-of-plumb means "not in proper vertical alignment"

out-of-universe refers to a perspective or view from the real world, in contrast to a perspective from within the fictional world

outsider art is art produced by self-taught artists

oven chips are frozen French fries prepared in the oven

over easy pertains to an egg that is flipped over gently when the white is nearly cooked and fried on the other side, with the yolk still being somewhat liquid

over the hill first meant "escaped from custody," and later that a person has passed life's high point and has begun to go downhill

over the top originated in World War I, when it was used to describe troops in the trenches charging over the parapets to attack the enemy

to **over-empty** is to make too empty

an **oxbow lake** is crescent-shaped and forms when a river changes course by flowing across the neck of land of an oxbow

an **Oxford comma** is the one before "and" in a series such as "red, white, and blue"

oxtail soup is actually made from stewed beef tails

oy gevalt means "uh oh!," an expression of worry at the realization of negative consequences or the recognition of something that is adverse

{ an **oyster part** is that of an actor who appears and speaks or acts only once }

oyster white is any gray-tinted off-white of a neutral shade

oysters Rockefeller, baked in a sauce of butter, spinach, watercress, shallots, celery, and seasonings, was created at Antoine's in New Orleans around the turn of the twentieth century and named for U.S. industrial magnate John D. Rockefeller

the **ozone layer** absorbs a large part of the sun's ultraviolet rays

{ P }

the **Pacific Basin** is Hong Kong, Singapore, South Korea, and Taiwan

the **Pacific Ocean,** "peaceful ocean," was so named by Magellan because it seemed so calm after the storms near Cape Horn

the **Pacific Rim** is broadly a region including every country whose coastline touches the Pacific Ocean

pack a punch is of U.S. origin from the 1920s, as is **pack it in**

pack rat is an allusion to the animal's habit of collecting and accumulating nesting material

package deal dates from the 1950s

the euphemism **package goods** was created when liquor became legal just after Prohibition

a **package store** is so called because it sells alcoholic beverages in containers to be consumed elsewhere

Malay padi "rice" gives us **paddy field**

paddy wagon comes from that nickname for Irishmen and their being a target of law enforcement when rounding up miscreants

page view is a website page that has been viewed by an individual; it is a measure of how many times a web page is requested from a server, a statistic valuable in online advertising

pain in the neck is a euphemism dating from the 1970s

a **paint chip** is a card showing a color or range of related colors available as paint (especially for walls)

originally, **paint the town red** carried the connotation of destruction—of bloody encounters

the **painted turtle** has red, yellow, and black markings along the border of the carapace and on the plastron

a **pair of compasses** is the proper name for the instrument used to draw circles and arcs and measuring distances between points (two arms linked by movable joint, with a pencil attached to one arm)

paired fins are the pectoral and ventral fins of fish, corresponding to the fore and hind legs of the higher animals

> **palazzo pants** are a type of loose-fitting, wide-legged women's trousers

a **palette cup**, often in a pair, is for clamping to the edge of a palette for holding turpentine or another medium

a **palette knife** is used to mix oil paints

pall mall was originally the name of a game—a distant cousin of croquet imported from Italy to London

palm off means "to deceive or defraud someone with something inferior"; **pawn off** has become a variant

Palm Sunday was once Fig Sunday, as figs were eaten to commemorate Jesus's cursing a barren fig tree

when efforts by gold prospectors were unsuccessful, they would say that the attempt had failed to **pan out**

the **panama hat** is in fact from Ecuador, where it was made from the palmlike plant called *jipijapa*

pancake beret and French beret are synonyms

the **Panchen Lama** is the Tibetan lama ranking after the Dalai Lama

a **Pandora's box** is a process that generates many complicated problems as the result of unwise interference in something

a **panel van** is a delivery van without side windows or rear seats

panic button originated during World War II when planes might have to be abandoned by crew members if damage to the plane was too extensive

panna cotta ("cooked cream") is a type of crème caramel, a cold, light, molded eggless custard flavored with caramel, possibly served with caramel or raspberry syrup

the **Pap test** is named for its originator Dr. George Papanicolaou (1883–1962)

a **papal bull** is the seal put on the pope's official documents

a **paper clip** has three bends and four legs

paper cuts is a type of picture cut into paper

another way of saying "Kleenex" is **paper handkerchief**

a **paper tiger** is a nation that seems powerful but in reality is weak, an expression likely Oriental in origin

papier-mâché is literally "chewed paper," but it was probably an invented term for this modeling technique

papiers collés ("pasted papers") are pictures made from bits of paper that have been glued together in an artistic color or form

par excellence contains the idea of quintessential and is not as assertive as saying "supreme"

par value is the value printed on a share certificate—also called **face value**

paradigm shift is an acceptance by a majority of a changed belief, attitude, or way of doing things—a fundamental change in approach or assumptions

a **parallax second** is a unit of length used to measure the distances of stars from the Earth; defined as the distance from the Earth of a star that has a parallax of one arc second

parallel construction is a process that happens because an affix is recognized but not fully understood for its original meaning

parchment paper is greaseproof and heat-resistant paper used for baking, and is treated with sulfuric acid to make it this way

pari-mutuel (1881) is from French, "mutual wager"

to **park the biscuit** is to sit down

the U.S. term **parking lot** is found in print by 1924

parking meters set atop pipe standards contain self-starting timers

Parkinson's disease is from French *maladie de Parkinson* (1876) and named for English physician James Parkinson (1755—1824), who described it (1817) under the names "shaking palsy" and "paralysis agitans"

Parkinson's Law (1955, first in *The Economist*) was named for its deviser, British historian and journalist Cyril Northcote Parkinson (1909–1993): "work expands to fill the time available for its completion"

parlor car refers to a railroad passenger car that has individual reserved seats and is more comfortable than a day coach

a **parlor grand piano** is intermediate between a concert grand and baby grand

Parma ham (or prosciutto) is a seasoned, salt-cured, unsmoked Italian ham with dense reddish-brown flesh, from Parma, Italy

Parmigiano-Reggiano is a premium aged, hard, dry cow's-milk cheese produced in the areas of Reggio Emilia, Bologna, Mantova, Modena, or Parma

parochial school (1755) is a school established and maintained by a religious body

part and parcel uses parcel in a sense no longer current: a constituent or component part, so the phrase is a reduplication

in a **partial eclipse**, in which the penumbra of the shadow falls on the observer, only part of the sun is obscured

a **partial protein** is any protein lacking one or more essential amino acids in correct proportions as necessary for good nutrition and health, true of many plant foods; also called incomplete protein

partially hydrogenated oil is a liquid oil that has only been through partial hydrogenation and is semi-solid, with a consistency like butter

a **participial adjective** is one that is a participle in origin and form, as burned, cutting, engaged

particle board is board made from sawdust mixed with glue, then pressed at a high temperature to bond them

parti-colored is from party "divided"

parting shot is from "Parthian shot," so named because of a trick used by Parthians of shooting arrows backward while fleeing

to the National Weather Service, **partly cloudy** (what we think of as **partly sunny**) is 3/8–5/8 cloud cover; mostly cloudy is 6/8–7/8 cloud cover; and cloudy is 8/8; there is no difference between "partly cloudy" and "partly sunny," the latter of which does not exist as a technical meteorological term

a **partners' desk** is a large desk with space for two people to sit opposite each other

parturient amnesia is forgetting pregnancy and childbirth not long after it is over

party favor started out as something given as a mark of favor; especially a gift such as a knot of ribbons, a glove, etc., given to a lover, or in medieval chivalry by a lady to her knight, to be worn conspicuously as a token of affection; then it became something given to a bride, at a coronation, and at a party meaning your showing up at the party meant you were favored by the host/hostess and this was a gift for you

a wall common to two adjoining buildings or rooms is a **party wall**

pas de deux can be used figuratively for a complicated maneuver carried out by two people or groups

pass out, "lose consciousness," is attested in 1915, probably from a weakened sense of the earlier meaning "to die"

passe-partout, "a master key," is from 1675, literally "pass everywhere"

passing fair started out meaning "extremely beautiful"; in **passing strange**, passing means "exceedingly"

passing the buck comes from card games in which a marker (a piece of buckshot, etc.) was placed before the poker player who was to deal the next hand

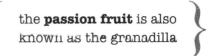

the **passion fruit** is also known as the granadilla

passive smoking (1971) may be a translation of German *Passivrauchen*

our **passive vocabulary** contains lexemes known but not used

passive voice is a verb or form of a verb which expresses the effect of the action of some agent, e.g., I am taught, she is loved, the picture is admired by all

past master, "true expert," was originally (eighteenth century) passed master

pasta fagioli, pronounced fa-ZHOOL, is an Italian bean and pasta soup served with sausage

pasteurized milk has been heated to a prescribed temperature for a specified length of time to destroy or check bacteria

a **pastry wheel** (or **pastry jagger**) is a handled tool with a thin, sharp wheel used for marking and cutting rolled-out dough

a **patch pocket** is sewn onto a garment's outer surface

patent leather got its name from the U.S. Patent Office, as the leather's finish was once protected by patent

paternity leave became a term by 1973

the attribution of human emotions to elements of nature—describing a rainy day as sad—is called **pathetic fallacy**

patron saint derives from the sense of patron, "man of status or distinction who gives protection and aid to another person in return for deference and certain services"

a **patterned form** is a word or phrase modeled on another, e.g., viewership from readership, Gray Panther from Black Panther

pax romana is an uneasy peace, as one imposed by a powerful state on a weaker or vanquished state

pay dirt was first a mining term for earth that yielded a profit to the miner

pay through the nose may be connected to the idea of a nosebleed, being "bled" for money

the **pea jacket** derives from Dutch *pij* (pronounced pea), a heavy water-repellent wool

peaches and cream originally meant "high living"

{ pink cheeks and creamy skin are a **peaches-and-cream complexion** }

the **peach-faced lovebird** is the largest of the lovebirds and very tame

the **peak visual** is the image most recalled by the audience in each crescendo of moment-by-moment pictures, an image most likely to be recalled long after viewing an ad and therefore most likely to contribute to a brand's long-term image

peanut butter is not butter, but it spreads like butter

in vaudeville days, audiences ate peanuts the way moviegoers now eat popcorn, and the term **peanut gallery** is related to this

pear-shaped tones denote a full-bodied vocal sound

pease porridge (or pudding) was dried peas boiled in a pudding cloth with some flour, salt, and pepper

pecking order describes the social hierarchy of birds, where a dominant bird may peck a weaker or lower-status bird, but not vice versa—and once this is established, there is little fighting within the group; pecking order (1927) is a translation of German *Hacklist*; the metaphorical use is not recorded before the 1950s

peculiar institution is an obsolete euphemism from the late 1700s for slavery

pedal pushers (c. 1940) was the term for slacks that extended to the mid-calf, worn by girls and women, originally used when cycling

peel out is hot-rodders' slang (1952), perhaps from peel, "blade or wash of an oar," or it may be from the aircraft pilot phrase peel away, "veer away from formation" (WWII) or from earlier slang peel it, "run away at full speed" (1860)

peeping Tom comes from a story of someone in Coventry, England, peeping to look at Lady Godiva

the **pelagic region** is the open ocean waters

pelican crossing is a rough abbreviation of pedestrian light-controlled crossing

pell-mell, "confusedly," is from French *pêle-mêle*, which is from the stem of the verb *mesler*, "to mix, mingle"

Peltier cooling is the process of cooling computer components via the Peltier effect (heat generated by the passage of the current in one direction will be absorbed if the current is reversed)

the **pelvic floor** is the muscle base of the abdomen, attached to the pelvis

> **penny-wisdom** is wisdom or prudence in small matters

people mover (1971) is an odd term devised for any of various (especially automated) systems or vehicles for transporting large numbers of people, usually over short distances

pepper spray is a liquid of oleoresins from capsicum (cayenne pepper) put in aerosol form to be used for self-defense against an attacker

a **peppering shower** is one in which rain descends like pepper from a shaker

Pepsi-Cola is a U.S. patent filed September 23, 1902, by Caleb D. Bradham (1867–1934), pharmacist and drugstore owner of New Bern, North Carolina, and the name probably comes from pepsin (1844), name of a fermin in gastric juice used medicinally for cases of indigestion, as early Pepsi ads touted it as a digestive aid

per annum, "by the year" (1601), **per capita**, "by the head" (1682), and **per diem**, "by the day" (1520), are from Latin

per capita is a way of expressing the averaging-out of a figure across a group

per se means "by itself, through itself"

one's **perceptual set** is one's mental predisposition to perceive one thing and not another

perfect binding is a method of book binding that invlves gluing instead of sewing

a **perfect rhyme** is one in which the final accented vowel and all succeeding consonants or syllables are identical, while the preceding consonants are different, e.g., great, late; rider, beside her; also called full rhyme or true rhyme

a **perfect storm** is a weather pattern involving the collision of a northeaster, a large high pressure system, and unusually cold Canadian air pushing down plus moisture and warm air pushing up from a hurricane to the south to create a "once-in-a-lifetime" storm

the **performing arts** include drama, dance, and music

perfume or **parfum**, is 20–40 percent oil and the highest concentration; **eau de toilette** is 10–18 percent oil, and cologne or **eau de cologne** is 3–9 percent oil

period of time is unnecessary when either period or time will do

{ the properties of elements repeat themselves periodically—hence, the **periodic table** }

perpetual motion is an incessant motion conceived to be attainable by a machine supplying its own motive forces independently of any action from without

perpetual snow is that which accumulates on the highest reaches of a mountain and never melts

persistence of vision is the phenomenon that makes it possible for pictures to "move"; since a motion picture is really a set of still photographs shown rapidly, this phenomenon allows one image to remain briefly on the retina so that the next overlaps it, and the images appear to move

persona grata is a person who is pleasing to others; **persona non grata** is a person "not pleasing (unacceptable, unwelcome)"

the **personal computer** came on the scene in 1976

personal organizer (1985) was first a loose-leaf portable notebook, but the term came to be applied to a handheld computer

the first record of the term **personnel department** was 1943, shortened to **personnel** in 1960, and replaced by **human resources** in the 1960s/1970s

pet de nonne is another term for fritter

in many **pet names**, there is a change of M into P; Margaret to Peggy, etc.

Peter Pan collars got their name from having been the type worn by Peter Pan in illustrations in the book of the same name

the **Peter Principle**, formulated by Laurence J. Peter, is the theory that all members of an organization will eventually be promoted to a level at which they are no longer competent to do their job

the term **petit four** is literally "small oven" and may have come from cooking these tiny cakes in a low oven at a low temperature

a **petite maison** is a love nest or a residence maintained for a mistress

the **petri dish** was named for German bacteriologist Julius Petri (1852–1922), who first devised it c. 1887

the very short but very wide pants worn by fishermen can be called **petticoat trousers** or waders

phantom rain is rain that passes through hot, dry desert air and evaporates before hitting the ground

Phi Beta Kappa is an undergraduate honorary society (1776) derived from the initials of Greek *philosophia biou kybernetes*, "philosophy, guide of life"

Philadelphia lawyer (1788) refers to Andrew Hamilton's successful defense in 1735 of John Peter Zenger against sedition and libel charges for his publications about William Cosby, the governor of the New York Colony

the Phoenicians invented the first **phonetic alphabet**

a **picnic ham** is a cut of pork from the upper portion of the foreleg extending into the shoulder; it is not a true ham, as true ham is just from the back leg

the **philosopher kings** are the elite whose knowledge enables them to rule justly

photographic memory or **eidetic memory** is the ability to recall previous images with vividness bordering on actual visual perception; such people are called eidetikers

phrasal verbs like take up, guard against, pile on, and turn out are word formations created mainly to express figurative and idiomatic meanings

physical sciences are concerned with inanimate natural objects, which differentiates them from life sciences

pia mater, the delicate innermost membrane of the brain and spinal cord, is Latin for "tender mother"; the arachnoid membrane encases it, and the dura mater encloses these

a **piano word** is one in which all of its letters can be played as notes on a musical instrument (cabbage)

pickin' a cherry is slang for running a red light

pickle-herring means a clown or buffoon and comes from a humorous character in a seventeenth-century German play

a **pick-up** or pick-up dinner is one made up of leftovers

pico de gallo is a combination of diced tomatoes, onions, chilies, and cilantro

pie in the sky originally belonged to the lyrics of a pro-union song written for the Industrial Workers of the World (1911)

pie weights are used to keep a pie tart or pastry crust from bubbling up, curling, or shrinking when blind baking it

the original context for **pièce de résistance** (piece of resistance) is what one is able to resist by eating the big dish—pangs of hunger

piece of cake first appeared in 1936 in an Ogden Nash poem

a **piecrust table** has a scalloped edge like that of a pie crust

a **pied à terre** is a small town house or rooms used for short residences (1829) from French, "foot on the ground"

on a **pierced earring**, the back is called the **friction nut**

pig iron is so called because a pig is an oblong mass of metal formed by molten metal run from a furnace and allowed to solidify

pig Latin is transposing the initial consonant of a word to the end and adding -ay after it, so went becomes *entway*

pig's breakfast means a complete mess that someone has made

pigs in clover is an emblem of contentment

a **pig's whisper** is a loud whisper, meant to be heard

a **pile driver** originally was a bucking horse that comes down with all four legs stiff

the fuzzy side of **Velcro** is the **pile**, or **loop tape**, and the nubby plastic side is the **hook tape**

pileated as in **pileated woodpecker** means "capped," as it has a red cap

a **pillow sham** is a decorative covering for a pillow

a **pilot hole** is a small hole drilled or hammered for the insertion of a nail or screw, or for drilling a larger hole

pilot light (1881) is a small flame kept burning continuously, as in a gas stove or furnace, to relight the main gas burners whenever necessary or desired

Pima cotton is from Pima County, Arizona, but developed from Egyptian cotton

pimento loaf is bologna containing chopped pimentos

pin money was originally money given to women to buy pins and later meant money for incidentals

PIN number is redundant, as N stands for number

piña (as in **piña colada**) is "pineapple" in Spanish or Portuguese, originally from Latin *pinea*, "pine cone"—and piña colada is Spanish for "strained pineapple"

pince-nez, folding eyeglasses, are from French, literally "pinch-nose"

a **pinch bowl** is a small bowl for holding individual servings of condiments or sauces

pinch cake refers to any of various quickly-made desserts made from unbaked Pillsbury (biscuit) dough, with butter (or margarine), sugar, cinnamon, or other flavorings, and baked in the oven

a **pine nut** is the same as pinon seed

pine straw is a term for dead pine needles

Hawaii earned the name of **pineapple paradise**

{ **Ping-Pong** is a trade name for table tennis and was invented as an echoic term for the sound of the ball }

pink collar refers to secretarial and other jobs more typically held by women

pink lemonade is pink-colored lemonade created by adding food coloring or a juice like grenadine or grape

pink noise is random noise with equal energy per octave, so it has more low-frequency components than white noise

pink spiders is an early variant of pink elephants

piñon and pignon seeds are the same thing

pinot noir means "black," **pinot gris** or **pinot grigio** is "gray," and **pinot blanc** is "white"

pinto beans are named for Spanish *pinto* "spotted, painted"

pious as a house cat means pretending to be pious

pipe down is a boatswain's piped signal to turn in for the night

pipe dream originated with opium smoking

piping hot either means hot as water that pipes or sings when it boils or refers to frying food being so hot that it makes a hissing or piping sound

pip-pip is a slangy salutation current in Britain from c. 1907–1923 said by lexicographer Eric Partridge to be in imitation of a bicycle horn noise

pis aller means "the worst that can happen"

pita bread is a flat, unleavened bread made from wheat flour; the rounds are cut in half, and may be made into pockets or used with a dip

a **pitched roof** is a roof built at an angle

a **pith helmet** was originally made from the dried pith of a tropical plant

{ **pizza bone** refers to the thick, generally curved, end piece of a slice of pizza }

since pizza is Italian for "pie," **pizza pie** is redundant

a **place mat** goes under a place setting, a **table service** (tableware consisting of a complete set of silver or dishware) for one

plain sailing probably comes from plane sailing, a way of determining a ship's position based on its movement on a plane (flat surface)

the **Plains states** are North Dakota, South Dakota, Nebraska, Kansas, Oklahoma, and sometimes Texas

plan ahead is redundant

Plan B derives from military jargon

a **plan chest** is a chest for storing large, flat papers like plans and maps

a **plane projection map** is when you see the Earth from the top or bottom, one hemisphere at a time

plano-convex means flat on one side and convex on one side; **plano-concave** is flat on one side and concave on the other

the **plantar pad** is the larger pad of a cat's foot; the **digital pads** are on the toes

a **planter wart** is so called because it occurs on the sole of the foot (Latin *planta*, "sole of the foot")

a **plasma screen** is a thin, high-definition television or computer display created with pixel-sized, gas-filled cells that emit different colors when electric current is connected

plaster of Paris is so called because it is prepared from the gypsum of Paris, France

the **plastic arts** include ceramics and sculpture

plastic explosives were described by 1906

plastic surgery dates to 1837 and "plastic" is used in the sense of "molding, shaping"

platinum blonde comes from a Jean Harlow film of that name (1931)

platonic year is a period of time determined by the revolution of the equinoxes, or the space of time in which the stars and constellations return to their former places in respect to the equinoxes

to **play a good knife and fork** is to eat well

to **play gooseberry** meant to act as a chaperone to lovers

to **play out of the cabbage** in golf means to shoot from an obstructed or disadvantageous position

> **play the field** comes from horse racing where one bets on all the horses except the favorite

playing fast and loose is from *Antony and Cleopatra*

playing the advantages means "cheating"

to **plead guilty** means one owns up to the offense; **pleading no contest** is not admitting or denying guilt but simply waiving the right to trial by jury

pleased as punch refers to the puppet show *Punch and Judy* (from 1600s)

plein-air, from the French phrase *en plein air*, "in the open air," is an art style developed among French Impressionists c. 1870

a **plenary session** is a session of a conference at which all members attend—normally held either at the beginning of a conference to discuss general issues, or at the end of a conference to announce progress

plenty as blackberries means to be plentiful, abundant

the **Plimsoll mark** is the load line on a ship, named for Samuel Plimsoll (1824–98) by whose efforts the Merchant Shipping Act of 1876 was introduced

a **ploughman's lunch** is cheese, bread, and a pickle

plug-and-play pertains to the addition of new hardware or software through automatic detection and configuration; by extension, anything characterized by ease of installation and use

plum job relates to the 1600s British term "plum" for one thousand pounds, meaning a serious amount of money

plum pudding was so named because it was originally made with plums and the word was retained to denote "raisin," which became the main ingredient; Christmas pudding is the "rich" one, with raisins, currants, dried fruit, etc., while suet pudding has just raisins

plumber's friend and **plumber's helper** are synonyms for plunger

plural marriage and **celestial marriage** are terms for polygamy

plus fours got their name (c. 1920) from the fact that such trousers were made four inches longer than standard knickerbockers or shorts, which came to just above the knee

plutonic rocks are granite, porphyry, and some other igneous rocks, supposed to have consolidated from a melted state at a great depth from the surface

poached egg is derived from French *poche* "bag," as the yolk of the egg appears in the "pocket" of white when it has been cooked

a **pochade box** is a compact or small portable painting studio in a box

pocket billiards is another name for pool

a **pocket veto** is when a U.S. President refuses to sign a bill that is passed by both Houses

a **pod hotel** is a style of hotel developed in Japan featuring very dense occupancy with room to sleep and little more

pod person is a term for a conformist, especially one who lacks personality or originality

poet laureate has the plural poets laureate

poetic justice is a term first recorded in 1679 in a poem by John Dryden

poet's day is a weary worker's term for Friday—"push off early, tomorrow is Saturday"

pogo stick came onto the scene around 1921 but is of uncertain etymology, possibly "pole" and "go"

point blank comes from the notion of standing close enough to aim (point) at the blank (white center of a target) without allowance for curve, windage, or gravity

point break is a type of surfing wave found off a coast with a headland

the **point guard** in basketball directs the team's offense

a **point man,** as in one who leads a military patrol in formation in a jungle, etc., is from 1944

the **point of sight** in a perspective drawing is the point assumed as that occupied by the eye of the spectator

ballet shoes with strengthened toes are called **pointe shoes**

points in the paint refers to (basketball) points scored from within the free-throw lane

pointy head, "intellectual," is an analogy with egghead

the saying to remember for **poison ivy** is "leaves three, let it be"

polar circles are two circles, each at a distance from a pole of the earth equal to the obliquity of the ecliptic, or about 23–28 degrees; the northern is called the Arctic circle, and the southern is called the Antarctic circle

in **polar tundra**, thaw only lasts four to five months; the **polar ice cap** has permanent ice cover

a **polarized plug** is an electrical plug with one prong larger than the other to prevent improper plugging into an outlet

pole position refers to pole as the term for the inside fence on a racecourse

political correctness (PC) can be an insult, accusation, moke, or the name of an effort to change a society by means of wide-ranging but often small-scale cultural reform; politically correct was used in the late eighteenth century to mean "correct from a political point of view"

a **political map** shows the boundaries of cities, states, and countries

polka dots were named for the once-popular dance (as they decorated clothes worn at the height of polka's popularity)

polyunsaturated fats' main sources are seeds, nuts, grains, vegetables, cooking oils, fish, and oils such as corn, grapeseed, safflower, and sunflower

pommes frites are fried potatoes

in **pomp and circumstance**, circumstance means "large numbers of people standing around"

pom-pom (1899), a name of imitative origin, soldiers' slang from the Boer War; the unrelated word meaning "ornamental round tuft" (originally on a hat, etc.) is first attested 1748, from French *pompon* (1725), of unknown origin

a **pony beer** is a small beer bottle or glass, often holding four to seven ounces

pony in the barn is an exciting and real prospect, something to be legitimately excited about

pony up, "to pay up," is from pony, meaning "a small sum of money"

a **Ponzi scheme** is an investment scam by which early investors are paid off from the contributions of later ones (1957) and refers to Charles Ponzi, who perpetrated such a scam in United States, 1919–20

pooh-bah is the name of the "Lord High Everything Else" in Gilbert and Sullivan's *The Mikado* (1885)

a **pool noodle** is a long, slender tube or rod extruded from buoyant foam and usually brightly colored that is used for swimming pool play

pool table got its name from "pooled" betting money put on the table for counting it out

pooper scooper is a U.S. expression dating from the 1970s

pop art refers to "popular" and to explosiveness

pork barrel was originally a barrel kept by farmers with a reserve supply of meat

port of call dates to 1838

a **porte cochere** is a roofed structure extending from the entrance of a building over an adjacent driveway and sheltering those getting in or out of vehicles

porter beer is a heavy, dark-brown ale made with malt browned by drying at a high temperature

a **portfolio manager** or investment manager invests money on behalf of a group or individual clients

Portland cement is named after a place in Dorset, England, which was first quarried for the limestone in this

portmanteau words are arbitrary combos like smog (smoke + fog) and chortle (chuckle + snort)

positive affectivity is the extent to which an individual habitually experiences positive moods like joy, interest, and alertness

positive psychology is the scientific study of the strengths and virtues that enable individuals and communities to thrive and find happiness

post-and-beam means constructed using a framework of upright and horizontal beams

post meridiem, "after noon" (1647), is from Latin

a **post road** was one with a series of post-houses or stations for post-horses established; a road on which mail was carried

poster paint is also called gouache

the **posterior rugae** of a human is the deep slender ridge between the two buttocks

by 1910, **post-impressionism** described a school of painting best exemplified by Cézanne, Gauguin, and Van Gogh

the place where you put things on a bulletin board is the **posting surface**

post-modern (1949) was originally used in architecture writing; the specific sense in the arts emerged in the1960s

post-mortem is a shortening of post-mortem examination and was first recorded in 1850

post-operative, "occurring after a surgical operation," was seen in 1889; the short form post-op is attested from 1971

post-partum (1844) is Latin, "after birth"; post-partum depression was first attested in 1929

pot stickers are a type of Chinese dumpling filled with ground meat, vegetables, etc., and fried, steamed, or both

potato bread is a type of bread made with mashed potatoes

the **potato chip** is also called the **Saratoga chip** since it was supposedly invented by a Native American chief in Saratoga, New York

> **potato crisp** is the British term for potato chip

potato printing is a craft method in which a raw potato's flat end is cut into a design, dried, inked or painted, and used to press the design on paper; also, a design or picture made with this craft method

potential energy is that stored in a stretched bow, and **kinetic energy** is that of the arrow in flight

potpourri fishing is a type that offers a variety of species or in which more than one fishing method can be used

a **potter's field** is a burial ground for destitute or unknown people

potting soil is a mixture of loam, peat, sand, and nutrients and is used as a growing medium for plants in pots

poudre douce (mild spice) was from medieval times, a mixture of sugar, ginger, and cinnamon

poudre fort (strong spice) was from medieval times and included various peppers, cloves, nutmeg, mace, cinnamon, ginger, and possibly other spices

pound cake is made of about one pound each of sugar, flour, butter, and eggs; pound cake in British English is Madeira cake

is alternatively called octothorp(e), crosshatch, gridlet, double cross, **pound sign**, and cross of Lorainne—and was originally a map symbol for a village surrounded by eight fields (*thorpe* is Old Norse for farm)

B.S. Rowntree first used the term **poverty line** in a 1901 book

powder blue was originally powdered smalt and its color, which was deep blue

a **powder room** was originally a room on a ship where gunpowder was stored

powdered sugar is the same as **confectioners' sugar**

power lifting involves the bench press, squat, and dead lift; **weight lifting** involves the press, clean and jerk, and snatch

power yoga is a type of yoga incorporating ujjayi breathing and a series of postures designed to affect the body and mind in positive ways

powers that be comes from Romans in the Bible

the quality that distinguishes between a **practical joke** and an ordinary joke is that it depends upon some "practical" action by the person perpetuating the joke

{ a **prairie chicken** is actually a grouse, and a **prairie dog** is a ground squirrel }

prairie eel is fried rattlesnake

a **prairie oyster** is a raw egg, flavored with some kind of liquid, and swallowed whole as a hangover cure

prairie squirrel is another name for the gopher

prairie strawberries are beans, **Pilgrim marbles** are Boston baked beans, and **lumberjack strawberries** are prunes

a **praise sandwich** is criticism prefaced by and followed by compliments

Tibetan Buddhists use **prayer flags** and **prayer wheels**, both inscribed with prayers

mantis is Greek, meaning "prophet, seer," and the insect got this name for holding its legs like it is praying; **praying mantis** is actually redundant

precatory words are words of recommendation, request, entreaty, wish, or expectation, employed in wills, as distinguished from express directions

the **precious stones**—emerald, sapphire, diamond, and ruby—are valued for their brilliance, durability, and rarity

a **predicate adjective** is an adjective that follows both the noun that it modifies and an auxiliary verb, e.g., complicated in "grammar is complicated"

pre-emption was literally "the right of purchasing before others," from Latin; and **pre-empt** (v.) is an 1855 back-formation, with **pre-emptive** from 1959

a **preexisting condition** is a medical condition that exists when new insurance goes into effect, and often is not covered

preferred stock is stock whose holders are guaranteed priority in the payment of dividends but have no voting rights

pre-owned (1964) is an automobile dealer's euphemism for "used"

prepared mustard is an American mixture generally made of powdered mustard, water, vinegar, sugar, and turmeric

a before-dinner drink is a **preprandial libation**

{ **presently** means "soon, shortly, before long," while **at present** means "at the time of speaking" }

on a CD, the surface that contains the recording is the **pressed area**

a **pressure cooker** is an airtight metal pot that uses steam under pressure at high temperature to cook food quickly—with a removable safety valve (on older models) that attaches to the lid or a built-in valve with easy to read pressure markings (newer models)

pressure points are places where arterial bleeding may be stopped by pressure

for wood, **pressure-treated** means wood compressed under great heat to increase hardness and resistance to moisture and decay

pret a porter is from French *prêt-à-porter*, "ready-to-wear"

prevailing winds come from the direction that is predominant or usual for a particular place or season

prick-song is the musical line or counterpoint that accompanies the main melody—or a song with all the notes written down

pride of place is now commonly used to denote an unsurpassed position

pride of the desert is the camel

prima donna, "principal female singer in an opera," is from Italian prima donna "first lady"; the meaning "temperamental person" was first recorded in 1834

prima facie (c.1420) is Latin for "at first sight"

the **primary auxiliary verbs** in English are: be, do, and have; modal auxiliaries are: can, could, may, might, must, shall, should, will, would; the list of twenty-three auxiliary/ helping verbs is: am, are, be, being, been, can, could, did, do, does, had, has, have, is, may, might, must, shall, should, was, were, will, would

in medicine, **primary care** is basic, not specialized

in dyes, pigments, and paints, the **primary colors** are red, yellow, and blue—which mix to make the **secondary colors** of orange, green, and purple

primary consumers are usually herbivores that feed on other herbivores, **secondary consumers** are carnivores that feed on herbivores, and **tertiary consumers** are carnivores that feed on other carnivores

the **prismatic layer** is the middle layer of the shell of certain mollusks, consisting chiefly of crystals of calcium carbonate

{
a **primary source** is a direct source of information or research, a document not amended by a third party
}

prime meridian is the meridian from which longitude on the earth's surface (and hence time zones) is reckoned; originally, it was variable (being a meridian on which magnetic variation of the compass was zero in a certain latitude) until the meridian passing through the Royal Observatory at Greenwich, England, was adopted internationally as the zero of longitude in 1884

prime rib is not graded "prime," but is taken from the rib primal; it is also called **beef rib roast**

prime time (1964) on TV is 8–11 p.m.

primeval forest is a large forest unaffected by humans

primo vomo is the principal male singer in an opera

primordial soup (c. 1529) is a solution rich in organic compounds in which life on earth is supposed to have originated

primrose path was first penned by Shakespeare (1604)

Prince Charming is from French, *Roi Charmant*, the name of the hero of Comtesse d'Aulnoy's "L'Oiseau Bleu" (1697), adopted into native fairy tales including "Sleeping Beauty" and "Cinderella"

the eye part of **private eye** started with the letterhead of the Pinkerton detective organization

pro bono is short for Latin *pro bono publico*, "for the public good"

pro forma is a noun meaning "invoice" and an adjective/adverb phrase meaning "as a formality"

pro rata is Latin, "according to the calculated (share)"

pro tempore, Latin, "for the time (being)," was abbreviated to pro tem by 1835

pro-active was in the language by 1971 when referring to persons or policies but by 1933 in a psychological sense

a **probatory term** is a time for taking testimony

process art is art created primarily as a physical record of the creative process

the word **pro-choice**, favoring a right to abortion, dates to 1975

Procrustean bed, a bed like that of Procrustes, means something done to ensure conformity—from Procrustes, the name of an Attican robber who stretched and mutilated his victims in order to make them fit the length of his bed

product placement is the appearance of a product or service in a broadcast program or movie, paid for by the manufacturer to gain exposure for the product or service

program music (descriptive music) depicts or suggests a subject, like a story, to create a mood

progressive dinner is a social event based on eating different courses of a meal at different homes

progressive lens is an eyeglass or contact lens with a range of focal lengths from near to far distances

a football is a **prolate spheroid**

the word **pro-life**, opposed to abortion, was first attested in 1976

Promised Land was the land of Canaan, as promised to Abraham and his descendants (Genesis 12:7, 13:15, etc.)

pronunciation spelling is spelling based on how a word is actually pronounced—like "gonna" for "going to"

the **proof in the pudding** is in the eating, i.e., a thing is tested by putting it to its intended use

a **proper adjective** is derived from a proper noun (American flag)

a **proper fraction** is less than one with the numerator less than the denominator, as 2/3

a **proper noun** is the name of a specific person, place, or thing

a **proprietary name** is registered as a trademark

pros and cons is an abbreviation of the Latin phrase *pro et contra*, "for and against"

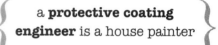
a **protective coating engineer** is a house painter

Proto-Indo-European is the unrecorded language thought to be the parent of all Indo-European languages

the mainland of Rhode Island is, properly, **Providence Plantations**

the hand's head line is also called the **proximal transverse**

Prussian blue is one of the iron blues, a dark-blue, crystalline, water-insoluble pigment produced by reacting ferrocyanic acid or a ferrocyanide with a ferric compound and used in painting

pseudo-science, a pretended or mistaken science, dates to 1844

psychic income is the nonmonetary, nonmaterial satisfaction that comes with a job

the **psychological moment** is the moment when the mind is most ready to receive suggestions from another

if a copyright or patent expires, the item becomes **public domain** a **public house** was first contracted to public and then to pub

Thomas Jefferson uttered the term **public relations** in 1807, but it did not establish itself until c. 1913 (PR recorded in 1941)

pudding rice is a short-grained rice used to make rice pudding

a **pudding ring** is made of facial hair consisting of a moustache and goatee

a **puddle jumper** is a small lightweight airplane used for short trips, such as for commuters

puffed wheat was introduced as a cereal in 1902 by Alexander Anderson

puffing pig is the common porpoise

a tiger's paw prints are called **pug marks**

a **pull hitter** in baseball is one who normally drives the ball in the direction of the follow-through of the bat

originally, **pull one's leg** meant to make a fool out of them, especially by outright cheating

pull out all the stops refers to the knobs and levers on a church organ that control the pipes; pulling out all the stops will result in the full range of pitch and maximum volume

pull the plug first referred to an old-fashioned type of toilet

pull the wool over someone's eyes goes back to when men wore powdered wigs; it was the practice of doing this to someone as a joke, so they could not see what was going on

pulled meat is any meat, usually pork butt or shoulder, but also chicken, smoked in a slow cooker until the meat pulls easily from the bone; also called pulled pork, pulled pig, pulled chicken

pump iron is of U.S. origin in the early 1970s

pumpkin pie was first called pumpkin pudding

pumpkin pie spice includes cinnamon, allspice, nutmeg, ginger, mace, and cloves

pumpkin time is the end of prosperity and a return to normal

punch buggy is a game in which the first player to call "punch buggy!" on sighting a Volkswagen Beetle gets to punch the other person

the holes in a sneaker are called **punch holes**

in **punch line**, punch means "point"—the point of a joke, skit, etc.

a **punch list** is a to-do list of items requiring immediate attention—or any list of significance

punitive damages are those awarded to punish, which are beyond simple compensation

the original punk in **punk rock** (1971) came from the adjective punk, "worthless, rotten"

pure color is a color or hue that is unmixed with other hues

pure science is one depending on deductions from demonstrated truths, such as math or logic, without regard to practical applications

when a tuning fork is struck, it vibrates with a single tone called a **pure tone**

purple haze is another term for LSD

a brilliant passage in an otherwise dull and uninspiring work is a **purple passage**, **purple patch**, or **purple prose**

purple state is any U.S. state that tends to be or is undecided in a general election

in flying, the envelope refers to the mathematically calculated parameters in which the mechanisms of an aircraft can perform safely (hence, **push the envelope**)

put through the hoop is an ancient marine phrase for a punishment for sailors involving an iron hoop

> **puttanesca sauce** is very spicy—flavored with garlic, dried chile peppers, capers, and anchovies

puzzle palace is a slang term for a place, especially a government department, where important decisions are made in great secrecy

a **Pyrrhic victory** is one won at such a high cost that it is really no victory at all

{ Q }

quadrille paper is paper marked out with (usually small) squares

a **quadruple double** is the achievement of a two-digit number of any four: points scored, assists, rebounds, blocks, or steals in a single basketball game

quality of life dates to the 1940s, when the expression was first recorded in the context of speculation as to how people would live their lives after World War II

a short or long mark over a vowel or diphthong is a **quantity mark**; **macron** is for long and **breve** is for short

there is irony in that **quantum leap** in physics is the minimum possible change, and in popular use, it means a big change or jump in concept

quantum mechanics is the branch of quantum physics that accounts for matter at the atomic level

quantum theory (1912) developed from ideas of Max Planck and Albert Einstein and was originally called quanta theory (1911)

a day beginning a new season or quarter is a **quarter day**

the **quarter horse** was so named for its ability to run high speeds in quarter-mile races

a **quarter light** is a small triangular side window in an automobile

a **queen dowager** is the widow of a king

the **Queensberry Rules** were drawn up in 1867 by Sir John Sholto Douglas (1844–1900), 8th Marquis of Queensberry, to govern the sport of boxing in Great Britain

when early scholars wrote in Latin, they would put the word **questio,** "question," at the end of a sentence to indicate this; an abbreviation gave way to a symbol eventually

qui vive (1726) is from French *qui voulez-vous qui vive?*, a sentinel's challenge, "whom do you wish to live, (long) live who?"—in other words, "whose side are you on?"

the **quick and the dead** means "the alive and the dead"

quick bread is any bread leavened with baking soda or powder instead of yeast and baked immediately, as muffins or biscuits —i.e., prepared with a batter instead of a dough

{ **quick time** is military marching at about 120 paces per minute }

quid pro quo is literally "something for something"

quod erat demonstrandum, QED, is literally "which was to be proved" and is put at the closing point of an argument

a **Quonset (or Nissen) hut** is a semi-circular, corrugated-metal hut, especially known from World War II, from Quonset Point Naval Air Station, Rhode Island, where this type of structure was first built, 1941

quotation marks are the youngest punctuation marks in English, about 300 years old

quote unquote dates from the 1930s and has its origin in the oral formula for quotation marks in dictation

{ R }

salad is sometimes called **rabbit food**

the rabbit is a symbol of fertility, so the **rabbit's foot**, the part of it in closest contact with the earth, became a good luck charm

to **rabbit on** is to chatter away

rabbit punch, a sharp blow to the back of the neck, is derived from the way in which a gamekeeper puts a rabbit out of pain

rabbit test was a pregnancy test (1927+) in which some of a woman's urine was injected into an unmated female rabbit and then later the ovaries of the rabbit were examined for the presence of corpora lutea, which indicated that the woman was pregnant; the term rabbit test was first recorded in 1949

race relations was first recorded in the title of a 1911 paper in *Political Science Quarterly*

rack of lamb is a roast of the rib section of lamb

rack rent gets its meaning from rack, as in "cause stress"

racking one's brain, figuratively stretching, is derived from the Tower of London's torture treatment

radio buttons in graphical display is a set of options from which only one may be selected at any time; it is any of a group of widgets in a graphical user interface that is used to select one of a group of options

radio silence is a status maintained where all fixed or mobile radio stations in an area stop transmitting (sometimes limited to certain frequency bands) the period of time during which this status exists

radio waves travel like rays of light, so taking their name from Latin *radius*, "spoke of a wheel; ray of light"

the decimal point is a **radix point**

the **Raggedy Ann** name was a blend of "The Raggedy Man" and "Little Orphan Annie," two James Whitcomb Riley poems

raglan sleeves, named for the 1st Baron Raglan (1788–1855) are cut so that the cloth from the outer cuff of the sleeve to the collar is in one piece—the seam running from the collar diagonally across or just below the shoulder to the armhole

ragtag and bobtail comes from the earlier tagrag and bobtail and means "the whole lot" or "riffraff"

ragu sauce is a meat sauce that is typically served with pasta (from French ragûter, "to stimulate the appetite"), and it usually contains ground beef, tomatoes, onions, celery, carrots, white wine, and seasonings

the change from saying **railway station** to **train station** is one that slipped into the language almost without anyone noticing it

a **rain band** is a dark band in the yellow portion of the solar spectrum near the sodium line caused by the presence of watery vapor in the atmosphere; it is sometimes used in weather predictions

rain forest (1903) is apparently a loan-translation of German *Regenwald*, coined by A.F.W. Schimper for his 1898 work *Pflanzengeographie*, and used first in the English translation of it

a **rain gauge** is also known as a pluviometer

rain pitchforks was originally used to express the notion of improbability, but now has the hyperbolic meaning of "to rain very hard"

rain prints are markings on the surfaces of stratified rocks, presenting an appearance similar to those made by rain on mud and sand, and believed to have been so produced

rain shadow is the leeward side of a mountain where little or no rain falls

a **rain stick** is filled with small pebbles

rainbow rotelle is a combination of tomato, spinach, and regular twirl-shaped pasta in the colors of the Italian flag

rainbow trout is a bright-colored trout native to the mountains of California, but now extensively introduced into the Eastern States, Japan, and other countries; also called brook trout, mountain trout, and golden trout

raining cats and dogs first appeared in a 1738 work, *A Complete Collection of Polite and Ingenious Conversation* by Jonathan Swift; in "raining cats and dogs," cats symbolize rain storms, and dogs symbolize wind storms

raise Cain is an allusion to the brother of Abel, traditionally the world's first criminal

a **raison d'etre** is a reason for being and can be applied to a person or thing

a **rake comb** has wide teeth and a fairly long handle; a **barber comb** is half wide teeth and half closely spaced teeth

ranch dressing is a creamy buttermilk-based dressing with garlic and other spices and herbs, developed at Hidden Valley Ranch in Santa Barbara in the 1950s

the **range hood** is a ventilation appliance over a stove for expelling or recycling fumes and odors

rank and file's meaning comes from a formation in which there is a rank of soldiers drawn abreast and a file of soldiers, which is one behind the other, and it first referred to privates and non-commissioned officers

the use of "rap" in the term **rap music** is probably a 1960s usage, "to indulge in repartee or street talk"

rara avis, "peculiar person," is from Latin meaning "strange bird"

a **rare book** is any book that is hard to find due to an early printing date, limited issue, special character of an edition or binding, or historical interest

rare-earth elements include any naturally occurring oxide of an element of the lanthanide series, usually lanthanum and frequently also scandium and yttrium

rarely ever is literally nonsensical

the spelling of **raring to go** is questionable, as it originally came from "rearing" or "roaring"; both meant "eager"

rat fink only dates back to 1964

the earliest **rat pack** was the Holmby Hills Rat Pack of Hollywood, consisting of Humphrey Bogart and his drinking friends

a **rational number** can be expressed exactly as the ratio between two other numbers—0.5 can be expressed as ½

a **ratoon crop** is one which grows from the remains of one already harvested (from Spanish *retono*, "sprout")

a **raw bar** sells raw oysters and other seafood

raw deal is a phrase dating to 1940

raw sienna is a brownish-yellow earth color obtained from a natural clay containing iron and manganese, one of the basic permanent artists' pigments

raw sugar is light brown and coarse, containing the natural molasses present in sugarcane

raw tea is harsh, not mellow

raw-gabbit refers to speaking confidently on a subject of which one is ignorant

a **ray flower** is a flat flower on the head of a composite flower, such as a daisy

the **Rayleigh scattering** is the scientific explanation for why the sky is blue: blue wavelengths of sunlight are scattered by air molecules in all directions, while yellow, red, and orange are not and pass to the earth unobstructed

barbed wire with points is **razor ribbon**

razzle-dazzle is an American slang reduplication of dazzle from 1889

the display cases for foods and beverages at the grocery store are called **reach-in freezers**

reaction time in nerve physiology is the interval between the application of a stimulus to an end organ of sense and the reaction or resulting movement

{ **read my lips** has been lurking in the American English slang vocabulary since the 1970s }

read the riot act is based on a ruling in 1714, during the time of George I, and implies strong disapproval of the actions of a person

a **ready meal** is any prepackaged fresh or frozen meal that only requires heating (often in a microwave) before being served, sometimes in its own packaging

any table or list that aids calculations is a **ready reckoner**

real estate originally meant "royal grant" in England, as all the land once belonged to the king, and the only way a person could obtain land was by royal grant

the first **real McCoy** was a sewing machine

reality television (1978) first was documentaries of ordinary people in everyday situations

the **rearview mirror** is the one inside the car

the **reason why** and "the reason is because" are both redundant

the **rebel yell** is the shrill, chilling shouts of Confederates as they advanced in the Civil War

receding colors—such as greens, blues, and violets—appear to be farther from the eye than others that are equally distant

recharge one's batteries dates from the 1920s

a **recognition mark** is a distinctive mark that makes an animal or bird easy to recognize by others of the same species

any **rectus muscle** (Latin) is a "straight" muscle

red alert is the state of maximum preparedness, yellow or amber is a high degree of readiness, and in between is orange alert for extreme readiness

red cent is an obsolete type of copper penny, first recorded in 1839

the rare **red coral** of the Mediterranean is actually blue

the **Red Cross** (c.1430) as the national emblem of England (St. George's Cross) was first; then, in the seventeenth century, a red cross was the mark placed on the doors of London houses infected with the plague; the red cross was adopted as a symbol of ambulance service in 1864 by the Geneva Conference

red dog originally meant a defensive tactic whereby a linebacker shot through the offensive line to hit the quarterback before the play got started

red earth is red soil found in tropical areas, containing oxidized iron

red goods refers to food products that are consumed quickly

a **red herring** is something introduced to distract from a more important or controversial issue

red ink, "financial losses," is from the red ink traditionally used to indicate debits in accounts (1929)

red letter day refers to the original practice of marking saints' days and holidays in red on almanacs and calendars

red pepper is another name for cayenne

the **Red Sea** is named for dying algae that turns its intense blue-green waters to red

the **red squirrel** is the chickaree

red state is any U.S. state that tends to vote for candidates of the Republican party in a general election

> **red tape** is so named because of the red or pink tape used to bind and secure official documents

red-eye, an airplane flight that deprives travelers of sleep, dates to 1968, from the red eyes of sleeplessness—but had an earlier meaning of "raw and inferior whiskey"

red-eye gravy is made from cooked ham and flour fried in coffee and water; **red flannel hash** is made with beets

red-handed (1819) is from the earlier red-hand, originally in Scottish legal writing presumably from the image of a murderer caught in the act, with blood on the hands

red-hot originally meant (c.1375) "heated till it glows red" (of metal, etc.); the meaning "lively, passionate" is recorded from 1608

red-hot mama came on the scene in 1926 as jazz slang for "earthy female singer" or "girlfriend, lover"

reed organ refers to an organ in which the wind acts on a set of free reeds, such as the harmonium, melodeon, concertina, etc.

re-entry, specifically of spacecraft, is from 1948

a **refectory table** is a long, narrow table—often for dining

refer back is a common redundancy

a **reference library** holds many reference books—not for loan but for use on site

referred pain is that felt in a part of the body other than its actual source

a **refractory word** is one with no common rhyme (orange, month, silver)

refried beans is a translation of Spanish *frijoles refritos*, but *refritos* means "well-fried," not "refried"!

refrigerator cookies require that the dough be chilled before the cookies are shaped and baked

the **region code** is a code used on DVDs to identify which region's DVD players it will play in

registered mail is for things with a high monetary value, and this mail can be insured

reinforced concrete has wire or metal bars embedded to increase its tensile strength; ferro-concrete (1900) became known as reinforced concrete (1902)

a **related word** is one that co-occurs frequently with another, as a collocation; also, a synonym, antonym, quasisynonym, hyponym, hypernym, or other semantically or conceptually associated word to another

a **relative adjective** is a pronoun used in an adjectival clause, e.g., "whose" in "the man whose time had come"

in archaeology, **relative dating** is the arrangement of artifacts or events in a sequence relative to one another but without ties to calendrically measured time; the arrangement of artifacts in a typological sequence or seriation

relative humidity is the amount of water vapor in the air, expressed as a percentage of the maximum amount that the air could hold at the given temperature

a **remainder mark** is a mark or stamp on a book (often on the bottom page edges) indicating a book was returned to the publisher unsold and then sold at a discount price

remote sensing is the scanning of the earth by satellite or aircraft to obtain information about it

remoulade sauce is mayonnaise, pickles, capers, anchovies, and herbs, and is from French *remola*, "large black radish," from a Latin word meaning "wild radish"

rere-banket was a second course of dessert

the **reserve price** is the lowest price that a seller is willing to accept for something being sold at auction

residual air is that portion of air contained in the lungs that cannot be expelled even by the most violent expiratory effort, from seventy-five to one hundred cubic inches

residual phenomena are the observed phenomena in a scientific experiment that a scientist cannot explain

resolving power is the ability of an optical system (eye, microscope) to separate images of objects lying very close together

resonate with actually means the vibrations of one thing match those of another

rest and relaxation is actually redundant

the term **remote control** existed by 1904 and the shortened version, remote, was used in print by 1966

art that seeks to depict the physical appearance of reality is called **representational art**, **objective art**, or **figurative art**

the **Reptilian Age** is that part of geological time comprising the Triassic, Jurassic, and Cretaceous periods, and distinguished as that era in which the class of reptiles attained its highest expansion; also called the Meszozoic Age

a **rest area** along a road is for just that, and there are usually restrooms; a **service area** provides more, like a gas station, restaurant, etc.

retail therapy is shopping as a leisure activity or comfort; also called shopping therapy the **reticular formation** is a network of neurons in the brainstem involved in consciousness, regulation of breathing, transmission of sensory stimuli to higher brain centers, and the constantly shifting muscular activity that supports the body against gravity

retroactive inhibition is a theory that later learning has a tendency to hinder the memory of previously learned material

the part of a lightning bolt that is bright and flashes is the **return stroke**

a **Reuben sandwich** is corned beef, Swiss cheese, and sauerkraut served hot and takes its name from Arnold Reuben (1883–1970), a restaurateur

to **reverse commute** is to travel to work opposite of the normal rush of traffic

reverse dictionary is a print or electronic dictionary in which one can search on a concept to find words and phrases related to or expressing that concept

reverse engineering is pirating a competitor's technology by dismantling or studying an existing product and then manufacturing a copy or improved version

revert back is redundant

on a tape measure, the button is a **rewind switch**

the **Rh factor** was named for the rhesus monkeys used in research to identify blood types

the **rhesus system** is the second most important blood group system in human blood transfusion, usually coded as "positive" or "negative"

{ the red nose of a drunk is called **rhinophyma** or **grog blossom** }

Rhode Island is Dutch for "red (clay) island"

a **Rhodes scholar** is a holder of any of the scholarships founded at Oxford in 1902 by British financier and imperialist Cecil Rhodes (1853–1902), for whom the former African nation of Rhodesia was named

a **rhumb line** is a line on a sphere that cuts all meridians at the same angle; the path taken by a ship or plane that maintains a constant compass direction

rhyme or reason is a phrase derived from French *ni rime ni raison*

rhythm guitar is a style of guitar playing in popular music consisting of the chord sequences over which a song or melody is sung

ribbon development is the building of houses along a main road, especially one leading out of town

rib-eye steak is a tender beef steak cut from the center (eye) of the rib cut of beef; also written rib eye steak, ribeye steak, and also called rib steak, Delmonico steak

rice bowl is a metaphor for the basic elements required to live; iron rice bowl is employment that is guaranteed for life

rice paper has no rice in it

ricochet words are hyphenated words, usually formed by reduplicating a word with a change in the vowel or the initial consonant sound, such as pitter-patter, chit-chat, riff-raff, wishy-washy, hob-nob, roly-poly, pell-mell, razzle-dazzle

ride shotgun (1963) is to travel as an (armed) guard in the seat next to the driver of a vehicle; hence, to act as a protector; to ride in the passenger seat of a motor vehicle

a **ridge runner** is slang for a southern U.S. mountain farmer or hillbilly

a **riding habit** is a woman's dress

riding roughshod first referred to horses wearing shoes with protruding nails to keep them from slipping on the battlefield

the **right brain** is the cerebral hemisphere to the right of the corpus callosum, that controls activities on the left side of the body and, in humans, usually perception of spatial and nonverbal concepts as well

right smart has nothing to do with cleverness but means "large amount or distance" and indicates mass, not a numerable quality

right wing started as a military term for the division on the right side of an army or fleet in battle array

in music, a **rim shot** is sound produced by hitting the rim and the head of a drum at once with a drum stick

a shallower round container used to serve individual portions of soup is a **rim soup bowl**

the **ring finger** is so called from Roman times, when they thought that a nerve from the fourth finger led directly to the heart and that a ring on that finger from one's beloved established a heart-to-heart connection

ringing the changes, figuratively speaking, now means trying every possible way of doing something

rings true first referred to a test for money's trueness—to make sure a coin was not counterfeit

> **rinky dink** (1912) comes from carnival slang, said to be imitative of the sound of banjo music at parades

a **Rip Van Winkle** is a person out of touch with current conditions, from the name of a character in Washington Irving's *Sketch Book* (1819–20)

ripple marks are parallel wavy ridges and furrows left on sand, mud, or rock by the action of water or wind

the **risorius of Santorini** is the muscle of facial expression running from the parotid fascia to the corner of the mouth, whose action draws out the angle of the mouth

a **river estuary** is the mouth of a river that is influenced by the tides

road rage (1988) led a rash of "rage" coinages

road to Damascus (from a Bible story) is a figurative term for a religious conversion or other major change in attitude, belief, or perspective

roaring forties is a sailor's name for the stormy tract of ocean between 40–50 degrees north latitude

a **roasting jack** is the device for turning a roasting spit

a **Robinson Crusoe** is a man without companionship, from the name of the eponymous hero of Daniel Defoe's fictional shipwreck narrative (1719)

rock and roll was a term used in connection with popular dancing from at least the 1930s, though as a music genre, not until 1954 (rock 'n' roll, 1955)

the **rock cycle** is the process by which rocks are formed, altered, destroyed, and reformed by geological processes and which is recurrent, returning to a starting point

Rock English, a mix of Spanish and English, is the language of the Rock of Gibraltar

a **rock garden** contains rock plants, those that grow on or among rocks

rock lobster is any one of several species of large spinose lobsters that have no large claws; also called spiny lobster or sea crayfish

rock salt is chloride of sodium (common salt) occurring in rocklike masses in mines, salt dug from the earth, or salt in large crystals formed by evaporation from sea water in large basins or cavities

a **rock sequence** is a set of rocks containing a variety of separate strata, with an overall lithology that can be used to interpret the paleoenvironment of deposition over a certain period

the **rocker panel** in a car is the bodywork below the passenger door

rocket surgery is any difficult task requiring intelligence or higher education (a blend of rocket science and brain surgery)

a **rocking chair job** (or **swivel chair job**) is one that requires little work

the **Rockwell scale** is a set of numbers representing the hardness of a metal

Rocky Mountain oysters are bull or ram testicles boiled and then sliced into ovals and fried, served with a spicy sauce

a **roller docker** is a food preparation utensil that looks like a small rolling pin with spikes, used to pierce pizza dough or pastry dough to prevent over-rising or blistering

rolling pin dates to 1589

rolling stock are carriages, locomotives, wagons, and other vehicles used on a railroad

{ a Roman actor and writer, Publilius Syrus, is credited with originating a **rolling stone gathers no moss** in the first century BC }

a **rolling stop** is when a vehicle driver slows down, but does not stop, at a stop sign

Rolls-Royce was registered in 1908 as a trademark, named for designers C.S. Rolls (1877–1910) and Sir Henry Royce (1863–1933), and in 1916 was extended to any product of high quality

a **rolltop desk** is also known as a **tambour desk**

roly-poly is probably a varied reduplication of roll

laitue Romaine, "Roman lettuce," was used for a leafy vegetable shipped through Rome to other places, now **Romaine** (or Cos) **lettuce**

a **roman à clef** is historical people and events in a work of fiction a **Roman candle** is a cylindrical firework that projects a series of colored balls of fire

the **Roman Empire** includes the lands and people conquered by Rome from c. 27 BC till AD 476 (the fall of Rome); the Holy Roman Empire encompassed a much smaller territory and dates from Charlemagne (AD 800) or Otto the Great of Germany (AD 962) and ended in 1806, when the title Holy Roman Emperor was officially renounced

a **Roman holiday** is enjoyment or profit derived from others' discomfort or suffering

romance languages are the languages that stem from Latin, the language of Rome

a **roo bar** is an Australian term for a metal bar on the front of a car or truck that prevents the vehicle from being damaged in the event of a collision with an animal

a **rood screen** (rood, "crucifix") is a screen in a church that separates the nave from the choir or chancel

room temperature is the average normal temperature of a living room, usually thought of as around 20 degrees C (68 degrees F) or slightly above

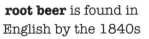
root beer is found in English by the 1840s

a **root cellar** is any excavation where root vegetables are stored

root hog or die started as an expression for turning hogs out into the woods or onto the prairies to get their own sustenance

the **root run** is the space over which the roots of a plant extend

root vegetables include the carrot, beet, and rutabaga

root-bound describes a plant whose roots have outgrown their container, thwarting new growth

the **Rorschach test**, also known as the inkblot test, is named for Hermann Rorschach (1884–1922), a Swiss psychiatrist

the **Rosetta Stone** was discovered in 1798 at Rosetta, Egypt, and is now in a British Museum; its trilingual inscription helped Jean-François Champollion decipher Egyptian demotic and hieroglyphics in 1822, which opened the way to the study of all early Egyptian records

Rosh Hashanah is Hebrew for "head of the year"—as it is the Jewish New Year

rotisserie league is a group of imaginary teams that the participants own, manage, and coach, with games based on statistics generated by actual players or teams of a professional sport—from La Rotisseries restaurant in New York, where it was invented

of clothes, **rough dry** means "dry, but not smoothed or ironed"

roughing-in is the installation of plumbing and electrical wiring

round robin originally referred to a grievance presented by seamen to their captain, called round because of the circular sequence of names, but the source of robin has been lost; as a kind of tournament in which each player plays the others, it is recorded from 1895

a **row house** is part of an unbroken line or series of houses

{ a **royal flush** in poker is an ace, king, queen, jack, and ten of one suit }

rub out might go back to Native Americans' sign language, in which "kill" is signed by a kind of rubbing motion

rub-a-dub (1787) is echoic of the sound of a drum

rubber cement (c. 1890) is an adhesive made by dissolving unvulcanized rubber in a solvent like benzene or naphtha

rubber ear is synonymous with the cold shoulder

the figurative sense of **rubber stamp** was first used by William Howard Taft

a **Rube Goldberg** is a needlessly complicated gadget for performing a simple function

Rubik's Cube (1980) was named for teacher Ernö Rubik, who patented it in Hungary in 1975 with its twenty-seven cubelets

rule of thumb is most likely an allusion to the fact that the first joint of an adult thumb measures roughly one inch, quite literally a rule/ruler of thumb

rule the roost first was rule the roast, as it referred to the master of the house, who sat at the head of the table

a **ruling pen** is a type of pen used in graphic design and calligraphy for drawing precise lines of various thicknesses

rumble strips is a series of coarse-textured ridges on or along the sides of a road to warn of a stop or alert drivers who have driven off the road surface

rummage in **rummage sale** comes from French *arrumage*, "to stow cargo in the hold of a ship"

mengamok is a psychiatric disease in which a man can go crazy and start killing others; this became the figurative English phrase, **run amuck** or **run amok**

a run is the quantity of something produced at one time, and the **run of the mill** is the material produced from a mill before it has been sorted or inspected for quality; the figurative use is from 1930

a **run-on sentence** is an ungrammatical construction in which two or more independent clauses are improperly joined without a conjunction or appropriate punctuation

some use the expression **run the gantlet** to mean "to suffer severe criticism or tribulation"

a **runaway truck** is one having braking problems, especially on steeply graded roads, and in need of a runaway truck ramp, runaway truck lane, emergency escape ramp, or truck arrester bed

a **runcible spoon** is a three-pronged fork curved like a spoon and used as a serving utensil

runner-up originally was "a hound that comes in second in the final heat," one that ran through the races up to the last one with being defeated

the original **running boards** extended from bow to stern on canal boats—which men walked along, propelling the boats with poles

{ facts at the bottom of
a book's pages are called
running feet }

a **running head** is a heading printed at
the top of every page (or every other page)
of a book

a sense of **running mate** is a horse entered
in a race in order to set the pace for another
horse which is intended to win

running start alludes to the long jump

run-off, "precipitation water drained by
streams and rivers," dates to 1892; the
meaning of "deciding a race after a tie" is
from 1873, and the electoral sense is first
attested in 1924

a **rush candle** or rush light Is a candle of
feeble power made by dipping the pith of a
rush in tallow or other grease

Russian dressing is not Russian, but
originated in the United States; it is known
as Marie Rose sauce in Europe

Russian roulette comes from Russian officers in the Czar's court before and during the
1917 Revolution

{ S }

a **sabbatical year** originally was a year during which land remained fallow, observed every seven years by the ancient Jews; now this has transferred to a rest or absence from other occupations, professions, or activities

the **sacher torte** was created in Vienna by Franz Sacher (c 1832)

sacré bleu is basically "holy cow!," but in French it means "holy blue" literally, a euphemism for sacré Dieu, "holy God"

sacred cow was originally U.S. journalists' slang (1910), meaning "copy that is not to be changed or cut"

sad sack was originally the name of a cartoon character invented by George Baker in 1942

saddle shoes were named for the brown or black "saddle" across the middle

Sadie Hawkins (1939) is from the name of a character in a U.S. cartoon strip *Li'l Abner*, by Al Capp (1909–1979), and refers to a day in early November in which women take the lead in romantic matters

safe sex and **sell-by date** are terms first recorded in 1973

it's **safe-deposit box**, not safety

safety school is a term for the least-desired choice of college or university of a student—the student thinks that this school is very unlikely to reject his or her application, and only applies to the school just in case he or she is rejected by all other colleges that he or she applies to

Saint Vitus's dance is chorea, so called from the supposed cures wrought on intercession to this saint

a **salad bowl** is the one used to toss and serve salad; a **salad dish** is a container used to serve an individual portion of salad

salad days (when one is "green") is from Shakespeare's *Antony and Cleopatra*

salad greens include lettuce, escarole, endive, watercress, arugula, etc.

the **salami technique** is any way of carrying out a plan by means of a series of small imperceptible steps, like successive thin slices of salami

the **salchow jump** in ice skating is named for a Swedish skater

Salisbury steak was named for a Civil War doctor who promoted eating shredded beef three times a day

in the strictest sense, only a person or group can **sally forth,** and the original sense was to rush forth from a besieged place against the enemy

the houses on Cape Cod and the New England islands are mainly **salt boxes**—a type of house generally two full stories high in front and one story high in back, the roof having about the same pitch in both directions so that the ridge is well toward the front of the house

salt cellar is redundant, meaning "salt cellar for salt," as cellar has no connection with underground rooms but is from Anglo-Norman *saler,* "salt cellar"

a **salt flat** is simply a flat expanse of land covered with a layer of salt

saltwater taffy is a taffy sometimes made with seawater but more generally made with salted fresh water

Sam Hill, a euphemism for "Hell," is from 1839 but of unknown origin

same difference is literally comparing the difference between one pair of things with the difference between one or more other

pairs; the idiomatic use is a verbal shrug or signal of indifference

same old six and seven is the same old routine, story, etc.

a **sand bath** is a bath of sand in which laboratory vessels to be heated are partly immersed, and is also used for eyeglasses adjustment

{ an Oklahoma rain is a **sandstorm** }

the **sandwich generation** is people in their thirties and forties who are raising their children but also taking responsibility for their aging parents

sang-froid, the ability to stay calm, cool, and collected, literally translates to "cold blood"

sans serif means the characters of a font have no line extensions at the end of a stroke

sans-culotte was the lower-class republican of the French Revolution, literally "without breeches," usually explained as referring to the class whose distinctive costume was pantaloons (long trousers) as opposed to the upper classes, which wore culottes (knee-breeches)

Santa Claus is a contraction of the Dutch "Sant Nikolaas," the patron saint of children

Saran Wrap is technically plastic film

satellite television (1966) originally was the use of an earth-orbiting satellite to relay television signals from one country to another

saturated color is a color not diluted with white, a pure unmixed color like those of the spectrum

saturated fat is primarily derived from animal meat, dairy products, and some tropical plant oils, such as palm and coconut

with **Saturday night special**, the allusion is to the use of the weapon in the barroom and street fights of the weekend

a **saucier pan** is a short and differently shaped version of a sauce pan—often used for preparations requiring more repetitive motions, such as whisking or stirring

sausage dog means dachshund

sauté pan is a wide pan with sloping or straight sides and a single long handle for cooking foods quickly in a small amount of fat; also called *sauteuse*, *sautoir*

sauvignon blanc is a white grape grown primarily in France and California

to **save face** (1898) was originally used by the English community in China, with reference to the continual devices among the Chinese to avoid incurring or inflicting disgrace

saving grace dates to 1910

{ **savoir faire** can only be used as a noun in English, though it is a pair of verbs in French }

savoir vivre is literally "knowing how to live" or knowing how to get the most out of life

a **scale drawing** is one whose dimensions are of the same ratio as those of the object drawn

a **scaled question**, usually part of a questionnaire, is one in which the response is chosen from a range of values, e.g., "rate the usefulness of this feature from zero to ten"

quotes made with finger gestures are called **scare quotes**

school colors are usually two colors chosen to represent a particular school; also, an article of clothing in the school colors

school of fish derives from a Germanic verb meaning "to distinguish, to tell apart," thus implying a corporate number of individual animals

a **school tuna** is one that is 20–100 pounds when caught

sciatic in **sciatic nerve** is from Greek, meaning "relating to the hips, hip joints"

science fiction became an important term around 1929

science park is an area set aside for office buildings that house scientific or technological research and development firms

a **scientific name** is the recognized Latin name given to an organism, consisting of a genus and species, according to a taxonomy; also called binomial name

a **scissor's bite** is the distance it cuts in a single stroke

scorched earth policy is a military strategy of burning or destroying all crops and resources that might be of use to an invading enemy force

on golf clubs, there are **scoring lines**

the **Scotch egg** is a hard-boiled egg enveloped in sausage meat and then fried

Scotch whisky is a protected trademark and has to be matured at least three years in charred oak casks; all its ingredients must be Scottish

scot-free is from Old English *scotfreo*, "exempt from royal tax"

when England and Scotland united under one king, the London police took up residence on land that had been known as **Scotland Yard**

the **Scoville scale** is a gastronomic measure of the "heat" of peppers, chilies, curries, and other forms of highly spiced food; an ordinary chili pepper is 5,000 degrees on the Scoville scale and a really hot one is around 8,000 degrees

scrambled colors are oil paints lightly mixed on the palette so the original hues can still be seen in streaks or swirls

{ **screaming gin and ignorance** is a British term for bad newspaper writing }

a **screen shot** is a reproduction of the current display on a computer screen, saved as a graphics file; also written screenshot; also called screen capture

scrimmage, as in **scrimmage line**, is a corruption of skirmish

script doctor is a person who analyzes, critiques, edits, and fixes screenplays and scripts

scut work (origin unknown) dates to only 1960

sea change first meant (in Shakespeare) "a change brought about by the sea," and it came to mean "a major change"

a lobster was once called a **sea crayfish**

sea cucumber is a slimy relative of the sea urchin; and it is boiled, dried, and smoked to make beche-de-mer ("worm of the sea"), used for soups in China

a fog that comes from the sea is a **sea fret**

the **sea monkey** is a heraldic animal and a proprietary name for brine shrimp (*Artemia salina*)

a **sea nettle** is a large stinging jellyfish

sea salts have a softer, fresher flavor and are used as finishing salts to enhance food flavor

sea-dog meant "harbor seal" and then "old sailor" about 250 years later

sea-lion was first a kind of lobster, and then a fabled animal; after 1697, it was applied to various species of large-eared seals

a **seam pocket** opens on the side seam of a garment

a **search box** is box for entering text which will be used for a search in a database, on the Internet, etc.

search engine optimization is the process of choosing targeted keywords and keyword phrases related to a website so the site will rank high when those terms are part of a Web search; abbreviation SEO

season creep is a small but significant tendency for spring to start earlier and for autumn to end later, the result of global warming

seasonal dimorphism is the condition of having two distinct varieties that appear at different seasons, such as certain species of butterflies in which the spring brood differs from the summer or autumnal brood

by a historian, an encyclopedia article, or a critical essay

second-class was first recorded in 1837 and second-class citizen is recorded from 1942

a **section sign** is the typographical character (ß), used mainly to refer to a particular section of a document, such as a legal code

{ **second-guess** (1941) is a back-formation from second-guesser (1937) and was originally baseball slang for a fan who loudly questions decisions by players, managers, etc. }

your **second cousin** is a child of your parent's first cousin

second nature (1390) is from Latin *secundum naturam*, "according to nature," from Aristotelian philosophy and contrasted to phenomena that were *super naturam* ("above nature," such as God's grace), *extra naturam* ("outside nature"), *supra naturam* ("beyond nature," such as miracles), *contra naturam* ("against nature"), etc.

second sight is the apparent power to perceive things that are not present to the senses

in medieval times, an archer always carried a **second string** in case the one on the bow broke

second wind first meant a condition of regular breathing regained after breathlessness during long-continued exertion

the **secondary colors** are green, orange, and purple

a **secondary source** is information or research that is derivative, such as a comment

security blanket as a metaphor has its origin in the comic strip *Peanuts* by Charles Schulz

a **sedan chair** is an enclosed chair carried on poles

the **seder plate** holds the six symbolic foods of the Passover meal

to **see monkeys** is to be overcome by the heat while working

see red probably comes from the old belief that a bull seeing a red flag becomes enraged

a **seismic wave** is an elastic wave in the earth produced by an earthquake or by artificial means; a seismic sea wave is a tsunami

the term **self-help** dates to 1831

the **selfish gene** is the concept of viewing genes as if they were the primary drivers and beneficiaries of the evolutionary process; a gene that exploits the organism in which it occurs as a vehicle for its self-perpetuation

sell someone down the river originally referred to the early practice of selling troublesome slaves to the owners of sugar cane plantations on the lower Mississippi

sell-out as "corrupt contract that sacrifices public for private interest" is from 1862

sell-through is the ratio of the quantity of goods sold by a retail outlet to the quantity distributed by it

seltzer water is the same as mineral water

a **semantic field** is a set of related words or phrases, for example, "verbs of perception," "nouns of art objects"

the **semiprecious stones** come just after the precious and are prized for their beauty and durability: amethyst, lapis lazuli, aquamarine, topaz, tourmaline, opal, turquoise, and garnet

semi-sweet chocolate is generally a little sweeter than bittersweet chocolate

semolina flour is made from durum wheat and used almost exclusively for pasta

send-up, "a spoof," is British slang, 1958, from the earlier verb phrase send up, "to mock, make fun of" (1931), from send + up, perhaps a transferred sense of the public school term for "to send a boy to the headmaster" (usually for punishment), which is attested from 1821

senior citizen is first seen in print in the 1930s

a **sentence adverb** (like "incidentally") is one that qualifies an entire sentence rather than a single word

sentence sense is the ability to recognize a grammatically complete sentence

a **sentential function** is an expression that contains one or more variables and becomes a declarative sentence when constants are substituted for the variables

{ the line down the center of the tongue is the **septum linguae** }

sequential art is a form of art where the content is presented in a series of artistic items positioned in a specific order to convey its message or effect

the **serial comma** is the second comma in "potato salad, pasta salad, and Waldorf salad"; the serial comma is a comma preceding the final conjunction in a list of three or more items; also called Harvard comma, Oxford comma

the term serial has been applied to murderers since at least the early 1960s, but the term **serial killer** (1981) came later

a **serial number** is so called as it shows the position of an item in a series

servants' quarters in Victorian days were usually referred to as "below stairs"; "above stairs" was the realm of the family

in tennis, **service game** is a game in which a particular player serves

a **service mark** is a proprietary term, such as Blue Cross and Blue Shield, American Express, or Planned Parenthood, that is registered with the Patent and Trademark Office

a **service pack** in computing is an update to a customer's software that may fix existing problems or deliver product enhancements

service road and frontage road are synonyms

a **serving suggestion** is about how a particular food could be served, used especially on the packaging of ready meals where the illustration is markedly different to the contents

a **set phrase** is one that is unvarying and having a specific meaning such as "raining cats and dogs"; a set phrase can be one like "make amends," the only use/context of the word "amends"

a **set piece** is a thing that has been carefully or elaborately composed or planned, e.g., speech, writing, but also something like a fireworks display arranged to form a design

one's **set point** (for happiness) is a genetically determined level of happiness, to which one returns after positive or negative emotional experiences

set/get off on the wrong foot goes back to the Romans and their superstitions about left-handed things being evil

set-in sleeves are sleeves made separate from the body of the garment for later attachment to the armholes

the **seven deadly sins** are pride, covetousness, lust, anger, gluttony, envy, and sloth

the **Seven Dwarfs** are Happy, Sleepy, Doc, Bashful, Sneezy, Grumpy, and Dopey

the **Seven Seas**, a term by 1872, are the Arctic, Antarctic, North Atlantic, South Atlantic, North Pacific, South Pacific, and Indian Oceans

the **seventh art** is the art of the cinema

seventh heaven may originate with the Koran's top of the seven-tiered heaven

seven-up, the children's game, is from 1830; with capital initials as the proprietary name of a brand of carbonated drink, it is attested from 1928

the **seven-year itch** (1899) began as some sort of skin condition (sometimes identified with poison ivy infection) that either lasts seven years or returns every seven years; then the "urge to stray from marital fidelity" is attested from 1952

{ **Seville oranges** are bitter tasting and have a flattened appearance and rough skin }

sex discrimination, though coined in the United States by 1916, did not reach widespread use until the 1960s

sex drive (1918), **sex object** (1911, first a technical term in psychology), and **sex symbol** (1911) have been in use for close to one hundred years

Shangri La, the imaginary earthly paradise, was the name of Tibetan utopia in James Hilton's novel *Lost Horizon* (1933); in Tibetan, *la* means "mountain pass"

a **shape poem** is a poem written in such a way that the lines form a pattern, usually related to the subject matter of the poem

the **shar-pei**'s name is from Chinese, *sha pi*, literally "sand skin"

Sheer Thursday is a synonym for Maundy Thursday

a **sheet cake** is a simple one-layer cake that is either topped with frosting or has other ingredients rolled into it

sheet lightning appears as a broad sheet-like illumination of parts of a thundercloud, caused by the reflection of a lightning flash

sheet rock is pre-hardened plaster of Paris (gypsum) sold in large sheets and used as a wall surface in building construction; originally a trade name, it is also called by the generic term wall board

a **shell game** is a sleight-of-hand swindling game resembling thimblerig but employing walnut shells or the like instead of thimble-like cups

shepherd's pie (once cottage pie) got its name from the meat it originally contained—lamb or mutton

a small black-and-white check pattern is **shepherd's plaid**

{ a **shield law** is one that protects journalists from having to reveal confidential sources }

shih tzu, the dog breed from Asia, is from Mandarin Chinese *shizi gou*, "lion dog," because it was bred with the features of the traditional Chinese representation of a lion

shilly-shally is from the earlier "shill I, shall I," a fanciful reduplication of "shall I?"

shin splints is a painful condition of the front lower leg associated with tendonitis, stress fractures, or muscle strain, often occurring as a result of running or other strenuous athletic activity, especially on a nonresilient surface; the term is still used by athletes, but no longer used by most doctors because it is too vague

ship's bells are the strokes on a ship's bell every half hour to mark the passage of time; in each of the day's six watches of four hours, one bell marks the end of the first half hour, eight bells marks the end of the watch

ship's company is the crew of a ship between peak and off-peak times

Henry Wadsworth Longfellow coined **ships passing in the night** in his 1863 poem "The Theologian's Tale"

Shirley Temple is a children's mocktail made with lemon-lime soda and grenadine syrup and topped with a cherry

shirred eggs are baked in butter with salt and pepper

shish kebab takes its name from Turkish *sis*, "skewer," and *kebap*, "roast meat,"—also spelled shish kebob, shish cabob—and the pieces of meat themselves are called kebabs

a bungee or other elastic cord with hooks on the ends is a **shock cord**

shoepeg corn is an heirloom variety of sweet corn with kernels tightly formed on the cob that does not grow in straight rows but in irregular, jagged groupings and is named for the small wooden pegs that held shoe soles in place during the 1800s; it has small and narrow-shaped kernels that are white in color, providing a slightly sweeter, milky flavor than the traditional yellow sweet corn kernels

shoo-fly pie is so named from the need to shoo flies away from the molasses confection

a **shooting star** is actually the luminous trace produced when a meteorite burns up as it enters Earth's atmosphere

a **shooting stick** is a walking stick with a handle that unfolds to form a seat and a sharp end that goes in the ground

shop time is the time for which a vehicle or machine is out of service for repair or the time spent by a foundry or machine shop to make a custom item

a **shore cliff** is a steep, rock-faced shoreline shaped by a sea

{ **short commons** is a term for the insufficient allocation of food }

short crust is lighter and crispier than regular pastry crust

the **short game** in golf involves approach shots and putting

a **short order** is an a la carte serving of one dish; a **short stack** is one or two pancakes instead of a regular stack

short pastry has some sort of fat added to make it soft and flaky

short ribs are a cut of beef consisting of rib ends between the rib roast and the plate

short sauce refers to potatoes, turnips, onions, pumpkins, etc.

shrift means "absolution, penance" and **short shrift** first meant a brief space of time allowed to a criminal to make his confession and receive absolution before being executed

shortbread, **shortcake**, and **short pastry** are made with shortening—"short" in this case meaning that the added fat makes the dough crumble easily

a **shortened form** is an abbreviated form of a multisyllable word, like auto from automobile

short-sleeve is first recorded in 1639 in an ordinance of Massachusetts Bay colony, forbidding "short sleeves, whereby the nakedness of the arm may be discovered"

being **short-waisted** means having a proportionately short upper body

short-wave (1907) is a radio wavelength less than 100 meters

a **shot glass** or jigger is traditionally 1.5 fluid ounces

the **shotgun approach** is the use of breadth, spread, or quantity in lieu of accuracy, planning, etc.

shovel prune is to dig up and dispose of a plant; also written shovel-prune

a **shovelful of work** is "very little work"

a **show barn** is a building for exhibiting cattle and other domestic animals, such as at a county fairgrounds

show-and-tell as an elementary school teaching tool is attested by 1948

show-off, "a display" (noun), is attested by 1776, and as a person who makes an ostentatious display, attested from 1924; the verb is first recorded in 1793

Shredded Wheat was introduced in 1892 by Henry D. Perky of Denver

violets actually shrink as if they become shy, giving us the term **shrinking violet**

shrub celery is the crisp, thick leafstalk of the celery plant, used as a vegetable or eaten raw

the button you push on a camera to take a picture is the **shutter release**

shuttle diplomacy refers to international negotiations conducted by a mediator who frequently flies back and forth between the negotiating parties

Siamese twins is a term originating with the famous Siamese twins Chang and Eng (1811–1874)

a **side chair** has no arms

side effect was first recorded in 1884, though the medical use is from 1939

the **side plate** is a plate smaller than a dinner plate, used for bread, etc.

side-dressing is fertilizer placed in or near a row where plants are growing

a **sidereal month** is the time it takes for the Moon to make one complete orbit of the Earth, approximately 27.3217 sidereal days or 27 days 5 hours 55 minutes and 49.44 seconds

side-slip is a term for an illegitimate child

sidestream smoke is that from a cigarette that passes into the surrounding air, not the smoker

{ **sidewalk surfing** is skateboarding, especially as a means of transportation }

the end of the telescope held to the eye is the **sight hole**

sight reading is to read, play, or sing without previous practice, rehearsal, or study of the material to be treated

the **signature block** is the typed or printed name and title of a person appearing below a signature at the bottom of a letter

the **silent butler** is the container used to collect table crumbs in fancy restaurants

as a metaphor for the departed, the term **silent majority** dates to the nineteenth century, then took its present meaning around 1955

Silicon Alley denotes a group of Internet-related companies in New York City

Silicon Valley (1974) originally and specifically applied to the Santa Clara Valley, southeast of San Francisco

silk-screen printing is a method of reproducing colored artwork using a cut stencil attached to a stretched, fine-meshed silk screen

Silly Putty is a silicone-based substance

silly season is any slow news period characterized by trivial news or no news a **silly straw** is a drinking straw with a fixed, amusing shape that includes loops

silver bullet (c. 1808), meaning "very effective, almost magical remedy," comes from the belief in the magical power of silver weapons to conquer foes, which goes back at least to ancient Greece, as in the Delphic Oracle's advice to Philip of Macedon

Milton's "Comus" contains the first reference to a cloud having a **silver lining**

silver lining first appeared in the 1915 wartime song "Keep the Home Fires Burning" (I. Novello and L. Gilbert)

silver plate is metal with a thin coating of silver

originally, all movie screens were given a reflective surface by the application of metallic paint—hence, **silver screen**

silver thaw is a glassy coating of ice on the ground or other surface, caused by freezing rain or refreezing of thawed ice

simnel cake is a rich fruit cake with a layer of marzipan on top, eaten especially at Easter or during Lent

Simon Legree was the cruel slave dealer in an anti-slavery novel by Harriet Beecher Stowe, hence a cruel employer that demands excessive work from the employees

the **simon-pure** is from Simon Pure, the name of a Quaker who is impersonated by another character (Colonel Feignwell) in part of the comedy *A Bold Stroke for a Wife* (1717) by Susannah Centlivre, English dramatist and actress; the real Simon Pure is dealt with as an imposter and is believed only after he has proved his identity

a **simple fruit** is an indehiscent fruit derived from a single ovary having one or many seeds within a fleshy wall or pericarp, e.g., grape, tomato, or cranberry

unlike **simple interest** which is paid only on the principal, **compound interest** is paid also on the previous interest earned

simple syrup is sugar and water cooked over low-to-medium heat while stirring till the sugar is dissolved and the mixture is clear

simplified Chinese is that written using simplified characters, and is used in the People's Republic of China and Singapore

sine die, "indefinitely," is Latin, "without (fixed) day"

sine qua non, "an indispensable condition," is Latin for "without which not"—and has more force than "essential," as without it you will not get what you want

to **sing small** is to have little to say for yourself

single flower denotes a flower with but one set of petals, as a wild rose

unblended whiskey is called **single malt** and contains whiskey from one distillery at one age; blended Scotch contains whiskeys from various distilleries

sippy cup refers to any spill-proof cup for toddlers

sis-boom-bah is a cheerleading chant from 1867, an echoic phrase imitating the sound of a skyrocket flight (sis), the burst of the fireworks (boom), and the reaction of the crowd ((b)ah)

sister languages are related because they descend from a common ancestor (proto-language)

foresters use **site index** to indicate a measurement of the capability of an area for growing trees

sit-in in reference to session musicians dates to 1936; 1937, in reference to union action; and 1941, in reference to student protests

a person's **sitting height** is the measurement of the distance from the supporting surface to the top of the head

{ **sit-ups**, a kind of physical exercise, date to 1955 }

sitz bath originated in Germany from *sitz* (seat) and *bad* (bath)

six of one, half dozen of the other has been traced to an 1836 novel by Frederick Marryat

the **six perfections** in Mahayana Buddhism are the six virtues that the bodhisattva must practice in their avowed pursuit of bringing all beings to enlightenment through bodhicitta; they are dana (munificence), sila (ethicality), ksanti (patience), virya (determination), dhyana (meditation), and prajna (wisdom)

the **sixth sense** is intuition or clairvoyance

sixty-cycle hum is the sound generated by the alternation of current in electronic devices

the **sixty-four dollar question** on the U.S. radio quiz (1942) became the **sixty-four thousand dollar question** on television (1955)

a **skateboard deck** is the flat part of a skateboard on which the rider stands

skeleton key (c. 1810) is a minimal key designed to fit many locks by having the interior of the bit hollowed

a **skid flip** in tenpin bowling is a bowl where the ball skids a long way before it starts to roll

skid row (1931) is from skid road, "track of skids along which logs are rolled" (1851); the sense was extended to "part of town inhabited by loggers" (1906), then, by hobos, to "disreputable district" (1915)

skim milk has no cream in it; the original form was skimmed milk

a **skin flint** was once one who, in trying to save money on flint for making fire, would split a piece down to its final layer, or "skin"

a **skirt steak** is a boneless cut of beef from the lower part of the brisket (skirt meaning "the diaphragm or midriff of an animal")

the **skunk eye** is a facial expression of distrust or dislike (also **stink eye** or **hairy eyeball**)

sky-parlor is an attic

before any turn of the tide, there is a time of **slack water** or **slack tide**

a **slanging match** is a prolonged exchange of insults

a **slash pocket** is one to which access is provided by a vertical or diagonal slit in the outside of the garment, as opposed to a **patch pocket**, a flat pocket sewn to the outside of a garment

slate gray is a dark bluish-gray color

{ **slide fastener** is an old term for zipper }

a pliers' articulating axle is the **slip joint**

a **slip knot** can be undone by a pull

Sloane Ranger, "fashionable but conventional young woman of London," is from 1975, from Sloane Square, near Chelsea, with a play on Lone Ranger

the first reference to **sloppy joe** is from 1961, in the *Burger Cook Book*: sloppy joes consist of ground beef, onions, celery, sweet pickle relish, brown sugar, Worcestershire sauce, chili sauce, vinegar, green pepper, hamburger buns

a screw with a single groove in the head is a **slotted head**

deep depression can be called the **slough of despond**

a **sloven's year** is a wonderfully prosperous year when even a poor farmer has good crops

slow food is any dish or meal cooked with care and attention to detail, often according to traditional recipes and using few or no new appliances like microwaves

slush fund originated in the British Navy, as it was formerly customary on war vessels to use slush and other refuse to raise a fund for the benefit of enlisted men; slush in this sense was fat, grease, and other refuse from the cook's galley

a **small beer** is one of only slight alcoholic strength

a **small capital** is the same height as a lowercase letter

small fruits are currants, raspberries, strawberries, etc.

the **small hours** are midnight or 1:00 a.m. to dawn, when the numbered hours are "small"

the **small intestine** is the duodenum, jejunum, and ileum

smallest room refers to the toilet, lavatory, loo, or bathroom

small-time was originally theater slang for lower-salaried circuits, or ones requiring more daily performances

the **Smart Car** was launched in 1998 in Europe

a **smart card** (1980) is different from a credit card in that it has a microprocessor

smart money is money bet by those in the know (1926), and earlier than that it meant "money paid to sailors, soldiers, workers, etc., who have been disabled while on the job" (1693)

curved and straight quotes are also sometimes referred to as **smart quotes** and **dumb quotes**, respectively; these names are in reference to the name of a function (found in word processors like Microsoft Word) that automatically converts straight quotes typed by the user into curved quotes

Smith & Wesson is the proprietary name of a type of firearm from the gunsmith firm of Horace Smith (1808–93) and Daniel B. Wesson (1825–1906) in Springfield, Massachusetts (1860)

Smithfield ham, originally from Smithfield, Virginia, is a lean country-cured Virginia ham that goes through elaborate curing, seasoning, smoking, and aging

smoke screen was first used as a form of military camouflage

Smokey Bear, "state policeman," dates to 1974 truckers' slang, in reference to the wide-brim style of hat worn by state troopers

a **smoking gun** is a piece of incriminating evidence that is incontrovertible

the **smoking point** is the temperature at which fats in cooking oils begin to break down, creating smoke as the oil is cooked

smooth jazz is a modern form of jazz first developed in the 1970s that blends in elements of rhythm and blues

smooth muscle is short and involuntary

Snakes and Ladders evolved at the beginning of the twentieth century from an Indian game called *moksha patamu,* "heaven and hell"

snap beans are so named because the pods are broken into pieces to be eaten

snapper-back is another term for the center in football

snare drum is probably named for Dutch *snare,* "harp string"

the shield around a salad bar is the **sneeze guard**

a **sniff test** is a "reality check" of a new idea or venture, consisting of very basic questions about whether the idea makes sense or has any chance of being feasible

a drive-up mailbox is called a **snorkel box** because of the curve of the drop slot

the **Snow Belt** or **Frost Belt** comprises the Midwest and Northeast; the **Sun Belt** is the South and Southwest

snow berm is a ridge of snow graded up by a plow

snow broth is snow melted and trodden into slush

snow crystals you see on windows are actually **stellar crystals**

a **snow groomer** is a truck or other vehicle, either with tracks running along both sides or dragging equipment behind, used to maintain ski hills and groom (pack down) snow

the allusion of **snow job** is that of an object concealed under innocent-looking snow

a **snow park** is an area of a piste created for snowboarders and skiers to do tricks

snow peas have flat, edible pea pods that contain tiny peas; **sugar snap peas** or **sugar peas** are a cross between snow peas and garden peas; both are eaten in the pods and do not require shelling

{ **snow showers** only occur when the air temperature is lower than 32 degrees F }

snowball's chance in hell dates from the 1950s

snow-bones are patches of snow still seen in furrows, ridges, or ruts after a thaw

a **soaker hose** is one with hundreds of tiny holes from which water trickles into a garden or yard

soap box, first a box for holding soap (1660), later referred to a wooden crate in which soap was packed and which was a makeshift stand for a public orator since at least 1907; also used by children to make racing carts (1933)

soap opera goes back to the early days of radio suspense serials, which were mainly sponsored by soap-makers; in soap opera (1939), the "opera" part is an echo of the earlier "horse opera" (a Western, 1927)

social Darwinism is an application of Darwinism to the study of human society, specifically a theory in sociology that individuals or groups achieve advantage over others as the result of genetic or biological superiority

social engineering is the application of sociological principles to specific social problems

a **social insect** is any insect that shares shelter, defense, and food, and reproduces cooperatively

P.A. Sorokin coined the term **social mobility** in 1925

social philosophy deals with the ethical values of a society

social security is a term coined by Winston Churchill in 1908, but it did not come into widespread use until the 1930s

social worker (1904) derived from the term social work (1890)

socialized medicine is a system of medical care that is financed and administered by the state

the **Socratic method** is a teaching technique in which a teacher does not give information directly but instead asks a series of questions, with the result that the student comes either to the desired knowledge by answering the questions or to a deeper awareness of the limits of knowledge

{ **soda pop** is flavored soda water }

soda water does not contain soda but is either carbonated water or a solution of water, sodium bicarbonate, and acid

soft answer is a phrase of Biblical origin

soft in the term **soft drink** means nonalcoholic (especially carbonated) as opposed to alcoholic "hard"

soft fruit is fruit that grows on bushes, such as berries, strawberries, and currants, as contrasted with "top fruit"

soft g is the "g" sound in "gem," "giraffe," and "generation," as distinct from the hard "g" in "get" and "give"

soft goods refers to textile products, as clothing, fabrics, and bedding

soft landing is a term for the best possible result in a difficult situation

a **soft market** is one in which prices are falling because supply exceeds demand

soft water is free of unwanted chemicals like iron and sulfur

a **soft-shell crab** is one (especially blue) that has recently molted and has a new shell that is soft and edible

software program is a redundancy

soi-disant means "self-styled" or "so called"

a **solar day** is the time it takes for a place on Earth directly facing the Sun to make a complete revolution and return to the same place facing the sun: twenty-three hours, fifty-six minutes

some pumpkins is an important or impressive person

someone's name is mud originates with Dr. Samuel Mudd, who got into big trouble for treating the injuries of John Wilkes Booth after he assassinated President Abraham Lincoln

son of a gun is nautical in origin, as women commonly gave birth beneath the guns of a ship

sonic boom (1952) was a familiar sound (shock waves in the air around a supersonic aircraft) in the early 1950s when aircraft makers were obsessed with breaking the sound barrier (1939)

sonic branding is the use of a specific sound or piece of music to identify or reinforce a product, brand, or organization

in a **solar eclipse**, the Moon passes between the Sun and Earth so the Moon's shadow falls on the Earth

solar flowers are flowers which open and shut daily at certain hours

the **solar plexus** is Latin for "sun" and "something woven"—as the network of nerves in the area of the belly are like the rays of the sun

the **solar wind** is a continuous flow of charged particles from the Sun, permeating the solar system; **stellar wind** is a steady or unsteady outflow of material from the surface of a star

sol-fa is from Latin for two notes of the musical scale and is related to *solfeggio*, "use the sol-fa system"

sotto voce is an expressive way of saying "confidentially" or "in an aside"

soul food is a term dating from the 1960s

a **soul patch** is a small growth of male facial hair just below the lower lip and above the chin

sound bite (1980) came into prominence in the 1988 U.S. presidential election

the **sound hole** is an aperture in the belly of a stringed instrument

a **sounding balloon** is used to collect atmospheric data up to an altitude of 20 miles

a **soup bunch** is a small bunch of vegetables set aside to make soup

soup to nuts comes from the early twentieth century, when the first course was traditionally soup and would be finished with a serving of nuts

soup-and-fish refers to the attire white tie and tails

sour cream is cream that has been deliberately fermented with certain bacteria

sour grapes comes from Aesop's fable "The Fox and the Grapes"

southern-fried means coated in flour, egg, and bread crumbs and then deep-fried

wild oats are relatively worthless weeds, so **sowing wild oats** would be "planting a worthless crop"

soy milk is soaked, ground, and cooked soybeans which become a milky liquid

soy in **soy sauce** translates to "salted bean oil"

the **soya bean** is the oil- and protein-rich seed of the soybean plant

the **space age** was christened with that term in 1946 (along with space vehicle)

a **space blanket** is often made of a plastic material covered with a reflective metal agent and is designed to reduce heat loss from a person's body following trauma

{ **space junk** is debris from spaceships and satellites that remains in Earth's orbit }

space shuttle was coined in a fictional context in 1960, then applied to a real vehicle in 1969

to call a **spade a spade** is based on gardening, not poker

a **spading fork** is the garden implement with long tines used for loosening soil

spaghetti alla carbonara is spaghetti in a sauce of cream, eggs, Parmesan cheese, small pieces of bacon, and vegetables, such as peas

spaghetti Bolognese is spaghetti in the style of Bologna

spaghetti squash has flesh that forms translucent spaghetti-like strands when cooked

spaghetti suit to astronauts denotes their long underwear, made of tubes

the Japanese equivalent of a **spaghetti western** is a **sukiyaki western**

Spanish America is applied to only that part of Latin America where Spanish is the chief language

a **Spanish olive** is a young green olive that is soaked in lye then fermented in brine for six to twelve months

spanking new originally described a fresh, lively breeze

spare ribs (1596) get their name from spare meaning "absence of fat" or perhaps from German *ribbesper*, "spare ribs"

the **spare tire well** is the depression in the trunk of an automobile where the spare tire is stowed

sparkling water is a name for several types of carbonated water on the market with deceptively similar descriptions: some are naturally effervescent mineral waters, some are artificially effervescent mineral waters, and some are artificially carbonated, but not mineral, waters

sparkling wine is the generic term for any wine that is naturally or artificially effervescent; **Asti Spumante** is artificially effervescent wine from Asti (spumante, "sparkling"), while champagne is naturally effervescent wine from Champagne

sparrow dominoes is another name for the game of mah-jongg

sparrow-fart is daybreak, very early morning

a **spear carrier** is either an actor in a walk-on part or someone else who is an unimportant participant is something

Special English is a 1,500-word vocabulary and short, simple phrases without the idioms and clichés of colloquial English used by broadcasters, who speak at about two-thirds the speed of conversational English

special ops dates only from the late twentieth century

the uncapitalized second part of a Latin classification name (genus) is the **specific epithet** or **trivial name**, such as *Acer saccharum* (sugar maple)

a **speech bubble** is a rounded outline containing words, representing speech in a cartoon

a **speech community** is a group of people largely alike in the language they use

a **speech tag** is an attributive phrase for reported utterances, e.g., "he said" for dialogue

{ the small punching bag used by boxers is called a **speed bag** }

speed dating is a type of matchmaking service where participants meet for seven to eight minutes each before moving on to another participant, ultimately making a list of those they are interested in dating; it is said to have started in the U.S. Jewish community (2000)

sperm whale is a shortening of spermaceti whale—so called because the waxy substance in its head was mistaken for sperm

the medical term for an ice cream headache is **spheno pulatine ganglio neuralgia**

spic-and-span comes from spick-and-span-new (1579), "new as a recently made spike and chip of wood," from spick, "nail," and span-new, "very new"

in **spill the beans**, first recorded in 1919, spill means "divulge," a usage dating from the 1500s

spin a yarn is nautical in origin from making and repairing ropes, which involved twisting long threads, or "yarns," while telling tales

spin doctor, a person who publicizes favorable interpretations of the words and actions of a public figure, is a term that came around about 1984

a **spirit level** is filled with alcohol (spirit) or ether

the little statue on a Rolls-Royce grill is named **Spirit of Ecstasy**

the little sink next to the dentist's chair is the **spit sink**

spitting image, from "spit and image," likely started as the statement "He's the very spirit and image of father/mother"

a **splat mat** is a waterproof and easily washable sheet used to collect food dropped by a small child while eating, or otherwise to protect easily soiled surfaces

a **split infinitive** example is "to boldly go where no man has gone before!" where the infinitive is "to go," and it has been "split" by the adverb "boldly"—considered poor style but not bad grammar

the **split pea** is a dried variety of a yellow or green pea

J.J. Thomson was the first person who **split the atom** (1909)

a **sponge bath** is an all-over washing of the body with a sponge or washcloth instead of a bath or shower

sponge cake is made of egg yolks and sugar beaten until fluffy, and then beaten egg whites are folded in; the eggs are the only leavening agent in the cake

{ **spoon bread** is soft cornbread served with a spoon and is also called egg bread or butter bread }

a **sporting house** is a term for a house of ill repute

sport-utility vehicle should be hyphenated, as should **all-terrain vehicle**

spotted dick (or spotted dog) is a steamed British pudding of suet and raisins or currants

spouse-breach is adultery

spread-eagle is literally "splayed eagle," a heraldic term; the meaning "person secured with arms and legs stretched out" (originally to be flogged) is attested from 1785

spring a leak first referred to ships, describing the way the timbers sprang out of position and let in water

a **spring chicken** is a young fowl ready for eating, which was originally in the spring

spring festival is another term for Chinese New Year

spring onion is another term for the scallion

spring rolls traditionally have a lighter, more delicate pastry wrap and are smaller than egg rolls

when the Sun and Moon are either on the same or opposite sides of the earth, the highest tides result, which are called **spring tides**

a **springform pan** is a tall, round baking pan with a clamp on the side which releases the sides from the bottom, allowing a cake to be easily removed when done

spumoni ice cream is an Italian style of ice cream of a very fine and smooth texture, usually containing layers of various colors and flavors and chopped fruit or nuts

Spy Wednesday is the Wednesday immediately preceding the festival of Easter, so called in allusion to the betrayal of Christ by Judas Iscariot

a **squall line** is a line or extended narrow region within which squalls or thunderstorms occur, often several hundred miles long

in **square deal**, square means "fair, adequate, satisfying"

to have **square eyes** is used to describe someone addicted to television

square meal may derive from the square platters used for serving meals on ships

a **square pyramid** is a three-dimensional geometric figure with a square base and four triangular sides that connect at one point, such as the Great Pyramid of Giza

a **square root** (c. 1557) is a divisor of a quantity that when squared gives the quantity

{ **squaw winter** is a brief cold snap preceding Indian summer }

a **squawk sheet** is a brief report written up by a pilot or driver about anything needing inspection, correction, or repair in an airplane, truck, or car

squeeze box is an informal synonym for accordion or concertina

squint media is any visual media, as television broadcasts, offered on small devices, such as cell phones and PDAs

a **squirrel cage** is one with a cylindrical framework that rotates as a small animal runs inside it; now, figuratively, any situation that seems to be endlessly without goal or achievement

squirrel-headed is narrow-minded

Sri Lanka was formerly Ceylon

stage diving is the practice of jumping from the stage in a rock concert to be caught and carried aloft by the crowd

stage phoning is an attempt to impress others by talking on a cell phone in a dramatic or animated manner

a **stage whisper** is a way of speaking that uses a lot of breath so the voice projects into the theater and sounds like a loud whisper

a **stag-headed tree** has dead branches at the top

stained glass, transparent colored glass formed into decorative mosaics, has existed since at least 1791

stained-glass ceiling is any unofficially acknowledged barrier to advancement in the clergy or in other fields on the basis of religious beliefs

stainless steel (1917) is a chromium-steel alloy (usually 14 percent chromium) used for cutlery, etc., so called because it is highly resistant to rust or tarnish

a **stair turret** is a turret filled by a winding staircase

the dented end of a tomato is the **stalk end**

stamping ground originally referred to a location frequented or frequently returned to by animals

stand by (c.1250), "to await, support," was an order to hold one's self in readiness and in that meaning recorded from 1669

stand for (1567) meant "represent, be in place of" and then "endure, undergo" (1606) and "tolerate" in 1626

stand pat derives from an adverbial use of pat, the obsolete "to strike accurately"

to **stand up** (someone) "fail to keep an appointment" is attested from 1902

standard deviation is a measure of the scattering or dispersal of data—calculated by taking the square root of the average of the squares of the individual deviations

standard transmission refers to a transmission that is operated manually with a gear lever and a clutch pedal

a **standing army** is a permanent army maintained in time of peace and war

the **standing part** in knot tying is the main section of rope, as opposed to the free end

the term **stand-up comedy** only dates from the 1960s

the **Stanford-Binet** intelligence test was first published in 1916 as a revision and extension of the Binet-Simon intelligence tests, from Stanford University and Alfred Binet (1857–1911)

a **staple puller** is the device designed to remove staples from paper, typically a small device with a spring-loaded hinge and four curved metal members resembling teeth

a **star cloud** is a region where there appears to be numerous stars close together

the six-pointed figure consisting of two interlaced equilateral triangles (hexagram), used as a Jewish and Israeli symbol, is the **Star of David**, or Magen David, or Mogen David

stark naked is a corruption of start naked, from Anglo-Saxon *steort*, meaning "tail"—as it described being naked to the tail

Stars and Stripes for the American flag is attested from 1782, and Stars and Bars as a name for the Confederate flag is attested from 1863

start from scratch comes from giving handicaps to some competitors in racing; a contestant who starts from scratch (a line scratched in the turf or gravel) is the one who has no special advantage

a **starter marriage** is a first marriage that lasts under five years and produces no children, where divorce is expected to "trade up" to someone better

state-of-the-art (1967) comes from the earlier "status of the art" (1889)

state's evidence usually refers to a participant or accomplice in a crime who gives evidence to the prosecution, especially in return for a reduced sentence

when you see a bird floating on a warm thermal of air, that is **static soaring**

the **stations of the cross** mark the stages of Jesus's journey to his crucifixion and burial

statuary marble is any white, crystalline, saccharoidal marble suitable for sculpture

the **Statue of Liberty** was originally called "Liberty Enlightening the World"

status quo is Latin, literally, "the state in which"

the **statute** or land mile is 5,280 feet

steak Diane (c. 1957) is pan-cooked thin slices of tenderloin steak with seasonings, especially Worcestershire sauce

steak fries are large, thick, flat or wedge-shaped French fries

steal (someone's) thunder is from the 1700s when a person invented a machine to make stage thunder, which then went on to be used by others

a **steam room** has moist air; a **sauna** has dry air

a **steam table** has pans of boiling or simmering water under the food, so it is kept hot

stellar wind is a stream of ionized particles ejected from the surface of a star

stem cells are unspecialized cells that can go on to produce any type of specialized cell in the body

a **step-thru** refers to having an open space in an otherwise solid object through which a person can step or walk, e.g., a motor-scooter has a *step-thru* frame

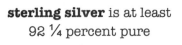

sterling silver is at least 92 ¼ percent pure

stick-in-the mud is based on the notion of "to stick in the mud, to be content to remain in an abject condition"

sticky rice is a short grain variety that sticks together when cooked

sticky wicket is an allusion to cricket, when a pitch dries after rain

the plural of **still life** is still lifes

a **stinky pinky** is a noun paired with a rhyming adjective (fat cat)

in **stir fry**, small pieces of food are cooked in a small quantity of oil over high heat for a brief period of time, stirring constantly

stir-crazy (1908) is from stir, meaning "prison," probably from Start Newgate (1757) prison in London

stock in **stock car** is from the standard or stock chassis used for such cars

stock market as a place where securities are bought and sold is from 1809; the original "stock market" (c.1350) was a fish and meat market in the City of London on or near the later site of Mansion House, so called perhaps because it occupied the site of a former stocks

stocking cap and **toboggan cap** are synonyms

the **Stone Age**, characterized by the use of stone tools and implements, is further divided into the Palaeolithic, Mesolithic, and Neolithic periods

with **stone crab**, only meat from the huge claws is consumed; the claws are removed and the crab is returned to the water so it can regenerate new claws

stone fruits (with stony endocarp) are cherry, peach, nectarine, apricot, plum, olive, mango, and date

stool pigeon comes from the original use of a pigeon fixed to a stool as a decoy

stoop labor is agricultural work done mostly in a stooping or squatting position

{ **stoop ball** is a baseball-like game played against a building or the steps of a stoop in place of a batter

a **stoop-gallant** is either an event that would humble a vain person or a fatal disease that knows no class boundaries

a **stop list** is a set of words automatically omitted from a computer search or index, usually the most frequent words, which would slow down processing or make results less satisfactory

the button you push to lock and unlock an umbrella's position is the **stop wire**

a **stopper knot** is a knot in string or rope to keep it from sliding through an opening

a **storm beach** is an expanse of gravel or sand thrown onto the coast by a storm

a **storm cuff** is a tight fitting one to prevent wind, rain, snow, etc. from getting inside a coat

a **storm door** is an extra outside door to prevent the entrance of wind, cold, rain, etc., usually removed in summer

a **storm lane**, or **tornado alley**, is a narrow belt that receives more than its fair share of storms, such as in the Midwest

a **storm surge** is a rise in the normal level of the sea along a coast due to the effects of a storm

storm troops (1917) was first a general term (from German *sturmtruppen*) for "shock troops," meaning highly trained soldiers for leading attacks

straight and narrow is a Biblical allusion from Matthew 7:14

straight from the horse's mouth comes from the way to tell a horse's age, by studying the teeth

in **straight pool**, the shooter may attempt to pocket any ball on the table; the object is to reach a set number of points determined by agreement before the game

straight up designates an alcoholic drink without a mixer or a chilled drink without ice, such as a martini; also called neat

the skin on the soles of your feet is the **stratum corneum,** "horny layer"

a **strawberry friend** is a freeloader, one who visits only when the strawberries are ready for picking

stream of consciousness is a term dating to 1855

striated muscle is long and voluntary, comprising all of the skeletal muscles

strictly for the birds (1950s) refers to horse manure, which is only good for picking over by birds

strike the set in theater is to dismantle a set completely

the earliest citations for **string along** are dated 1901

string beans are so called for the stringlike fibers along their sutures

strip steak is from the top loin muscle of the short loin, the most tender portion of beef; this goes by many names: **New York strip steak**, **boneless top loin**, **strip loin**, **hotel style steak**, **boneless club steak**

stud poker was first stud-horse poker, a variety that came about around 1879

a **studio apartment** is one containing a spacious room with large windows, which is or resembles an artist's studio; more recently, a small one-roomed apartment

Sturm und Drang is literally "storm and stress" from the late eighteenth-century German romanticism period, taken from the title of a 1776 romantic drama by poet Friedrich Maximilian von Klinger (1752–1831)

styptic in **styptic pencil** means "having the power of contracting organic tissue" and "arresting hemorrhage"

sub rosa, "privately, secretly," is Latin "under the rose," which was regarded as a symbol of secrecy

the **subject clause** is a clause that is the subject of a sentence, e.g., "The cat with no tail" in "The cat with no tail ran across the road"

in Miami, a **submarine sandwich** is called a **Cuban sandwich**, and in Maine, it is called an **Italian sandwich**

a **subordinate clause** or **dependent clause** cannot function as a sentence: his father, who is a drummer, wants him to play in the jazz band

a **subterranean stream** is a watercourse that flows through underground cavities

the permanent teeth that erupt to replace baby teeth are called **succedaneous teeth**

{ Mark Twain first used the term **sudden death** in 1865, in referring to rotgut whiskey }

sugar nippers were used for cutting loaf sugar into lumps

the **sugar pea** and **string bean** are fruits but the individual peas and beans are seeds

a **sugar shack** is a building where sap from a sugarbush is boiled down to make maple syrup

sugar snap peas are a cross between snow peas and garden peas and are eaten in their pods

the brown flecks on banana skins are **sugar spots**

sui generis refers to something so new, bizarre, or rare that it defies classification

sui juris is "legally competent to manage one's own affairs"

summer complaint is a term for any diarrheal disorder occurring in summer, especially when produced by heat and indigestion

summer sausage is a dried or smoked sausage that does not need refrigeration

summer squash are soft-shelled with thin edible skin and seeds: crookneck, pattypan, yellow squash, zucchini

summer stock is a term based on stock company, "a company who regularly act together at a particular theater"

a **summum bonum** is a supreme moral objective which should guide choices, actions, etc.

sun grins are the seeming smiles of someone whose eyes are not protected from bright sun

sun salutation is a series of twelve yoga postures performed in a single graceful flow with each movement coordinated with the breath; also called surya namaskar

sun shower (sun showers) is a rain shower while the sun is shining

Sunday artist is a term for an amateur artist who paints on Sundays only

Sunday school words are oaths and curses

the term **Sunday supplement** (in a newspaper) first occurred in 1905

sun-dried tomatoes are chewy, flavorful dark-red tomatoes made so by drying them in the sun; they are often packed in oil

surf kayaking is riding waves as a surfer while seated in a kayak

surf 'n' turf is an entrée of a serving each of seafood and meat; also written surf n' turf, surf and turf

the **surface boundary layer** is the lowest layer of the earth's atmosphere up to one kilometer

surface coal refers to cow dung, sometimes used as fuel

surface tension is the force that keeps drops of liquid, such as water, together, with the liquid's molecules pulled toward each other and the surface behaving like an elastic skin

surviving spouse is the Department of Defense term for widow or widower

to **swallow one's teeth** is to retract a statement

to say that someone **swallowed the dictionary** is to accuse them of using many long words

swan dive was once swallow dive, a forward dive in which the arms are extended sideways to simulate the outline of a swallow until just before entry into the water

swan song is based on an erroneous myth that a swan sings right before it dies

SWAT team stands for Special Weapons and Tactics team

{ the second hand on a clock is also called a **sweep hand** }

sweet and sour sauce and dishes usually combine sugar and vinegar in the flavoring

sweet corn is considered a vegetable rather than a grain

sweet potato is an informal name for the ocarina, a musical instrument

the **sweet potatoes** and yams in the stores are the same vegetable; true yams are not sold anywhere except a handful of specialty grocers—sweet potatoes are inside every yam can; black slaves brought to North America saw the resemblance of the sweet potato to their native plant, the true yam or *nyami* (a tuber with a sweetish taste); hence, our misnamed sweet potato

the **sweet spot** is dead center of the club, paddle, or racket face, or on a baseball bat or golf club, the precise spot that will deliver the maximum mass behind the ball

sweet tooth dates to 1390

Jonathan Swift gave us the phrase **sweet-ness and light**, describing bees as furnishing mankind with the sweetness of honey as well as the light from beeswax candles

Swiss Army knife originated in Ibach, Schwyz, Switzerland, in 1897, but despite efforts in the United States, the term is not a protected designation of origin and any knife can claim to be a Swiss Army knife

{ **Swiss chard** is a variety of beet, taking its name from French chardon, "thistle" }

Emmental or Gruyère are more specific names of **Swiss cheese**

Swiss steak is not from Switzerland but rather refers to an English cooking technique, "swissing," which tenderizes meat

a **switch plate** or **cover plate** is the flat piece that covers the wiring behind a light switch

swizzle sticks (1879) can be used to flatten the effervescence of a cocktail

in **sympathetic magic**, a supernatural connection is assumed between something that is or was closely associated with a person

a composite weather map of a broad region is a **synoptic chart**

Szechwan cuisine is a hot, oily, and spicy style of Chinese cooking; also called Szechwan-Hunan cuisine, also written Szechwan, Sichwan, Sichuan

{ T }

T cushion is the technical name for the removable cushion in a stuffed chair, which looks like a broad, squat "T"

Tabasco sauce was developed more than 125 years ago from a hot pepper that originated in Tabasco, Mexico

tabby cats get their name from a kind of fabric called tabby, since their striped or brindled coats of gray or tawny hues look like this fabric

another name for a coffee-table book is a **table book**

table d' hote, literally, "table of the host," means a complete meal with specified courses for a set price—and means the same as **prix fixe**

table mountain is another term for a mesa or plateau

table tennis is often called by its trademarked name, **Ping-Pong**

table wine is any wine of moderate quality suitable for drinking with a meal

a **tableau vivant** is a silent and motionless group of people arranged to represent a scene or incident

a **tablet chair** is one with an expanded arm for a writing surface—also used in schools as a desk

tabloid was originally a trademark (1884) for a small medicine tablet, and it evolved into the term **tabloid journalism** (1901) for small-format newspapers with sensational stories

tabula rasa is, literally, "scraped tablet"

the **tack coat** in road-making is a thin coating of tar or asphalt applied before a road is laid to form an adhesive bond

a **tackle block** is the pulley over which a rope runs

tackling a horse is harnessing it, especially to a wagon, etc.

tae kwon do is Korean for "art of hand and foot fighting" or "way of the hands and feet"

taedium vitae is more than world-weariness or ennui—but hints at a disgust with life

in visual design, a **tag cloud** is a type of display for weighted tags, with more frequently used tags depicted in a larger font or otherwise emphasized, while the displayed order is generally alphabetical

t'ai chi (short for *t'ai chi ch'uan*) is Chinese for "extreme limit" or "great supreme absolute" and constitutes the source and limit of life force

the **tail covert** signifies any of the smaller feathers covering the bases of the main feathers of a bird's tail

a fin at the posterior extremity of a fish's body is the **tail fin** or **caudal fin**

the **Taj Mahal**, Persian for "the best of buildings," is a mausoleum at Agra, India, built c.1640 by Shah Jahan for his favorite wife; its use as a name denoting anything excellent is attested from 1895

because those members of the British Parliament who belong to the majority party take the front seats, those who are in the minority **take a back seat**

take a gander is a reference to the bird's long neck

take a powder comes from "take a runout powder," with powder meaning "impetus, rush; impetuosity"

take down a peg is from British Navy jargon (eighteenth century) when a ship's colors were raised by pegs, and the higher the peg, the higher the honor

to **take for the kitchen** is to withdraw from a conversation or to remain silent

{ to **take out the onion** means to fake deep emotion }

use **take place** for scheduled events; use **occur** when something is accidental

take to the cleaners was probably inspired by the advent of commercial dry-cleaning establishments

take with a grain of salt alludes to an unappetizing meal that might be made better with the addition of some salt

takeaway food in England is takeout food in the United States.

taking the cake once meant literally winning the prize of a cake, awarded in a cakewalk

talk turkey may have come from the efforts of turkey hunters to attract their prey with gobbling noises

talking point is a topic that will invite discussion or even argument

tall timber is a dense and uninhabited forest

a **tambour desk** is one with desktop-based drawers and pigeonholes; the small drawers and nooks are covered, when required, by reeded or slatted shutters which usually retract into the two sides, left and right

the **tam-o'-shanter**, formerly worn by Scottish plowmen, comes from Tam O'Shanter, the name of the hero in a poem of the same name by Robert Burns, written 1790

a face of a wooden board is a **tangential section**; the sides are **radial sections**; the ends are **cross sections**

tank tops were named after the tank suits of the 1950s, as one-piece bathing costumes worn in a tank (swimming pool)

tape record as a noun (1905) was replaced by **tape recording**

tape recorders (1932) originally used steel tape

{ "fish eggs" is a colloquialism for **tapioca pudding**, which they resemble }

taps, the bugle call for lights out, is also called **last post**

tartar sauce is a translation from French *sauce tartare*, with *tartare* originally being a dish covered with breadcrumbs and grilled and served with a seasoned sauce; somehow *tartare* was influenced by Tartarus, "the Greek underworld," but was not ultimately derived from it

a **task bar** is a strip along the bottom of a computer screen that indicates what is happening with a task, offers information like date, time, open applications, etc., and allows launching of applications

a **tasting menu** is a set of small portions of a variety of dishes, served in courses as a prix-fixe restaurant meal

Mark Twain first used the term **tax return** in 1870

a **taxi dancer** is so called because she goes from one partner to another at the beck and call of the customer

taxi squad, a group of players that practice with a team but do not play, is derived from the use by a certain football team owner of his reserve players as taxi drivers

Tay-Sachs, a fatal inherited disorder, was named for British ophthalmologist Warren Tay (1843–1927) and U.S. physician and neurologist Warren Sachs (1858–1944) who described it in 1881 and 1887, respectively

T-bone (1916) was so called from the T-shaped bone that runs through it

a **tea ball** is also called an **infusion ball** or **tea egg**—and holds loose tea or herbs in boiled water

tea caddy derives from Malayan *kati*, "21 ounces," as the tea was once packaged in 21-ounce boxes

a **tea rose** is so called because its scent resembles that of tea

teacher's pet dates from the 1920s

on a CD, the surface where the disc's identification code is engraved is the **technical identification band**

technicolor yawn is an informal term for vomiting, dating to the early 1960s

teddy bear is named for U.S. president Theodore "Teddy" Roosevelt, a noted big-game hunter, whose conservationist fervor inspired a comic illustrated poem in the *New York Times* of January 7, 1906, about two bears named Teddy, whose names were transferred to two bears presented to the Bronx Zoo that year; the name was picked up by toy dealers in 1907 for a line of "Roosevelt bears" imported from Germany

it is **tee ball**, not T-ball

tee off on someone is not connected to golf but comes from the expression "teed off" or "tick off"

a **teeter-totter** is sometimes referred to as a **tilting board** or **dandle board**

an umbrella that can become shorter is a **telescopic umbrella**

the **temporal case** is a noun case used to specify a time, usually expressed by the preposition "at," as in "at six o'clock," "at midnight," "at Christmas"

a few hundred years ago, a **ten-foot pole** was used as part of land-surveying equipment

ten-gallon hat does not refer to capacity but may be borrowed from Mexican-Spanish *sombrero galon*, "braided hat"

teriyaki sauce is a sauce made from soy sauce, sake, sugar, ginger, and seasonings and used as a marinade for meats that are then grilled, broiled, or fried; teriyaki translates to "gloss, luster" and "roast"

{ a downright lie is a **terminological inexactitude** }

in Italian, **terra cotta** means "cooked earth"; terra cotta is the noun, and terra-cotta is the adjective

terra firma is Latin for "solid ground"

terra incognita, "unknown or unexplored region," is Latin for "unknown land," and it appeared on the earliest maps to signify unexplored areas

tertiary color is any color obtained by mixing the secondary colors—as orange and green to make olive or khaki

tertium quid is Latin "third something," first used in alchemy for "unidentified element present in a combination of two known ones"

a **test pattern** on TV allows viewers to adjust the quality of their reception

a **tête-à-tête** is an S-shaped sofa on which two people can sit face to face

Texas butter is another name for gravy

Texmati rice is an aromatic white or brown rice that is a cross between long-grain and basmati rice

a **text box** Is a rectangular widget that accepts textual input

text message arrived about 1978, at first in the context of computer networks, and then in the 1990s as applied to cell phones

textured vegetable protein is a high-protein product made from processed soybeans that are formed into chunks or ground and flavored to taste like meat

the carrot and the stick refers to reward and punishment

the phrase **the other day** first meant "the second day"—either forward or backward

the Pill (1957) became a practical reality in the early 1960s

theatrical properties are items used in stage plays and similar entertainments to further the action

the term **theme park** was first recorded in 1960 and denotes an amusement park built around a central theme—like a fantasy land, future world, past age, or aspect of nature

a **theme restaurant** is any eating establishment designed around a concept, especially a sport, time or era, music style, etc.

the ball of the thumb is also called the **thenar eminence**

in **there's the rub**, rub refers to an obstacle or difficulty

a likely source for the phrase **think outside the box** is the mathematical nine dots puzzle

think tank was a term by the early twentieth century and first referred to a brain

third degree refers to the highest degree in Freemasonry—a very difficult test of proficiency, where a person going for the Third Degree had to submit to grueling examinations; the colloquialism originated in the United States in 1900

the **third estate** is the common people; the first is clergy; the second is barons and knights

the **third eye** or **eye of insight** is located in the forehead between the eyes and may be activated in meditation or yoga

a **third rail** is a subject like Social Security, considered by politicians to be too dangerous to discuss or modify

the first "empire" was the Holy Roman Empire (up to 1806); the second was the Imperial German state of 1871–1918, making the **Third Reich** of Hitler the third (from German *Dritte Reich*, "third empire")

{ **third tongue** is a term for a slanderer or backbiter }

third wave is a term coined in the early 1980s by U.S. futurist Alvin Toffler to denote the age of information technology as a development of the agrarian first wave and the industrial second wave

a **third way** is an option or alternative to two extremes

Third World is a translation of French *tiers monde*, a 1950s term coined by a demographer

in cartooning there are **thought balloons**, **idea balloons**, **maledicta balloons**, and **speech balloons**

culinary lore has it that **Thousand Island dressing** was named for the group of almost two thousand small islands of the St. Lawrence River

thread count is a measure of the fineness of fabric; the total number of vertical and horizontal threads in one square inch

the expression **three dog night** originated with the Eskimos and means "a very cold night"—so cold that one has to bed down with three dogs to keep warm

when the ropes of a three-sheeted (a rope or chain attached to the lower corner of a sail) craft are extended, the sails flap and the craft sails out of control like a drunkard—giving us the phrase **three sheets to the wind**

the names of the **three wise monkeys** are Mizaru (see no evil), Mikazaru (hear no evil), and Mozaru (speak no evil)

a **three-piece set** of furniture is a sofa and two armchairs

three-point landing is an aircraft landing in which the two wheels of the main landing gear and the tail or nose wheel touch the ground simultaneously

a **three-point turn** in a vehicle is forward, backward, and forward again in a series of arcs

throw down the gauntlet, "to issue a challenge," comes from the practice of a medieval knight throwing down his metal glove as a challenge to combat

throw in the towel comes from boxing, a sign of surrender

throw out the baby with the bath-water is from a German proverb that dates to 1512

the ticket dispenser of a toll booth is actually called a **ticket spitter**

tic-tac-toe (or **tick-tack-toe**) is the North American term for noughts and crosses

a **tidal island** is a piece of land that is connected to the mainland at low tide but separated at high tide

a **tidal wave** is caused by the gravitational effect of the Moon and is on the surface (no deeper than 30 feet), while a tsunami is triggered by an earthquake, landslide, volcano, or meteorite and extends from the surface to the ocean floor

a **tide day** or **tidal day** is the length of time between one high tide and the next (a little less than twenty-five hours generally)

a **tiger lily** is so called because its flower is orange with black stripes and splotches

throw your hat in the ring was from early boxing days when locals could enter a boxing match by throwing their hat in the ring

thrown for a loss comes from American football, while **lose ground** is probably a military metaphor and is not from sports

the alphabet notches in a reference book are the **thumb index**

a **thumbnail sketch** is one of very small proportions, and the origin of the term is attributed to English painter William Hogarth, who sketched a tavern scene on his thumbnail when no paper was available

tight ship is literally one in which ropes and rigging are tied and taut

tighty whities are men's white underwear briefs

tikka masala is a style of Indian dish in which the main ingredient (such as chicken) is marinated, cooked in a tandoor, and served in a masala sauce

tilt at windmills is an allusion to Don Quixote, who attacked windmills, thinking they were giants

time depth is the period of time over which a language, language group, or culture evolves

{ **time warp** is a concept that arose in the 1950s and originally applied to science fiction }

having a **tin ear** is having insensitivity to music or to sounds of a given kind, from the idea of metal being incapable of sensation

tin god is a slang expression using tin in its senses of "pettiness, insignificance," "pretension," and "contempt"

in **tin lizzie**, lizzie is a slang corruption of limousine

Tin Pan Alley was an actual place on the side streets off Times Square—getting that name from cheap tinny pianos used there during music auditions

Henry David Thoreau in 1839 was the first to use the form **tinker's dam**—tinkers had a reputation for damning everything

tip one's hand is of U.S. origin and alludes to a hand of cards held in such a way that others can see them

the **tipping point** is when there is a buildup of minor incidents and this causes someone to do something they have previously resisted— or the culmination of a build-up of small changes that effects a big change

Tirami Su is actually supposed to be two words

a **tirliry-puffkin** is a lightheaded, flighty woman, a flirt

tirra-lirra is the repetitive melodic sound made by a songbird, such as a robin or lark

tit for tat is probably borrowed from Dutch *tip for tap*, "blow for blow"

to boot comes from an Anglo-Saxon word *bote/bot*, meaning "advantage or profit" and this boot is now obsolete except in the expression "to boot"

to live short is a New England term for "to live in poor circumstances or an undesirable place"

the expression **to strike it rich** arose in the California mining fields in the 1850s

to the manner born is a phrase first found in Shakespeare's *Hamlet*

the phrase **to wit** literally means "to know" and is a shortened form of the now obsolete "that is to wit," which meant "that is to say; namely"

toast points are triangular pieces of toast, often without the crust, used as the base of hors d'oeuvres and canapés

the bread slots in a toaster are called **toast wells**

to-do (1570s) is from Old English to don, "proper or necessary to be done"; the meaning "disturbance, fuss" was first recorded in 1827

the **toe edge** is the sharp edge on the long side of a snowboard closest to one's toes, regardless of which way one is facing or riding

toe jam is any material that collects between the toes; also written toe-jam

a **toe loop** in ice skating is a jump, assisted by the toe pick, on which the skater takes off from a back outside edge and lands on the same edge

toe the line first had to do with lining up for a race

the indented space under kitchen counters is the **toe-hole** or **kick space**

together by the ears means struggling or quarreling

toilet water or **eau de toilette** is a dilute form of perfume

tollhouse cookies are named after the Toll House in Whitman, Massachusetts, the source of the recipe

Tom Collins is a drink named after a nineteenth century London bartender

a **Tom Swifty**/Swiftie is a sentence with a made-up quotation and a punning adverb after it

tomato paste is tomatoes cooked for several hours, then strained and cooked longer to reduce them to a thick concentrate; the difference between tomato paste, tomato puree, and tomato sauce is texture and depth of flavor (thicker = deeper flavor)

there are **tom-dogs** as well as tomcats

the **Tommy gun** is a Thompson short-barreled submachine gun named for its co-inventor John T. Thompson

tom-tom, "drum," (a set of two single-membrane drums on a drum set) was originally used in India and comes from Hindi *tam-tam*, probably of imitative origin

the movable arm of a record player is the **tone arm**

tone color is the same as timbre, the quality of sound that distinguishes one voice or musical instrument from another

a tongue of a wooden board is a projecting tenon along the edge of a board, to be inserted into a groove or mortise in the edge of another board, hence, **tongue and groove**

a **tongue-fence** is a debate or argument

{ to be **tongue-whaled** is to be severely scolded }

tonic solfa is a system of naming the notes of a scale: do re mi fa sol la ti

tonic water is a carbonated beverage flavored with a small amount of quinine, lemon, and lime

toodle-oo, a colloquial "good-bye" word, is from 1907 but of unknown origin

tools of ignorance is a term for a baseball catcher's mask, shin guards, and chest pads

tooth music is the sound of chewing

Tootsie Rolls were created by confectioner Leo Hirschfield and named for his daughter Clara, nicknamed Tootsie

top banana and **second banana** are terms that were reinforced by the soft, banana-shaped bladder club used by burlesque comedians to hit other comedians

when a book is closed, the top of the pages is the **top edge**, the side is the **fore edge**, and the bottom is the **tail edge**

top fruit is fruit that grows on trees, contrasted with soft fruit

a **top note** is the highest in a piece of music or in a singer's vocal range; it can also refer to the dominant scent in a perfume

a **top round** is a cut of meat taken from an inner section of a round of beef

top sirloin is a lean boneless cut from the tender top loin; also called sirloin tip, loin tip, and triangle sirloin, top sirloin

top ten was first recorded in 1958, top twenty in 1959

the **topic sentence** is the one expressing the main idea of the paragraph in which it occurs

a **topographic landscape** is a landscape in which the terrain and features of a specific scene are accurately depicted

a **topographic map** is a map showing the relief features of the earth's surface, usually by means of contour lines to show changes in elevation; also called topo map, topo quad, contour map

top-sider, a kind of casual shoe (1937), gets its name from topside in the nautical sense of "upper deck of a ship," where the rubber soles would provide good traction

topsy-turvy likely comes from "tops" and obsolete "terve," "turn upside down, topple over"

a chef's hat is a **toque blanche**

a **toric lens** is used to correct the vision of someone with astigmatism—curved in such a way as to have a different focal length along each axis

putting things **to-rights** is to set them in order

a **torque wrench** is a tool for setting and adjusting the tightness of nuts and bolts

in a **total eclipse**, the sun is completely obscured; in an **annular eclipse**, a narrow ring of the sun remains visible when the moon is over the sun

total recall is simply a really remarkable memory

totting up, "adding up, calculating," is the correct spelling

touch and go has a nautical origin: when a vessel is in relatively shallow waters so that its bottom occasionally touches the ground but then moves off without damage, that is called touch and go

> **touch wood** is the same as **knock on wood**

tour de force is, literally, "feats of strength"

what makes a **touring bike** different from other bicycles is its ability to carry gear on racks mounted to the front and rear of the bicycle frame

town car is another name for limousine

town planning as a topic existed by 1906

a **toy boy** is a male lover much younger than his partner

a **trace fossil** is a fossilized track, trail, burrow, boring, or other structure in sedimentary rock that records the presence or behavior of the organism that made it

{ a **trade book** is one produced by a commercial publisher for general readership (not book clubs, specialists, or libraries) }

trade wind refers to the old sense of trade, meaning "a regular or habitual course of action," as these blow habitually in the same direction; it is a consistent wind of 10–15 miles per hour

traditional art is art that is a part of the culture of a group of people, the skills and knowledge of which are passed down through generations from master craftsmen to apprentices

traffic calming is the deliberate slowing of traffic in residential areas via speed bumps or other obstructions

traffic block (1896) was first used and gave way to **traffic jam** (1917)

the term **traffic light** seems to have been coined by Rudyard Kipling (1912), though the ones we are familiar with came into being after World War I and were known first as traffic regulation lights (1920)

the fleshy cartilage between your ear and temple is the **tragus** and the downward notch is the **intertragic notch**

trail mix is usually dried fruits, oats or chocolate, nuts or seeds, and is a food mix thought to boost energy; one type is GORP, "good old raisins and peanuts," or "granola, which is oatmeal, raisins, and peanuts"

a **train shed** is a large structure sheltering tracks and platforms of a railroad station

train spotting is the hobby of collecting the numbers and names of locomotives seen at railway stations and other vantage points

trance dance is any ritual or spiritual dance that puts its performer into a trance-like state; or any ritual or spiritual dance performed to trance-like music

trans fat is a fatty acid that has been produced by hydrogenating an unsaturated fatty acid (and so changing its shape), and it is found in processed foods such as margarine, fried foods, puddings, commercially baked goods, and partially hydrogenated vegetable oils

transcendental meditation (1966) was popularized in the West by Maharishi Mahesh Yogi and involves the use of a mantra

a **transit lounge** is a waiting room at an international airport used mainly by passengers transferring from one flight to another without presenting themselves to customs or immigration officials

trans-oceanic, "situated across the ocean," (1827) came before "passing over the sea," recorded from 1868

a **transom window** is a small one, often hinged, above a door

transpiration stream is the flow of water through a plant

inactivity is different from **treading water**; in treading water the lack of direction, purpose, or aim is deliberate—it is active waiting

treasure trove is from French, literally meaning "found treasure"

a **Treasury bill** is a short-term obligation maturing in a year or less; a **Treasury note** matures in one to ten years, and a **Treasury bond** matures in ten to thirty years

a **tree ring** is any of the concentric rings of the cross-section of a tree trunk, representing a year's growth; the layer of wood produced by a year's growth in a woody plant; and is also called annual ring

trial-size is a small size of a product

{ a **trifold wallet** actually only has two folds }

a **triple threat** is someone who can act, dance, and sing well—or in football, a player who is good at running, passing, and kicking

triple-witching hour is when stock options, stock index futures, and options on such futures all mature at once—which happens quarterly and is usually accompanied by highly volatile trading

the **trivial name** or **specific epithet** is the uncapitalized Latin adjective or noun that follows a capitalized genus name in binomial nomenclature and serves to distinguish a species from others in the same genus, as human for *Homo sapiens*

Trojan condoms are so named for their strength

the pole sticking up from a bumper car is the **trolley pole**

a painting with photographic reality is a **trompe l'oeil**

trophy art is any work of art looted in time of war, especially in World War II

the **Tropic of Cancer** is above the equator; the **Tropic of Capricorn** is below it

tropical fish denotes any of numerous small, usually brightly colored fishes, indigenous to the tropics, and often kept and bred in home aquariums

a **tropical storm** is precipitation with winds between 37–74 miles per hour

truck farm refers to a meaning of truck, "commodities for sale," and later, "garden produce for market"

a **truck garden** is one from which vegetables, herbs, and flowers are sold at a market

true blue is from a fabric of Coventry, England, in the Middle Ages, prized for its durable blue dye

a **true bug** has mouthparts for piercing and sucking

the original **true colors** were shown in the flags of early sailing ships

true fact is redundant

true lobsters have claws, and spiny lobsters have no claws

true north is north according to the Earth's axis, not magnetic north

a **true rib** is one attached to the breastbone

a bed that rolls under another bed is a **trundle** or truckle bed

a **trunk call** is a call from one telephone exchange to another

a **try square** is a woodworking or a metal-working tool used for marking and measuring a piece of wood, with "square" referring to the primary use of the tool: measuring the accuracy of a right angle (90 degrees)

use **try to**, not "try and"

the **tsetse fly** comes via South African Dutch, from a Bantu language

T-shirt (1920) is an allusion to the shape it makes when laid out flat

tube steak is a hot dog; frankfurter

tubular bells is a set of tuned metal tubes of different lengths used as a musical instrument, suspended vertically from a frame and struck with a mallet to produce sounds or melodies

strictly speaking, **tuna fish** is redundant because tuna is always fish

the **tuning fork** was invented in 1711 by John Shore

turbinado sugar is raw, light-brown, coarse sugar that has been steam-cleaned, made from the first crystallization of cane juice, and retaining some molasses

a **turkey shoot** is a situation in which the aggressor has an overwhelming advantage

Turkish baths originated in ancient Rome

turn over a new leaf refers to the leaves, sheets of paper, of a book—particularly turning to a blank page in an exercise or copy book to start new work

turn the tables may come from backgammon as the game itself was once called tables and the two halves of the playing board are still called tables

to **turn turtle** is to flip something upside-down

turning point comes from chariot racing, as the place where the driver turned at each end of the stadium

the firefighter's coat is a **turnout coat**

tutti-frutti (1834) is from Italian, meaning "all fruits"

a **tuzzy-muzzy** is a nosegay of flowers (Old English *tus*, "cluster, knot")

a **twelve-step program** is a spiritually oriented program of recovery from addiction or compulsive behavior, especially that of Alcoholics Anonymous

twenty-three skidoo could be and was used to mean almost anything, from enthusiastic approval to dismissive rejection

twilight arch (or bright segment) is a faintly glowing band that is visible above the solar point during twilight

{ the area lighted by daylight just inside a cave entrance is the **twilight zone** }

the **Twinkie defense** is a legal case in which the criminal defendant's behavior is attributed to diminished mental capacity caused by a diet of too much sugar; by extension, any defense seeking to excuse someone's behavior by evading responsibility

a **twisted proverb** is a humorous variation or inversion of a familiar proverb, maxim, or slogan, e.g., "nothing exceeds like excess" (from "nothing succeeds like success")

two bits, "quarter," is from 1730; two-bit (adj.), "cheap, tawdry," was first recorded in 1929

there are a few phrases meaning "stupid; not all there," such as **two sandwiches short of a picnic, three bricks shy of a load**, etc.

two-by-twice means small in floor area

Type 1 diabetes (juvenile diabetes) has been known for some time but is treatable with insulin injections; **Type 2 diabetes** has only been known since 1935 and is also called slow-onset diabetes—treatable by change in diet, exercise habits, and weight loss

a **type founder** is a designer and maker of metal type

a **typewriter word** is one that can be typed on a single row of a typewriter or computer keyboard (e.g., typewriter)

{ U }

U-boat (1916, said to have been in use from 1913) is a partial translation of German *U-boot*, short for *Unterseeboot*, "undersea boat"

ugli in **ugli fruit** is simply a spelling variant of ugly

ugly duckling alludes to Hans Christian Andersen's fairy tale about a cygnet hatched with ducklings that is despised for its clumsiness until it grows up into a beautiful swan; the tale was first translated into English in 1846, and the term was used figuratively by 1871

ultima thule is a Latin term first used to describe an unidentified island in the fourth century BC

an **umbrella term** is a term used to cover a broad category of functions rather than a single specific item, e.g., cryptology is an umbrella term that encompasses cryptography and cryptoanalysis

Uncle Sam, symbol of the United States of America (1813), was coined during the war with Britain as a contrast to John Bull, and no doubt suggested by the initials U.S.

Uncle Tom for a servile black man has been somewhat inaccurately used in reference to the humble, pious, but strong-willed main character in Harriet Beecher Stowe's novel *Uncle Tom's Cabin* (1852)

under hand and seal means "ratified"

if one is **under hatches**, one is being kept under the deck of a ship

under the hammer indicates something is being auctioned

under the weather first referred to being at sea when the weather turns bad

under the wire, "just in time," is from horse racing, in which the wire marks the finish line

under wraps is from the 1930s and alludes to a new project, such as an innovative design or new model of a car, which is kept secret until completion

Underground Railroad, a network of U.S. anti-slavery activists helping runaways elude capture, is attested from 1852 but said to date from 1831, coined in jest by bewildered trackers after their slaves vanished without a trace

unearned income refers to income derived from investments, as opposed to wages

an **unforced error** in sports is a mistake made by the player and not due to the opponent's skill or effort

an **unholy alliance** is a coalition among seemingly antagonistic groups, especially if one is religious, for ad hoc or hidden gain

every URL (**uniform resource locator**) has a **communication protocol** (http), **server** (www), **second-level domain** (word-nerd), and **top-level domain** (com)

Union Jack (1674) was first a small British union flag flown as the jack of a ship, but it has long been in use as a general name for the union flag

{ **United Arab Emirates** was formerly Trucial Oman }

the **United Nations** (1942) was originally the Allied Nations who united against the Axis powers in World War II

university man is the British version of college graduate

in decision analysis, **unk-unk** is an unknown unknown, an uncertainty that is unanticipated in a formal decision model; by extension, a problem that has not and could not be anticipated

unsalted butter is preferred for cooking and baking

unsaturated fat is fatty acid that is in a liquid form at room temperature and is primarily taken from plants; this type of fat is generally referred to as an oil and is made up of two different types, monounsaturated and polyunsaturated

up a creek was popularized in an 1884 political campaign song titled "Blaine Up Salt Creek"

up for grabs was first referring to leftovers collected at the end of a lunch counter for the needy to grab

to be **up the spout** is in a hopeless condition or disastrous situation

up to snuff was first up to sniff, which meant that all senses were intact, and one was feeling fine

upper crust is a nineteenth-century term from a general metaphor of the upper crust of anything; being at the peak

the **Upper Midwest** (or Upper Middle West) states are Wisconsin, Minnesota, North Dakota, South Dakota, and Michigan

upside down was originally "up so down" (up as if down)

an **upside-down French apple pie** is cooked with its pastry on top and then turned over

upstage in theater is "toward the rear of the stage" and **downstage** is "toward the audience"; **stage left** and **right** are left and right as the audience views the stage

upsy-daisy (1711) is from up-a-daisy, a baby talk extension of up

up-to-date, "right to the present time," was the first use of the phrase, then "having the latest facts" and "having current styles and tastes"

urban legend comes from the book *The Vanishing Hitchhiker: American Urban Legends & Their Meanings* (1981)

an **urban myth** is a folkloric and often sensational tale about modern life that is repeated in the media and by other means, making it more believable to some; also called urban legend

USA Today is jokingly nicknamed McPaper (which preceded McJob)

the phrase **usual suspects** originates from a line in the film *Casablanca*

a **utility knife** is a knife with a small, sharp retractable blade

U-turn was first recorded in 1934

{ V }

the earliest record of the term **vacuum cleaner** is in the name of a company (1903); the abbreviated form vacuum was recorded in 1910

vade mecum, "go with me" in Latin, is a favorite book carried everywhere

Arizona is nicknamed the **Valentine state** for its date of entry into the Union, February 14, 1912

value-added tax is a tax levied on the difference between a commodity's price before taxes and its cost of production

vanishing cream is that which is readily absorbed by the skin

the **vanishing line** is the intersection of the parallel of any original plane and picture, one of the lines converging to the vanishing point

in a drawing, the **vanishing point** is when parallel lines show perspective, converging at a point on the horizon line

the end-of-show credit for a TV production company is the **vanity card**

a **vapor trail** is the trail of condensed water left by an aircraft at high altitude

another word for **varicose vein** is **varix** (plural varices)

variety meats are the entrails and internal organs of an animal

tomatoes and melons are actually **vegetable fruits**

vegetable sponge is another name for loofah

a **vehicle identification number** is a mandatory unique number assigned to each vehicle produced that is stamped into the metal on the dashboard on the driver's side (viewable through the windshield), on the engine block, and at least one other place somewhere on the body of the vehicle; if you say VIN number, that is redundant, since the N means "number"

velo binding is a type of document fastener using a narrow strip of plastic on the front and back and attached with thin plastic pegs through the pages; also called velobind

velvet revolution is a translation of Czech *Sametovà revoluce*, which was introduced to English by events in Czechoslovakia leading to the end of Communist rule in 1989

venereal disease is now called a **sexually transmitted disease**

in Venice, **Venetian blinds** (invented in Japan) are known as **Persian blinds**

venial sin does not deprive the soul of divine grace because it is either not a serious transgression or, if it was, it was not committed with full consent

a **verbal agreement** that is spoken is also an oral agreement

verbal diarrhea is also called logorrhea

a **verbal noun** is a noun formed from an inflection of a verb, such as "loving" in "loving is hard"

vertical market in business is all of the potential purchasers within a business sector; a market which meets the needs of a particular industry by producing similar goods or services, e.g., banking, insurance, transportation

a **vertical publication** is one whose editorial content deals with the interests of a specific industry, e.g., *National Petroleum Magazine, Retail Banking Today*, etc.

a **vertical symmetry letter** is an uppercase letter with left-right symmetry (A, H, I, M, O, T, U, V, W, X, Y)

a **vertical tasting** is wine tasting in order of year of vintage

an inanimate object that is the height of perfection can be called the **very dinky**

a **Very light** is a colored flare fired from a Very pistol, named after the American naval officer Edward W. Very (1847–1910)

vested interest often refers to one's special interest in protecting or promoting that which is to one's own personal advantage

grammatically, it should be **Veterans' Day** with a possessive apostrophe (i.e., a day for or belonging to veterans), but you will often find this holiday spelled without the apostrophe; the word veteran ultimately comes from Latin *veter/vetus*, "old" (which became *veteranus*, "of long experience") and the word's original meaning was that of an old soldier or one who had a long history of military service; our modern meaning in North America is any ex-serviceperson.

a **via media** is a middle way

a **via negativa** is a way describing something by saying what it is not

{ **vice versa** is a Latin phrase, literally "the position being reversed" }

the term **vicious circle** is used for those positive feedbacks where the trend is toward disaster

a **victory garden** started as a way to increase food production during a war

Vidalia onions are grown mostly in Georgia

video games are typically in arcade cabinets; the most common kind are uprights, tall boxes with a monitor and controls in front

vieux jeu means "out of date"

a **vintage car** is an old car, especially one built between 1917 and 1930

viral marketing is the distribution over the Internet of a service that becomes so immediately desirable that it leads to an enormous growth in traffic

virgin forest is that untouched by humans

a **Virginia ham** must be processed in Virginia to be so called

a **virtual office** is a business location that is simulated by telecommunications and computer links

virtual reality helps people practice difficult and dangerous activities, such as guiding spacecraft or developing surgical skills; the term originally was used by computer programmers in the 1980s

vis-à-vis (French "face to face") carries a suggestion of opposing forces, although it is generally used to mean "in connection with; about"

Vitamin R is a nickname for Ritalin, and **Vitamin V** for Viagra

viva-voce, "by word of mouth," is from Latin, meaning "living-voice"

vive la différence originally celebrated the distinctions between the sexes

vocal cords (not chords!) are also known as vocal folds

a **voice actor** is an actor who provides voices for animations, commercials, dubbed films, etc.

the **voice box** is the larynx

to adjust a wind instrument is to **voice it**

it is **voice mail** (and voice-mail message), not voicemail

the **Volkswagen Beetle** began production in 1938 (2003) and although the names "Beetle" and "Bug" were quickly adopted by the public, it was not until August of 1967 that VW themselves began using the name Beetle in marketing materials; it had previously been known only as either the "Type I" or as the 1200 (twelve-hundred), 1300 (thirteen-hundred), or 1500 (fifteen-hundred), which had been the names under which the vehicle was marketed in Europe prior to 1967; the numbers denoted the vehicle's engine size in cubic centimeters. The New Beetle began production in 1994.

volte-face (1819) is a reversal of opinion, from Italian *volta faccia* "turn face," from Latin *voltare faccia*

voluntary simplicity is a lifestyle that is less pressured due to a focus away from accumulation of goods and more toward nonmaterial aspects of life; also called downshifting

the original idea of **vox populi**, that the people's voice was all-powerful, has been lost and now it is used to mean "popular opinion"

{ W }

wah-wah (1926) in jazz slang refers to the effect on brass instruments made by manipulating the mute and is of imitative origin

wait state is when a computer is unable to process further while waiting for something to complete, like a data transfer

wake up and smell the coffee was first recorded in 1955, and it was popularized and may have been originated by the advice columnist Ann Landers

a maitre d' at the Waldorf-Astoria Hotel created the **Waldorf salad**

walk the walk means to act competently, like an expert

walkie-talkie (1939) was popularized in World War II army slang

in real estate, **walk-in-walk-out** means buying property as is

walk-on, a minor non-speaking role, was theatrical slang by 1902; as the actor who has such a part it is attested from 1946,

and the sports team sense is recorded from 1974

a **wall of honor** is a wall of inscribed names of heroes or heroines

Wall Street got its name from the half-mile wall built in 1653 for protection and situated where the financial district grew

Walpurgis night is from German *Walpurgisnacht*, "witches' revel," especially on *Brocken*, on May-Day eve

a **walrus mustache** is a thick drooping mustache resembling a walrus's whiskers

Walter Mitty, a "daydreamer," was the creation of James Thurber in 1939

a **wang-tooth** (Old English "to the side") is a molar

War Between the States was the first term used to refer to the U.S. Civil War (1861–1865)

war crime and **war criminal** are terms first recorded in 1906

a **war hawk** is an advocate of an aggressive policy on foreign relations, the term coming from the congressmen from the South and West, led by Henry Clay and John Calhoun, who wanted war against Britain in the period leading up to the War of 1812

warm colors are the yellows and reds of the color spectrum, associated with fire, heat, sun, and warmer temperatures; also called hot colors

a **warm front** is the leading edge of air advancing on and rising over a mass of cooler air

> **warm fuzzy** is a noun meaning a good impression or a feeling of comfort or trust

the first **warning tracks** on baseball fields started out as running tracks in Yankee Stadium and Cleveland Stadium; true warning tracks did not become standard until the 1950s

warp speed alludes to the use in science fiction, especially the speed used for interstellar travel in the science fiction television series *Star Trek*

a **warple** or **warple way** is a country lane

Oliver Cromwell was the inspiration for the phrase **warts and all**

wash drawing involves washes of watercolor laid over a pen or pencil drawing

to **wash one's hands** of something comes from Matthew in the Bible

a **wassail bowl** is one from which healths were drunk of the alcoholic drink wassail

when a ditch is dug, the excavated dirt left lying beside the ditch is a **waste bank**

a **watch cap** is a close-fitting knit cap with a turned-up cuff

the funny squared pocket inside a pants or jeans pocket is the **watch pocket** or **fob pocket**

water bed first referred to a bed on board a ship

water biscuits are bland, as they do not contain fat

a hose attachment that disperses rather than concentrates water (as a nozzle) is a **water breaker**

the **water cycle** is the constant circulation of water between atmosphere, land, and sea by evaporation, precipitation, and percolation through soils and rocks

water ice is another term for sorbet

watermelon was first **water melon**, first recorded in 1615

a **water sky** is described as the dark appearance of the underside of a cloud layer when it is over a surface of open water; an ice sky is the underside of a cloud layer that is white, rosy, or orange-colored, when it is over a surface of ice

water softening is the removal of calcium and magnesium ions from water, or their replacement with sodium, either by chemical reaction or by ion exchange

the **water table** is a vast expanse of underground water fed by rainwater filtering through the earth—and it supplies springs and wells

water works constitutes the system of supplying clean water to domestic and business properties; typically, water will be taken from a source, purified, pumped to local water towers or other reservoirs, and then gravity-fed to the consumers

a **watercooler moment** is a segment in a television or radio program that is controversial, shocking, or exciting enough to be discussed the next day, especially in the workplace as around the watercooler or a discussion of this segment

watering hole first referred to a pool where animals drank

the **wave base** is the maximum depth in water beneath which wave action is no longer perceptible

wax beans are golden yellow or purple versions of the green bean

a minor station on a railroad is a **way station**

weapon of mass destruction was a term in use by 1937

wearing your heart on your sleeve was customary among knights at one time—a scarf or handkerchief given by a damsel to her knight

weasel words are those used to make a good impression, but are ambiguous and lacking in forthrightness

weigh anchor means to haul it up so that a ship may sail

weight lifting is specifically the press, the clean and jerk, the snatch; power lifting is bench press, squat, and dead lift

a **well drink** is a mixed drink for which one does not specify the exact brand of liquor to be used; the opposite is a call drink

well-taken means "accurate, shrewd" of a comment or argument

Welsh rarebit (or Welsh rabbit), buttered toasted bread with melted cheese, milk, and Worcestershire sauce, may have been so called for its being a dish resorted to when meat was not available

the states of the U.S. **West** (or **Far West**) are California, Nevada, Arizona, Utah and sometimes Oregon, Idaho, New Mexico, and Wyoming

the **Western world** refers to all of the countries of the world other than those in Asia, taken as a whole

a bar with a sink is a **wet bar**

{ the last place on a newborn to dry is the small place behind the ears, hence, **wet behind the ears** }

wet blanket (early 1802) alludes to smothering a fire with a wet blanket

wet-aged beef is vacuum-packed in plastic and ages in its own juices; the texture becomes tender, but the flavor does not become concentrated

wheat beer is made with wheat instead of barley

wheat germ is the embryo of a seed or kernel of wheat, located at the bottom center of the kernel next to the stalk; it is covered by several layers of outer coating known as the bran layers, and it is highly nutritious, providing protein, fat, vitamins, and minerals

a **wheat penny** is a U.S. one-cent coin produced from 1909 to 1959, having a portrait of Abraham Lincoln on the obverse and a pair of ears of wheat on the reverse

a **wheel clamp** is a device locked to the wheel of a motor car to prevent it from being driven; normally used to enforce payment of a traffic violation fine

a list accompanying a graph or diagram is the **where list**

whipping boy, "scapegoat," is formerly from a boy raised with a prince or other young nobleman and whipped for the latter's misdeeds

a **whistle-stop tour** refers to a whistle stop as a station that a train stops at only on request, as when there are passengers or freight to be taken on or discharged—as those being the stops on a tour by a candidate as part of a political campaign

white ant is another name for the termite

a **white book** or **white paper** is an official publication of a national government, so named for its formerly being bound in white

white bread was coined c.1300

white bucks are white leather oxford shoes

a **white cap** is a small wave that breaks offshore due to the wind

white chocolate is a blend of cocoa butter and milk solids and sugar and vanilla; used in candy bars and baking and coatings, it is not technically chocolate because it contains no chocolate liqueur

white coffee is coffee with milk added

white collar originated in the United States by 1919; **blue collar** by 1950

white eggs come from hens with white feathers while brown eggs come from hens with reddish brown feathers

white elephants have enormous appetites, and the term has come to mean "useless, expensive possession"—or a possession that is more trouble than it is worth; the meaning of white elephants stems from a story about life at the royal court in Siam (Thailand)

white fish is any with pale flesh, such as cod, halibut

white gold was first the name for certain alloys of gold and silver, about five parts silver to one of gold; white gold now is different, containing the same percentage of fine or pure gold and base metals as any other ten to twenty karat gold—though the difference is that the alloys give the metal a white appearance

white goods are large electrical appliances like refrigerators and washing machines

white heat is the temperature or state of something that is so hot that it emits white light

a **white hole** is the theoretical/hypothetical opposite of a **black hole**, that is, instead of pulling things including light into itself, a white hole pushes thing out of itself

white hope, c. 1912, was originally in sporting use in reference to the quest for a white man capable of beating champion pugilist Jack Johnson

the **White House** was so painted to cover up fire damage done by the British in 1814; it was not officially called the White House until Teddy Roosevelt began printing its image on stationery in 1901

white knowledge is any information acquired without conscious effort

white lie (1741) is a consciously untrue statement which is not considered criminal

white light is apparently colorless light, like ordinary daylight, containing all the wavelengths of the spectrum at equal intensity

white lightning, "illegally distilled whiskey," is an Americanism dating to around 1910

a list of favored people or things is a **white list**

white magic is that used only for good purposes

{ **white meat** is the pale meat of poultry, rabbit, or veal; red meat is from beef or lamb }

a **white night** is either a sleepless night or one where it does not get dark, as in high latitudes in summer

white noise is noise made from a blend of all audible frequencies

white sugar is purified sugar

though **white supremacy** appeared in print in 1902, it lay dormant until the late 1950s

white tea is made from the young, silky, white-haired buds growing on the same tea shrub that produces green and black tea; white tea needs little processing and therefore is very high in polyphenols and antioxidants

white tie is white bow tie with tails and means formal evening dress

the term **white trash** dates to 1831

a **white wedding** is one in which the bride is still a virgin

the **white-light district** is a theatrical or amusement district

whole (or **broad**) **cloth** referred to any full-sized piece of cloth not yet cut to make clothes

whole grain is any grain that has been hulled to remove the outer husk, cleaned, and possibly roasted; **whole wheat** uses all parts of the wheat berry in the flour, including the bran, germ, and the endosperm

the **whole kit and caboodle** is redundant

whole language is a philosophy of reading and writing instruction that emphasizes interpreting meaning from the context of everyday literature

whole milk contains not less than 3.25 percent fat and not less than 8.25 percent nonfat milk solids

whole nine yards started out as U.S. military slang in the 1960s, perhaps from concrete mixer trucks, which were said to have dispensed in this amount—but there are many other theories about its origin

whole wheat is flour or bread ground or made from the full wheat berry

the radius of a **wide area network** can be half a mile or more

a **widow's peak** is a V-shaped point formed by the hair near the top of the human forehead, from the superstition that it is a sign of early widowhood

Wiener schnitzel is literally "Vienna cutlet"

the **Wiffle ball** (1950s) is a variant of the word "whiffle"

the **wild blueberry** is any of several species of blueberry, of the genus *Vaccinium*, having blue berries, that are not normally cultivated

wild oats are inferior weeds that will not bear fruit, so sowing wild oats is wasting time on an activity that will not bear fruit

wild rice, the seed of a tall aquatic grass rather than a true rice, was earlier called water oats, water rice, and Indian rice

a **wildcat strike** is one called by the employees without the supervision of their union and without a vote of the union membership

the **wildtrack** or room tone consists of the barely audible noises that make up a background sense of quiet

will-o'-the-wisp is from earlier "Will with the wisp" (1608), from the proper name and wisp, "bundle of hay or straw used as a torch"

willy-nilly is a contraction of "will I, nill I" or "will he, nill he" or "will ye, nill ye," literally "with or without the will of the person concerned"

wilted greens means they are gently sauteed until the leaves soften

wild card's figurative sense came from its literal use in poker

wild goose chase (1592) was first attested in *Romeo and Juliet*, where it evidently was a figurative use of an earlier (but unrecorded) literal sense in reference to a kind of follow-the-leader steeplechase

wild marjoram is another term for oregano

win place or show has become synonymous with first, second, and third

a **wind band** is a band of wind instruments or a collective term for the wind instruments of an orchestra a tree deformed by wind is called a **wind cripple**

a **wind farm** is an area of land with a large number of electricity-generating windmills or wind turbines

Harold Macmillan, the former British prime minister, institutionalized the phrase **wind of change**, but it first appeared in 1905

a measurement of the cooling effect of a given temperature and a given wind speed is the **windchill index** or **windchill factor**

a **winding cloth** or winding sheet is a burial shroud

window ledge is the same as windowsill

the term **window of opportunity** is based on the image of seeing an opportunity through an open window and seizing it before it shuts

window treatment is a term that covers all the accessories required to decorate a window, e.g., shades, curtains, draperies, blinds, and rods

a **Windsor chair** (named for the place in England) is a wooden chair having a high spoked back, outward-slanting legs connected by a crossbar, a saddle seat, and arms

wine cooper is an old name for a person who samples, bottles, and sells wine

a **wine cradle** is a basket (etc.) used to hold wine at a slant

wing chairs (a high-backed armchair with projecting sidepieces) were designed originally to protect the sitter from drafts

a **wing collar** is a high, stiff shirt collar with turned-down corners

wing it comes from theatrical jargon, referring to the hurried study of lines by an understudy in the wings or to the help given by a prompter who stands in the wings of a theater

the mirrors on the sides of a vehicle are **wing mirrors**

a **wing nut** is also called a **butterfly nut**

{ **wing tip** shoes have a design resembling the shape of a wing }

winged words are highly significant ones

a bow tie's ends are called the **wings**, and the middle is the **crosspiece** or **cross knot**

the **winter banana** is actually an apple

winter squash have hard skins and firm, dense flesh: acorn, butternut, golden nugget, hubbard

a **winter storm warning** indicates that a severe winter storm has started or is about to begin

winter storm watch means there is a possibility of a winter storm

a **winter weather advisory** is issued once snow or sleet is in progress and indicates it is an inconvenience not a danger

wisdom teeth are so called because they appear around the age of twenty

to **wish a whaler greasy luck** means to wish a good voyage with plenty of oil

wish book is the term for the now almost defunct, mail-order catalog

wishy-washy (1693) "feeble or poor in quality," is a reduplication of washy, "thin, watery," and the meaning "vacillating" was first recorded in 1873

{ a multifaceted mirrored ball is a **witch ball** or a **disco ball** }

witch doctor once referred to a magician among African tribes whose business it was to detect witches and to counteract the effects of magic

witch hazel was first *wych* hazel (cf. wych elm) as *wych* was used in names of trees with flexible branches, from a Germanic root meaning "bend"

by 1640 **witch hunt** existed in the literal sense; the extended sense is attested from 1932

witches knickers is the term for disposable bags caught in trees

witching hour is a term for midnight, the time when witches are active and magic takes place (a phrase derived from Shakespeare)

within compass means "within moderation"

with-its are the other things served at dinner besides the entrée

without ballast indicates one is without any steadying influence

wolf in sheep clothing comes from Matthew in the Bible

a **wolf whistle** is characterized by a rising and falling pitch and implies that the whistler is "hungry"

woman-tired is the same as hen-pecked

women's liberation (1966) and **women's lib** (1969) were largely abandoned in favor of feminism (late 19th century)

women's movement was in print by 1902; **women's liberation** in 1966

Wonder bread got its name from a vice president who watched a hot-air balloon race shortly before the bread needed a name —and "wonder" is how he described the event and then the bread

a **wood engraving** is pretty much the reverse of a woodcut

in a tree, a **wood ray** is a conduit connecting the pith to the core and circulating nutrients horizontally within the trunk

Worcester grocers Lea and Perrins coined the term for their **Worcestershire** (also **Worcester) sauce**

a **word family** is any group of words within a language with a shared derivation, e.g., slay, slayer, slaughter, etc.

word of mouse is communicating via computer or electronics, as opposed to oral communication

a **word problem** is a math exercise in the form of a hypothetical situation with an equation to be solved

the revolutionary **word processing** and **word processor** arrived in 1970

word search is a puzzle consisting of letters arranged in a grid which contains a number of hidden words written in various directions

word-music is the musical quality of spoken language

a **word-pecker** plays with words

work ethic, especially with the words Protestant or Puritan added, is an attitude that idleness is improper and sinful

working memory is the contents of somebody's consciousness at the present moment or the memory for intermediate results that must be held during thinking

world city describes a city which has national and global significance as a center of trade, banking, finance, industry, and markets

the **world is my oyster** is from Shakespeare's *The Merry Wives of Windsor*

> English is a **world language**, known or spoken in many countries

world war was initially (1909) a theoretical term, probably a translation of German *Weltkrieg*, then applied to the 1914–1918 war during its first year

World War I was called the **Great War** until that of 1939–45

a fence with the rails crossed in a zigzag pattern is a **worm fence**

a **worm's eye view** is a perspective seen from below or from a low or inferior position

worry beads date from the 1960s and originated among the Greeks

would have is the correct phrase, not "would of"

the **wrong end of the stick** was originally the dirty or muddy one

wrought iron is an alloy containing little carbon, the composition of which produces a metal that can be readily worked or "wrought"

wu wei is letting nature take its course, working in harmony with natural laws

{ **X** }

X chromosome (female) and **Y chromosome** (male) are found by 1911

X-acto knife is trademark for a utility knife with a very sharp replaceable blade

X-ray is a translation of German *X-strahl*, from "X" the algebraic symbol for an unknown quantity, and *Strahl*, "beam, ray"; coined in 1895 by German scientist Wilhelm Conrad Röentgen (1845–1923), who discovered them

{ Y }

yabbadabba doo can be traced to an early twentieth-century popular novelty song about chimpanzees and baboons

yadda-yadda, "and so on," is from the 1990s and of echoic origin

Yale University took its name from an early British Colonial governor of Madras, India, who sent the school three trunks of madras, some books, and about $4,000

Yankee Doodle was a popular tune of the American Revolution, apparently written c.1755 by British Army surgeon Dr. Richard Schuckburgh while campaigning with Amherst's force in upper New York during the French and Indian War; the original verses mocked the colonial troops serving alongside the regulars, and the Doodle element just may have been, or hinted at, the eighteenth-century slang term for "penis"; the song naturally was popular with British troops in the colonies, but after the colonials began to win skirmishes with them in 1775, they took the tune as a patriotic prize and re-worked the lyrics; the current version seems to have been written in 1776 by Edward Bangs, a Harvard sophomore who also was a Minuteman.

in winter sports or mountain biking, a **yard sale** is a fall or wipeout

a **yellow brick road** is a metaphorical road to happiness, an allusion to the song in *The Wizard of Oz*

a **yellow dog** is a contemptible or cowardly person or thing

yellow jackets and hornets are actually types of wasps

yellow journalism is sensational chauvinism in the media and started with U.S. newspaper agitation for war with Spain, though originally it was a "publicity stunt use of colored ink" (1895) in reference to the popular Yellow Kid character in Richard Outcault's comic strip "Shantytown" in the *New York World*

yes man is a creation of sports' cartoonist T.A. Dorgan

yin yoga is a type of yoga practice focused on the connective tissues and joints, as opposed to muscles

Yom Kippur is from Mishnaic Hebrew *yom kippur* (in biblical Hebrew, *yom kippurim*), literally "day of atonement"

Yorkshire pudding is a popover made with unsweetened egg batter and baked till it is puffy, crisp, and golden like a popover; it is served with roast beef or prime rib

you are what you eat can be traced to Anthelme Brillat-Savarin's "Physiologie du gout" (1825)

young Turk is a term for a tyrannical or unmanageable man, based on the members of a party of Turkish agitators who brought about the revolution of 1908

{ **you're welcome** did not exist as a polite formulaic response to a thank you until 1960 }

yo-yo (1915) is apparently from a language of the Philippines; registered as a trademark in Vancouver, Canada, in 1932, though the toy itself is much older and was earlier known as bandalore (1824)

Yukon gold potatoes are a cross between wild yellow South American potatoes and North American white potatoes

yule log comes from an archaic term for Christmas, from Old English *geol*, "Christmas Day"

yuppie flu is a derogatory nickname for chronic fatigue syndrome (myalgic encephalomyelitis)

{ Z }

a **zebra crossing** is the striped area at intersections (etc.) where vehicles must stop to let pedestrians cross

an obsession with unfinished work is the **zeigarnik effect**

Zener cards is a set of twenty-five cards designed for use in psychological testing of extrasensory perception and psychic ability

zero hour is a military term first used in World War I for the exact time at which an attack or operation was to begin

a **zero-sum game** is a game in which the sum of the winnings by all the players is zero; a gain by one player must be matched by a loss by another player; poker is a zero-sum game if the house does not take a cut as a charge for playing

the term **zero-tolerance** dates to 1972

zodiacal light or false dawn is something seen about an hour before the sun rises—a faint light in the sky; it is the sun's light being reflected off the millions of particles of debris in space

parallel lines crossed with other lines to give the illusion that they are not parallel are called **Zollner's lines**

zoot suit is a rhyming formation on suit

zuppa inglese is, literally, "English soup" —but is an Italian version of an English trifle

{ About the Author }

Barbara Ann Kipfer, PhD is the author of many list and reference books. Barbara has an MPhil and PhD in Linguistics from University of Exeter, a PhD in Archaeology, an MA in Buddhist Studies from Greenwich University, and a BS in Physical Education from Valparaiso University. A lexicographer and part-time archaeologist, Barbara is the managing editor of Lexico LLC (Dictionary.com). Her websites are http://www.thingstobehappyabout.com and http://www.archaeologywordsmith.com.